W9-BTT-446

Working
With Child
Abuse and
Neglect

Interpersonal Violence:
The Practice Series
Jon R. Conte, Series Editor

Interpersonal Violence: The Practice Series is devoted to mental health, social service, and allied professionals who confront daily the problem of interpersonal violence. It is hoped that the knowledge, professional experience, and high standards of practice offered by the authors of these volumes may lead to the end of interpersonal violence.

In this series...

Working With Child Abuse and Neglect

A Primer

Vernon R. Wiehe

Interpersonal Violence:
The Practice Series

SAGE Publications
International Educational and Professional Publisher
Thousand Oaks   London   New Delhi

For information address:

SAGE Publications, Inc.
2455 Teller Road
Thousand Oaks, California 91320
E-mail: order@sagepub.com

SAGE Publications Ltd.
6 Bonhill Street
London EC2A 4PU
United Kingdom

SAGE Publications India Pvt. Ltd.
M-32 Market
Greater Kailash I
New Delhi 110 048 India

Printed in the United States of America

Library of Congress Cataloging-in-Publication Data

Wiehe, Vernon R.
    Working with child abuse and neglect: A primer/ Vernon R. Wiehe.
        p. cm.—(Interpersonal violence; v. 15)
    Includes bibliographical references and index.
    ISBN 0-7619-0348-8 (alk. paper).—ISBN 0-7619-0349-6 (pbk.:
alk. paper)
    1. Child abuse. 2. Child abuse—Treatment. 3. Child abuse—
Prevention. I. Title. II. Series.
    RC569.5.C55W49   1996
    616.85'8223—dc20   96-10040

96 97 98 99 10 9 8 7 6 5 4 3 2 1

This book is printed on acid-free paper.

Sage Production Editor: Gillian Dickens

Contents

Acknowledgments

Many persons and organizations provided assistance in writing this book. Organizations such as the National Clearinghouse on Child Abuse and Neglect Information and the National Committee for Prevention of Child Abuse and Neglect provided information on various practice and policy issues. I wish to express my appreciation to their staffs for their invaluable assistance in answering many questions and providing information.

I deeply appreciate the contribution to this book of the expertise of Joel Griffith, Kay Kile, and Ann Richards in the drafting of Chapters 5, 6, and 7, respectively. I am grateful to Linda Combs, who formerly was associated with the University of Kentucky Writing Center, for her guidance in editing the manuscript. Thanks go as well to Linda Burchell, Anna Grace Day, David Royse, and Melinda Smith. Their suggestions were helpful in the many revisions of the manuscript. Finally, my thanks go to my wife, Donna, whom I deeply love, for her support and encouragement.

Preface

Thousands of children annually are victims of child abuse and neglect. Daily, the media present accounts of children who have been physically abused or sexually molested by their parents or others. Reports of children neglected by their caregivers compound this woeful tale. To these problems must be added the plight of children who are emotionally abused, a form of child abuse that largely remains unrecognized in the public media. This book presents a historical perspective on child maltreatment and discusses its scope, theoretical perspectives for understanding the problem, and ways in which child abuse and neglect can be treated and prevented.

❏ The Audience

I have written this book with several audiences in mind. First, the book is directed to advanced undergraduate and graduate students in counseling, social work, nursing, and related mental health fields who have a basic foundation in helping skills. This book will assist you in applying this foundation of knowledge to working specifically with child abuse and neglect. You will find numerous references in the text to the knowledge you have acquired in these core courses, such as the roles one assumes in working with clients, theories for understanding complex social problems, and research methodology for evaluating treatment effectiveness.

A second audience to which this book is directed is mental health professionals new to the field of child abuse and neglect. Your training and knowledge of human behavior will serve as an excellent foundation on which to add specific knowledge aimed at helping you understand, treat, and prevent child abuse and neglect.

A third audience to which this book is directed is persons who may not have an education in a mental health discipline but are employed or are volunteering in the field of child abuse and neglect. This book will provide you with a theoretical understanding of factors associated with child abuse and neglect. From this theoretical understanding, you should be able to identify strategies for intervening in abusive or neglectful families or ways to prevent maltreatment in families at risk. I hope that the book also will stimulate you to read more about child maltreatment. Numerous references to the literature are provided throughout the book for this purpose.

❏ The Content

Knowledge about child abuse and neglect is developing at an explosive rate. Professionals in many fields, such as social work, medicine, nursing, psychology, psychiatry, criminal justice, and education, are addressing this social problem from their unique perspectives. Nearly every issue of the journals in these disciplines includes at least one article related to the subject of child maltreatment. Conferences at national and regional levels are being held at which professionals share new research findings and new treatment and preventive strategies in child maltreatment. Journals such as *Child Abuse & Neglect*, the *Journal of Family Violence*, and the *Journal of Interpersonal Violence* publish extensively in this subject area.

In the light of the rapid explosion of knowledge in child maltreatment, I faced the dilemma of what should be included in the book

and the way the book should be written. (Some may even argue that
the wealth of information on these two problems—child abuse and
child neglect—indicates the value of separate treatments rather than
discussion of both subjects within a single text.) First, I assumed that
most readers would have basic knowledge in understanding human
behavior or have access to individuals and resources with this information. Rather than repeat this knowledge, I emphasize applying it
to working specifically with child abuse and neglect. For example, I
give little emphasis to basic principles of interviewing clients. Interviewing techniques will be applied to the unique setting of working
with abusive and neglectful families. Similarly, emphasis is placed
on applying basic empirical research knowledge, already acquired,
to evaluating treatment effectiveness in child maltreatment.

Second, I chose to interpret the concept of working with child
abuse and neglect in a broad rather than a narrow sense. Rather than
focusing only on direct interventions with individuals and families
involved in child maltreatment, I chose to include information on
social policy issues relative to child maltreatment. Thus, I include
information on historical efforts in the United States to cope with this
problem, the politics of child abuse and neglect, the scope and impact
of the problem, and the prevention of child maltreatment. Successful
interventions in child maltreatment or efforts to prevent this problem
rest on effective public policies at the local, state, and national levels.

Third, I was confronted with the many differences in state statutes
relevant to child abuse and neglect, various models for delivering
protective and mental health services, and the differing structures of
the courts across the country. I therefore present information in a
general sense, noting that differences will occur across states and that
readers must become familiar with structures, statutes, and policies
in their communities.

Fourth, although individuals with various educational backgrounds
work with child abuse and neglect in many different settings, such
as child protective services agencies, courts, hospitals, schools, mental health centers, and state and federal legislatures, I wrote this book
primarily from the perspective of a mental health professional employed in a child protective services agency. Finally, I have followed
the principle that in the same way that graduation exercises are
identified as a "commencement"—namely, a beginning or a start—

so the reading of this book should represent a beginning or a starting point for the reader on the path of acquiring knowledge about child maltreatment. Thus, the book is titled *Working With Child Abuse and Neglect: A Primer.* Because it is intended as a starting point, the book contains numerous references to the published literature in this subject area and information on state and national organizations working in this field. Reading this literature or contacting these organizations, the latter listed in Appendix B, will provide a wealth of helpful information in understanding and intervening in child abuse and neglect.

This book is dedicated to the many individuals, often unrecognized for their untiring efforts, who work with the treatment and prevention of child abuse and neglect.

The Problem

Case Example

Mr. and Mrs. Roberts, a young couple in their late twenties, live in a large metropolitan community in a midwestern state. Mr. Roberts is employed as a bus driver, and Mrs. Roberts works part-time as a cook in a neighborhood restaurant.

Mrs. Roberts and her sister took Mike, the Roberts's 5-year-old son, to a local hospital's emergency room following what Mrs. Roberts described as "a fall from his bicycle." While examining Mike, a nurse noticed bruises on his back and a welt on his buttocks. Mike would not allow the nurse to touch his arm, which he carried close to his body as if it were in a sling. The nurse reported this information to the physician who was to complete Mike's examination.

The attending physician's examination confirmed the nurse's suspicion that Mike's injuries were unlikely to have occurred as a result of falling off his bicycle. The bruises and the welt appeared to have resulted from having been slapped repeatedly and possibly having been whipped with a belt. Although X rays revealed that Mike's arm was not broken, it apparently had been twisted. The physician and nurse shared their suspicions about the nature of Mike's injuries with Mrs. Roberts and her sister.

Although Mrs. Roberts initially persisted in her story that Mike had fallen off his bicycle, she later stated that her husband had some "old-fashioned ideas" about the way children should be disciplined. Mrs. Roberts's sister described her brother-in-law as having a "short fuse" when he was around children. Mrs. Roberts tearfully admitted that her husband "had lost his cool with Mike." She stated that she loved her husband and that she knew he loved their children. The attending physician expressed concern to Mrs. Roberts regarding the way Mike received the injuries. Explaining that a report had been filed with child protective services, the doctor stated the child would not be released until an investigation was initiated.

Case Example

Melissa is an 8-year-old girl living with her mother and uncle in a rural, isolated area of a southeastern state. Melissa's mother, a divorcee, is employed during the day as a waitress. Melissa's Uncle Paul, a former miner, is on total disability as a result of black lung disease. Paul, a single man in his forties, lived with his parents until their deaths. After their deaths, he moved in with his sister, Melissa's mother, to help his sister financially. She was not receiving child support payments from her former husband. Melissa attends second grade during the day. Her uncle cares for her in the late afternoon after she arrives home from school and before her mother returns from work.

Recently, Melissa began to have difficulty at school with even simple assignments her teacher gave her. Melissa became increasingly withdrawn and spent a large amount of time daydreaming. She would cry at seemingly insignificant provocations from her classmates or when her teacher would confront her about her lack of attention and failure to complete assigned tasks. Melissa's teacher described her as "retreating at times into a world of her own." The teacher shared her concern with Melissa's mother at a parent-teacher conference. Melissa's mother also had become aware recently that Melissa was not acting like her usual self at home. The mother, however, paid little attention to this observation after she told a friend about it and the friend responded that "kids go through phases."

Melissa's mother supported the teacher's request that a referral be made to the school guidance counselor. The counselor met with Melissa on three occasions, using storytelling and hand puppets to put Melissa at ease and to assist her in talking about herself. In the third session, Melissa revealed her fear of returning home from school to be alone with her uncle. She stated that her Uncle Paul was doing something she did not like. "When we watch TV together," she hesitantly stated, "he puts his hand in my panties while he rubs himself between his legs." The school counselor assured Melissa that it was appropriate and important that she had shared this information with her.

The guidance counselor discussed with Melissa's mother and the principal the information she had received from Melissa. The counselor filed a report with child protective services in accord with the state's mandatory reporting laws regarding child sexual abuse.

Case Example

Linda, age 17, appeared at the public health clinic for an examination of her 2-month-old infant, Cherise. Linda had received no prenatal care and delivered at a public hospital after being brought to the emergency room when she was in labor. Cherise had received no medical care since her birth. Following Linda's delivery in the hospital, she was referred to the public health clinic for medical care for herself and the baby. She had not received notices from the clinic about checkups for herself and the baby because initially her referral was lost between the hospital and the public health clinic. An appointment letter from the clinic was not forwarded to her following a change in residence.

The nurse examining Cherise immediately noticed that the baby was thin and frail. The baby's weight was considerably under the norm. The clinic nurses observed that the infant was very docile and listless. They also noted that the infant's mother, Linda, seemed depressed, unconcerned with the child, and preoccupied with her thoughts. Following the examination, the infant was diagnosed as being severely malnourished and was hospitalized.

A hospital social worker interviewed Linda as part of the admitting process for her child. A social history revealed that Linda became pregnant in her junior year of high school at the age of 17. She was living with her parents at the time in a small rural community in the southern part of the state. Linda's father was the preacher in a fundamentalist church he had started in the community where the family lived. When Linda's parents became aware of her pregnancy, they sent her to live with an elderly aunt in a large metropolitan city approximately 300 miles from her home. Linda's parents rejected her, stating that her pregnancy out of marriage was an embarrassment to the family. Although Linda left home to live with her aunt, she maintained contact with her boyfriend, Rocky, the baby's father.

Following the baby's birth, Linda moved out of her elderly aunt's home. The aunt, as Linda described the situation, had become "condescending to me and the baby." At the same time, Rocky dropped out of high school and moved to the community where Linda was living, seemingly to rescue Linda from her unpleasant living situation with her elderly aunt.

When work was available, Rocky worked for a moving company unloading moving trucks. At other times, when he was motivated, he would secure odd jobs by standing outside the employment office. He generally spent the time when he was not working and his evenings at a pool hall with friends he made through his moving company job. Rocky and Linda rented an efficiency apartment above a liquor store in a drug-infested neighborhood. Rocky had little contact with his own family. His father was in prison, and his mother was an alcoholic.

The hospital social worker evaluated Linda's care of Cherise as deficient and inadequate. Linda spoke of breast feeding, bathing, and changing the baby. These activities, however, did not appear to occur on a scheduled basis; rather, Linda cared for her baby based on how she felt. Linda indicated that she had not been feeling well since Cherise's birth. She spent large amounts of time watching television and sleeping. The baby had severe diaper rash. Linda reported that she was using disposable diapers but could not change the baby as often as necessary because she lacked funds to buy enough diapers.

Rocky appeared not to be involved with the baby and Linda, except for the first few days after the couple moved into their apartment together. He failed to provide adequate financial support for Linda and her baby because of his lack of stable employment.

The hospital social worker reported the case to child protective services.

The incidents of child maltreatment that are reported represent only the tip of the iceberg.

Mike, Melissa, and Cherise are three examples of the thousands of children each year, across the United States, who are victims of child abuse and neglect. Fortunately for these three children, their maltreatment became known to child protective services agencies in their communities and interventions occurred on their behalf. The incidents of child maltreatment that are reported represent only the tip of the iceberg of this serious social problem, which occurs in all types of families, from those residing in small rural communities to those living in large metropolitan areas.

This chapter will introduce the subject of child abuse and neglect. Various types and forms of child maltreatment will be identified and defined. The different forms of child maltreatment will be illustrated with case examples.

❏ Terminology

Although the term *child abuse and neglect* is used frequently, *child abuse* and *child neglect* are two different types of problems, each taking different forms. A more appropriate comprehensive term is *child maltreatment*, which can be divided into two major types: child abuse and child neglect. Three forms of child abuse will be identified: physical abuse, psychological maltreatment, and sexual abuse. Five forms of child neglect will be described: growth failure, physical neglect, abandonment and failure to provide adequate supervision, medical neglect, and educational neglect (Faller, Bowden, Jones, & Hildebrandt, 1981). Although the various types and forms of maltreatment will be identified, defined, and illustrated separately, in many instances they appear not in isolation but concurrently.

CHILD ABUSE

Child abuse occurs in three forms: physical abuse, psychological maltreatment, and sexual abuse.

Physical Abuse

Physical abuse consists of inflicting injury on a child through hitting, biting, kicking, slapping, and similar means. Injuries may also result from the use of an object such as a belt, stick, rod, or bat. This form of abuse generally involves willful acts of adults that result in injury to a child. Physical abuse also may result from parental actions not intended to injure or harm the child. This may occur in disciplinary situations in which a parent whips, beats, or uses other forms of corporal punishment.

A less known form of physical abuse is Munchausen Syndrome by Proxy, which consists of a parent's persistent fabrication of a child's illness, resulting in repeated diagnostic and treatment procedures (Schreier & Libow, 1993). Harm occurs to the child through the parent's fabrication of symptoms; alteration of laboratory specimens, such as urine or blood; and direct production by the perpetrator of physical signs or of disease itself (Jones, 1994).

Case Example

Kevin, age 6, was described by his teacher as a "quiet, blond, little boy." Police found him beaten to death in his mother's apartment. A coroner's investigation revealed that the child had experienced a severe concussion to the head. A neighbor, who was the apartment building manager, called police after the live-in boyfriend of Kevin's mother was seen hastily leaving the building. Kevin's mother was away at work at the time. The apartment manager became suspicious when he heard Kevin screaming and crying prior to the boyfriend's departure. The boyfriend, a drug dealer in the neighborhood and an expert in martial arts, later was arrested. In the investigation that followed the arrest, the boyfriend of Kevin's mother admitted "hitting Kevin around after he had smarted off."

Psychological Maltreatment

Psychological maltreatment, known also as emotional abuse, is defined as a behavioral pattern in which an adult attacks a child's self-esteem and social competence. This form of abuse is seen, for example, in verbal comments with the intent of ridiculing, insulting, threatening, or belittling the child. Emotional abuse may occur in isolation or concurrently with physical and sexual abuse. Psychological maltreatment is difficult to document because of the absence of physical evidence that often can be found in cases of physical abuse and sometimes in cases of sexual abuse. Some researchers, however, identify psychological maltreatment as the core component and major destructive force in all types of child abuse (Brassard & Gelardo, 1987).

Although psychological maltreatment generally is conceptualized as occurring between a parent or parent surrogate and child, this type of abuse also can occur at a societal level. Psychological maltreatment at this level is seen, for example, when children are victims of prejudice, cultural bias, or gender stereotyping, or are living in dangerous or unsafe environments (Ayalon & Van Tassel, 1987; Jones & Jones, 1987; Reschly & Graham-Clay, 1987; Telzrow, 1987).

Brassard and Gelardo (1987, p. 128) identify seven types of psychological maltreatment.

1. *Rejecting.* Treating a child differently from siblings or peers in ways suggesting a dislike for the child; actively refusing to act to help or to acknowledge a child's request for help.
2. *Degrading.* Calling a child "stupid," labeling as inferior, or publicly humiliating a child.
3. *Terrorizing.* Threatening to physically hurt a child or forcing a child to observe violence directed toward loved ones; leaving a young child unattended.
4. *Isolating.* Locking in a closet or, for extended time, in a room alone; refusing to allow interactions or relationships with peers or adults outside the family.
5. *Corrupting.* Teaching and reinforcing acts that degrade those racially or ethnically different; teaching and reinforcing criminal behavior; providing antisocial and unrealistic models as normal, usual, or appropriate via the public media.
6. *Exploiting.* Sexually molesting a child; keeping a child at home in the role of a servant or surrogate parent in lieu of school attendance; encouraging a child to participate in the production of pornography.
7. *Denying emotional responsiveness.* Ignoring a child's attempts to interact; mechanistic child handling that is void of hugs, stroking, kisses, and talk.

Case Example

Melinda, age 21, contacted a community outpatient mental health clinic regarding her frequent episodes of depression. A social history revealed that Melinda had been raised in an emotionally abusive family. She was the youngest of four children. Her father, a construction worker, drank heavily and frequently was unemployed. Melinda's mother supported the family by cleaning offices at night.

As a child, Melinda was tall for her age and overweight. Her siblings gave her the nickname "Moose," which she despised but they persisted in using. Her peers at school often would use this name. Melinda's father regularly called her Moose, despite her request that he not do so. Melinda's weight and height became the frequent object of jokes and taunts from her siblings, father, and peers.

At the age of 18, Melinda left home, moved to another city, and became self-supporting. At 21, she sought counseling for her low self-esteem and frequent bouts of depression, which were interfering with her ability to hold a job. She described to her therapist a childhood consisting of one emotionally abusive incident after another. She pictured herself currently as a "loner," having few friends and preferring to be by herself.

Case Example

The parents of 12-year-old Tom were surgeons. He and his parents lived in a beautiful, large, suburban home. A cook, a cleaning person, a gardener, and a full-time housekeeper worked for the family. Tom was arrested one day after school for shoplifting a 75-cent key chain. A juvenile court worker's investigation revealed that Tom sometimes would not see his parents for an entire week because of their work and social schedules.

Box 1.1 presents 17 operational definitions of child emotional maltreatment, demonstrating the variety of ways this form of abuse appears in families. These definitions resulted from an 18-month research project, funded by the National Center on Child Abuse and Neglect (NCCAN), in which professionals in five states developed operational definitions of psychological maltreatment based on their experiences in working with parents (Baily & Baily, 1986; T. Baily & W. Baily, personal communication, February 6, 1989). The statements, except for the final two (which are directed to preschool children), apply to latency-age children. With a few changes in wording, they also are applicable to pre-latency and adolescent children.

Sexual Abuse

The third form of child abuse, sexual abuse, may be defined as an adult's use of a child for sexual gratification. Sexual abuse may occur on a contact or noncontact basis. Contact forms of child sexual abuse include behaviors such as sexually touching a child or requesting a child to sexually touch an adult, attempted penetration, intercourse, and sodomy. Noncontact sexual abuse may include indecent exposure to a child, forcing a child to observe adult sexual behavior, or taking pornographic pictures of a child.

Sexual abuse occurring with a family member (blood relative, relative by marriage, live-in boyfriend) is referred to as incest or familial abuse. Sexual abuse by an individual outside the family is known as extrafamilial abuse.

Case Example

Betty Stone has two children, Tom, age 16, and Sarah, age 13. Betty's boyfriend, Bob, a disabled veteran, lives with the family.

Recently, Betty purchased for Sarah a book on the facts of life. Betty became concerned about Sarah's reaction when, several days later, she privately asked Sarah if she had read the book. Sarah reacted angrily, stomping down the hallway. In tears, she slammed the door to her bedroom.

Later, in a conversation with her daughter, Betty learned that her boyfriend, Bob, recently had been watching pornographic videos in their bedroom when Sarah returned home from school and before Betty came home from work. The bedroom door was open, and when Sarah inquired about what he was watching, Bob invited her into the bedroom to watch the movies with him, stating, "You might as well learn about this now." After watching the movies on several occasions, Bob asked Sarah if she wanted to see his erect penis. Sarah refused and left the room in tears. Later, Bob threatened Sarah, telling her that if she ever told anyone about what had happened, she would be in for "big trouble" with him.

CHILD NEGLECT

The second major type of child maltreatment is child neglect. Five forms of child neglect will be identified and defined.

Growth Failure

Growth failure occurs when parents neglect to meet a child's nurturance and nutritional needs. This condition is known as nonorganic

BOX 1.1

Operational Definitions
of Child Emotional Maltreatment

1. The parent shows little or no attachment to the child and fails to provide nurturance. The parent typically fails to call the child to meals, wake the child in the morning, recognize the child's presence, keep promises or agreements, or otherwise act as if the child is a member of the family.

2. The parent consistently singles out one child to criticize and punish, to perform most of the household chores, and to receive fewer rewards.

3. The parent has unrealistic expectations of achievement for the child and criticizes, punishes, ostracizes, or condemns when the child does not achieve far above normal abilities in areas such as school, arts, sports, and social status.

4. The parent makes inappropriate demands on and exploits the child by expecting the child to take care of the parent, to be a companion, to protect the parent from outsiders, and to perform household tasks or functions when the parent is unwilling to do so.

5. The parent expresses no affection toward the child and avoids and resists all physical closeness such as hugging, touching, or smiling.

6. The parent confuses the child's sexual identity by forcing the child to dress in clothing that is inappropriate for the age or sex of the child, resulting in ostracism.

7. The parent provides no stability or security for the child.

8. The parent exposes the child to maladaptive and harmful influences and forces or permits the child to engage in the same.

9. The parent does not permit the child autonomy or independent learning.

10. The parent denies the child the opportunity to learn from others by prohibiting the child from participating in social activities commonly engaged in by the child's peers, such as extracurricular activities or outside play.

11. The parent regularly denigrates and ridicules the child, stating, without foundation, that the child reminds everyone of a person who is offensive and is unacceptable to the family.

12. The parent sexually exploits the child by permitting or forcing the child to watch pornographic materials.

BOX 1.1

Continued

13. The parent uses excessive threats and physical punishments in an attempt to control the child.
14. The custodial parent undermines the child's attachment to the other parent by consistently refusing all legitimate opportunities or requests for visits between the child and the other parent, even when these are requested by the child, or by using the child as a spy, ally, or confidante in the parent's romantic relationships.
15. The parent consistently refuses to permit any professional to assess the child's problems and announces that the child is forbidden from participating in any remedial education or counseling services.

Preschool

16. The parent seldom responds to, stimulates, or shows affection toward the infant and rarely, if ever, holds the child during feeding.
17. The parent shows unrealistic expectations of the infant by regularly scolding and yelling at the infant whenever the child exhibits typical infant requirements, such as crying or needing to be fed, changed, or held.

SOURCE: Adapted from T. Baily and W. Baily (personal communication, February 6, 1989). Reprinted with permission.

"failure to thrive (FTT)" (Bullard, Glaser, Heagarty, & Pivchik, 1967; Drotar, Eckerle, Satola, Pallotta, & Wyatt, 1990; Evans, Reinhart, & Succop, 1972; Sturm & Drotar, 1989). The causes of nonorganic or environmental FTT are external to the infant. Nonorganic FTT accounts for approximately 70% of children diagnosed with FTT (Schmitt & Mauro, 1989).

Three types of nonorganic FTT occur: accidental, neglectful, and poverty related. Accidental FTT results from errors in formula preparation, deficient maternal diet resulting in inadequate breast-feeding, faulty feeding techniques, or erroneous parental perceptions of what constitutes a healthy diet for infants and children (Evans, Bowie, Hansen, Moodie, & van der Spuy, 1980). In neglectful FTT, a parent's psychosocial problems, such as depression, being overwhelmed with family and job responsibilities, marital problems, and substance abuse, prevent the parent from spending adequate time with the child, especially relative to emotional nurturance and proper feeding practices. Serious physical anomalies other than low weight and delayed development, such as abnormalities in sleeping, eating, motor ability, physical growth, and psychological functioning, may result from neglectful failure to thrive (Garbarino, Guttman, & Seeley, 1986; Powell, Brasel, & Blizzard, 1967). Children exhibiting these abnormalities often are identified as suffering from psychosocial dwarfism or deprivation dwarfism (Gardner, 1972). Poverty-related FTT, defined as malnutrition resulting from the unavailability of food or money to purchase food, rarely occurs in the United States except in transient or extremely isolated families (Schmitt & Mauro, 1989). Regardless of the type (accidental, neglectful, or poverty re-lated), nonorganic FTT is a type of child neglect and requires inves-tigation by a child protective services agency.

Case Example

Eighteen-month-old James was hospitalized at University Hospital following referral from a public health clinic. The purpose of the hospitalization was to evaluate him for chronic respiratory infections, weight loss, and cessation of growth over the previous 4 months. Following his admission to the hospital, the nurses noted that James seldom smiled. He appeared fearful of leaving his hospital bed, despite numerous play activities that were available to the children hospitalized in the unit.

Interviews with the mother, Rose, revealed a single parent with periodic bouts of severe depression. She spoke about her child in a detached manner, as if she felt little warmth and love for the child. Rose seemed unable to cope with the demands of caring for her son. She described how overwhelmed she felt at times, caring for the child when she did not feel well herself. She spoke of spending many hours in bed, leaving the child unattended, when she was depressed. Observations by hospital personnel when Rose visited James indicated that the mother seemed inattentive to the child's needs and was incapable of providing nurturance to the child.

Physical Neglect

Physical neglect is defined as parental failure to provide children with adequate food, shelter, sleeping arrangements, clothing, and general physical care.

Case Example

Mr. and Mrs. Joy lived in a school bus parked in a trailer park. The Joys moved from state to state, picking crops in season. They had two children, ages 3 and 4.

A neighbor living in a house with a backyard bordering the trailer park reported to the park manager that the children were playing in the neighbor's yard late at night without wearing adequate clothing. The neighbor also expressed concern about the bus's filthy condition and the family's lack of running water and toilet facilities. The children were reported by other neighbors to be filthy and often went from house to house begging for food. When the park manager seemed inattentive to these complaints, a neighbor anonymously reported the situation to child protective services and the health department.

Abandonment and Failure
to Provide Adequate Supervision

Abandonment and inadequate supervision include parental behaviors such as abandoning a child, expulsion of a child from home, not allowing a runaway to return home, and leaving a child alone without adequate supervision.

Case Example

Ms. Benton supplemented her welfare check by working as a cocktail waitress on weekends at a local bar. She had no family to care for her three children, ages 4, 6, and 8, nor did she feel she could afford a baby-sitter. She left her 8-year-old son in charge at home when she worked. She would padlock the door to the apartment from the outside to prevent the children from leaving the apartment. One night, the children were burned to death when a towel, placed too close to a space heater, caught on fire.

Medical Neglect

Medical neglect is parental failure to provide children with adequate medical care. Generally, charges of medical neglect focus on parents' neglectful behavior that may be serious or life threatening for a child, rather than their fear of not being able to pay for medical services or their lack of understanding the importance of specific medical treatment (Faller et al., 1981).

Case Example

A routine school examination revealed that 8-year-old Becky was having hearing problems. The examining nurse noted a severe ear infection. The school nurse informed Becky's parents about the seriousness of this problem in a telephone call and follow-up letter. Becky's parents were instructed to take Becky to a specialist or to seek help through the public health clinic.

Approximately one month later, Becky's teacher noted an increased deficiency in Becky's hearing in the classroom. The teacher consulted with the school nurse, who in turn contacted Becky's parents. The contact with Becky's parents revealed that they had ignored the earlier communications about Becky's ear problems and had not sought medical help for Becky as they had been requested to do. They excused their behavior on the basis that they assumed that the problem would go away.

Educational Neglect

Educational neglect occurs when parents fail to enroll children in school or an alternate means of education, keep children from school, fail to get children to school (waking them, getting them dressed, arranging for transportation), allow children to be chronically truant from school, or fail to assist children in completing educational tasks. Educational neglect generally applies to children under the age of 11 and children under the parents' control. Situations involving older children, in which the children defy parents' efforts to get them out of bed or in which the children leave home but skip school, are considered truancy rather than educational neglect (Faller et al., 1981).

Case Example

Dale, age 11, lived in a trailer with his father, a carnival worker responsible for the maintenance of rides erected in shopping centers. A police officer patrolling the shopping center repeatedly noticed Dale working with his father on the rides. The police officer questioned Dale's father about the young boy's failure to attend school. The father's response was that he intended to have Dale go to school but "had not gotten around to it." When the officer continued to observe Dale not in school, a report was filed with school authorities.

❑ Summary

Two types of child maltreatment exist: child abuse and child neglect. Three forms of child abuse occur: physical abuse, psychological maltreatment, and sexual abuse. Five forms of child neglect can be identified: growth failure, physical neglect, abandonment and failure to provide adequate supervision, medical neglect, and educational neglect. The different forms of neglect frequently are collapsed into fewer categories because of the overlap occurring in the definitions. This will be noted in the next chapter in the National Incidence Studies, in which child neglect is reported according to three major forms: physical, emotional, and educational.

2

The Scope of Child Maltreatment

How serious is the problem of child maltreatment? How many individuals are victims of its various types and forms? In this chapter, findings from several studies will address these questions.

❏ Studies on the Scope of Child Maltreatment

Several studies on child abuse and neglect present data on the scope of this problem. These studies report the extent to which random samples of adults have experienced child maltreatment as well as the number of reported incidents of child abuse and neglect.

THE RUSSELL STUDY

A sample in San Francisco formed the basis of a study determining the extent to which women had experienced incestuous and extrafamilial sexual abuse as children (Russell, 1986). The study defined incestuous abuse as any kind of exploitive sexual contact or attempted contact occurring between relatives, no matter how distant the relationship, before the victim turned 18 years of age. Extrafamilial abuse was defined as unwanted sexual experiences, ranging from attempted petting to rape, before the victim turned 14 years of age, and completed or attempted forcible rape experienced from ages 14 through 17. A marketing and public opinion research corporation drew the sample of 930 women

> *One woman in eight is incestuously abused before the age of 14, and one in six before the age of 18.*

for the study. Trained interviewers conducted in-person interviews with the respondents.

Russell found that 16% of the sample (152 persons) reported at least one experience of incestuous abuse before the age of 18. Twelve percent of these women (108) had been sexually abused by a relative before reaching 14 years of age. Abuse by a nonrelative was even more prominent, with nearly one third of the sample (31%, or 290 persons) reporting at least one sexual abuse experience before reaching the age of 18. Before these women had reached their 14th birthday, 20% (189) had been sexually abused by a nonrelative. Combining the two categories of incestuous and extrafamilial child sexual abuse, 38% (357) of the 930 women in the sample reported at least one experience of sexual abuse before reaching 18 years of age; 28% (258) identified at least one such experience before the age of 14.

If the findings reflect the prevalence of sexual abuse in the United States, then one woman in eight is incestuously abused before the age of 14, and one in six before the age of 18. The data also indicate that more than 25% of the population of female children have experienced sexual abuse before age 14 and more than one third by age 18.

THE FINKELHOR, HOTALING, LEWIS, AND SMITH STUDY

Men and women nationwide were surveyed to determine if they had experienced any form of childhood sexual abuse (Finkelhor, Hotaling, Lewis, & Smith, 1990). The Los Angeles Times Poll, a survey research organization, conducted this study by telephone, interviewing a sample of 2,626 men and women in the United States, 18 years of age or older. Interviewers obtained sexual abuse information by asking respondents if, when a child (age 18 or under), they remembered someone trying to have or succeeding in having any kind of sexual intercourse with them; any kind of experience involving touching, grabbing, kissing, or rubbing up against their body; someone taking nude photographs of them, exhibiting parts of their body to them, or performing a sex act in their presence; or any sexual abuse involving oral sex or sodomy.

Thirty-eight percent of the women and 16% of the men recalled a history of sexual abuse. The median age for sexual abuse was 9.9 years for boys and 9.6 years for girls. Approximately one fourth of the victimization occurred before age 8. Boys were more likely to be abused by strangers, girls by family members. One half of the offenders or perpetrators were authority figures in the children's lives.

A breakdown of the research results is shown in Table 2.1. The summary data presented earlier are based on combining the victims' responses indicating "yes" to any of the four items identified above.

THE STRAUS AND GELLES DATA

Two national probability samples of households were studied in 1975 (2,143 families) and 1985 (3,520 families) to determine rates of physical abuse of children and spouses (Gelles & Straus, 1987; Straus & Gelles, 1986; Straus, Gelles, & Steinmetz, 1980). Although these studies focused on violence among various family members, only parent-child violence is reported here.

Researchers used the Conflict Tactics Scales to measure violent behavior (Straus, 1979, 1981). This instrument asks respondents to think of events in the past year during which they were angry or had a disagreement with a family member and to identify how often they engaged in behavior classified as minor or severe violence acts. A child abuse index was formed from several acts.

Table 2.2 presents the findings from the 1975 and 1985 studies. The data indicate that, with the exception of two items composing the "severe violence acts" (items 7 and 8, "threatened with a gun or knife" and "used gun or knife"), the occurrence of each form of

TABLE 2.1 Responses to Questions About Sexual Abuse

Question	Men (%) n = 1,145	Women (%) n = 1,481
Sexual intercourse	9.5	14.6
Touch, grab, kiss	4.5	19.6
Nude photos, exhibition, etc.		
Photos	—	0.1
Exhibition	1.0	3.2
Performing	0.3	0.3
Other	0.3	0.1
Oral sex, sodomy	0.4	0.1

SOURCE: Adapted from *Child Abuse & Neglect, 14,* Finkelhor, Hotaling, Lewis, and Smith, "Sexual Abuse in a National Survey of Adult Men and Women: Prevalence, Characteristics, and Risk Factors," 19-28, © copyright 1990, with kind permission from Elsevier Science Ltd., The Boulevard, Langford Lane, Kidlington 0X5 1 GB, UK.

TABLE 2.2 Parent-to-Child Violence: Comparison of Rates in 1975 and 1985 (rates per 1,000 children ages 3 through 17[a])

Type of Violence	1975 n = 1,146[b]	1985 n = 1,428[c]	t for 1975- 1985 Difference
A. Minor violence acts			
1. Threw something	54	27	3.41***
2. Pushed/grabbed/shoved	318	307	0.54
3. Slapped or spanked	582	549	1.68
B. Severe violence acts			
4. Kicked/bit/hit with fist	32	13	3.17**
5. Hit, tried to hit with something	134	97	1.41
6. Beat up	13	6	0.26
7. Threatened with gun or knife	1	2	0.69
8. Used gun or knife	1	2	0.69
C. Violence indices			
Overall violence (1-8)	630	620	0.52
Severe violence (4-8)	140	107	2.56**
Very severe violence (4, 6, 8) ("child abuse" for this article)	36	19	4.25***

SOURCE: Adapted from "Societal Change and Change in Family Violence from 1975 to 1985 as Revealed by Two National Surveys," Straus and Gelles, *Journal of Marriage and the Family, 48,* p. 469, © copyright 1986 by the National Council on Family Relations, 3989 Central Ave. NE, Suite 550, Minneapolis, MN 55421. Reprinted with permission.
a. For two-caretaker households with at least one child 3 to 17 years of age at home.
b. A few respondents were omitted because of missing data on some items, but the *n* is never less than 1,140.
c. A few respondents were omitted because of missing data on some items, but the *n* is never less than 1,418.
*$p < .05$; **$p < .01$; ***$p < .001$ (two-tailed tests).

violence from parents toward children declined during the 10 years between studies.

Three possible explanations can be cited for the reduction in violence between 1975 and 1985. First, parents may have been more reluctant in 1985 to share with interviewers incidents of violence toward their children because of increased public attention to the problem of child abuse. Second, the difference may be the result of changes in data collection. The 1975 data were collected through telephone interviews and the 1985 data through in-person interviews. In addition, the response choice "never," not offered in the 1975 study, was added in the 1985 research. Third, a change in parental behavior toward children actually may have occurred between 1975 and 1985. This change may be due to a reduction of stress factors associated with violence in families as a result of couples marrying at a later age, couples waiting until later to have their first child, family size decreasing, or the economic climate improving. The decrease in parental violence toward children also may be due to increased parental awareness of child abuse, stemming from efforts of prevention and treatment programs (Gelles & Straus, 1987).

Several cautions should be raised regarding the Straus and Gelles data. This research did not include incidents of child sexual abuse or child neglect. These problems constitute a significant proportion of cases in child protective services agencies (Schene, 1987). The studies focused only on two-parent households and households with children 3 to 17 years of age. Violence toward children may occur with even greater intensity in one-parent households or in households with nonparental guardians. In addition, children under the age of 3 are at high risk for maltreatment (Cohn, 1987).

NATIONAL INCIDENCE STUDIES

The National Incidence Studies (National Center on Child Abuse and Neglect, 1988a, 1988b) represent two major efforts of statistical data collection involving reported cases of child maltreatment. The first National Incidence Study, referred to as NIS-1, was completed in 1980. The second (NIS-2) was conducted in 1986.

Community professionals collected data for these studies in 29 counties in 10 states regarded as representative of the entire country.

Community professionals included child protective services workers and key respondents in other agencies such as schools, hospitals, and police departments. Key respondents served as "sentinels" by watching for cases during the data collection period that met the study's definition of child maltreatment. Those cases fitting the standardized definitional criteria for the study were counted and used as the basis for the national estimates.

The NIS-2 study in 1986 used two sets of child maltreatment definitions. The first set corresponded to the definitions used for NIS-1 and reflected the number of children experiencing demonstrable harm as a result of maltreatment. These definitions allowed for comparisons between the 1980 and 1986 studies to determine if statistically significant changes had occurred. The second set of definitions, or revised definitions, was broader and more inclusive. Children who were endangered by maltreatment or placed at risk for harm but not necessarily yet harmed were included in the revised definitions (National Center on Child Abuse and Neglect, 1988b).

Nearly one million children across the United States, or an estimated 14.8 children per 1,000, were victims of child abuse and neglect in 1986. This represents a significant increase from 1980, when more than 600,000, or 9.8 children per 1,000 (or nearly 1.5 million children nationwide) experienced maltreatment (see Table 2.3). Based on the

TABLE 2.3 National Incidence of Child Maltreatment

| | *Original Definitions* | | | |
| | | | *1980-1986* | *1986 Revised* |
Category	*1980*	*1986*	*Increase*	*Definitions*
Rate[a]				
Total countable	9.8	14.8	5.0*	22.6
Total				
Total countable	625,100	931,000	315,900[b]	1,424,400

SOURCE: Adapted from *Study Findings: Study of National Incidence and Prevalence of Child Abuse and Neglect: 1988* (DHHS Publication No. 20-01093), National Center on Child Abuse and Neglect. Reprinted with permission.
NOTE: Data for 1986 reflect corrected figures reported in *Technical Amendment to the Study Findings—National Incidence and Prevalence of Child Abuse and Neglect: 1988* (Sedlack, 1990).
a. Per 1,000 children in the population.
b. Total number of children rounded to the nearest 100; not adjusted by population totals.
*p < .05.

TABLE 2.4 Distribution by Type: Abuse and Neglect

| | Original Definitions | | | |
Category	1980	1986	1980-1986 Increase	1986 Definitions
Rates[a]				
Abuse	5.3	8.1	2.8*	9.4
Neglect	4.9	7.5	2.6	14.6
Totals[b]				
Abuse	336,600	507,700	171,100	590,800
Neglect	315,400	474,800	159,400	917,200

SOURCE: Adapted from *Study Findings: Study of National Incidence and Prevalence of Child Abuse and Neglect: 1988* (DHHS Publication No. 20-01093), National Center on Child Abuse and Neglect. Reprinted with permission.
NOTE: Data for 1986 reflect corrected figures reported in *Technical Amendment to the Study Findings—National Incidence and Prevalence of Child Abuse and Neglect: 1988* (Sedlack, 1990).
a. Per 1,000 children in the population.
b. Total number of children rounded to the nearest 100; not adjusted by population totals.
*$p < .05$.

revised definitions, an estimated 22.6 children per 1,000 experienced abuse or neglect in 1986.

Table 2.4 presents a breakdown of these data into the two major types of child maltreatment: abuse and neglect. Fifty-two percent of the cases (8.1 children per 1,000) included under the original definition involved abuse, and in 48% (7.5 per 1,000), the maltreatment was defined as neglect. This means that 507,700 children were abused in 1986 and 474,800 children nationwide were neglected. Using the revised definitions, neglect constituted 61% of the cases (14.6 per 1,000) and abuse 39% (9.4 per 1,000). These data reverse the pattern presented by the original definition: More children potentially faced maltreatment through neglect under the revised definitions of 1986.

Table 2.5 presents a further breakdown of the data by type and form of abuse. (The rates per 1,000 in Table 2.3, when summed, do not agree with the totals presented in Table 2.2 because cases involving both abuse and neglect are included in both categories.) Under the original definitions for 1986, the most frequent category of abuse was physical, followed by emotional, and then sexual. Educational neglect was the most frequent, followed by physical and emotional. Similar patterns occurred in 1986, with the revised definitions, except

TABLE 2.5 Distribution of Child Abuse and Neglect Cases by Type

| Category | Original Definitions | | | |
	1980	1986	1980-1986 Increase	1986 Definitions
Child abuse				
Rates[a]				
Physical abuse	3.1	4.3	1.2*	4.9
Sexual abuse	0.7	1.9	1.2*	2.1[b]
Emotional abuse	2.1	2.5	0.4	3.0
Totals[c]				
Physical abuse	199,100	269,700	70,600*	311,500
Sexual abuse	42,900	119,200	76,300*	133,600
Emotional abuse	132,700	155,200	22,500	188,100
Child neglect				
Rates[a]				
Physical neglect	1.6	2.7	+1.1	8.1
Emotional neglect	0.9	0.8	−0.1	3.2
Educational neglect	2.7	4.5	+1.8	4.5
Totals[b]				
Physical neglect	103,600	167,800	+64,200	507,700
Emotional neglect	56,900	49,200	−7,700	203,100
Educational neglect	174,000	284,800	+110,800	285,900

SOURCE: Adapted from *Study Findings: Study of National Incidence and Prevalence of Child Abuse and Neglect: 1988* (DHHS Publication No. 20-01093), National Center on Child Abuse and Neglect. Reprinted with permission.
NOTE: Data for 1986 reflect corrected figures reported in *Technical Amendment to the Study Findings—National Incidence and Prevalence of Child Abuse and Neglect: 1988* (Sedlack, 1990).
a. Per 1,000 children in the population.
b. Includes teenage perpetrators.
c. Total numbers of children rounded to the nearest 100; not adjusted by population totals.
*$p < .05$.

in the area of neglect, in which physical neglect was most frequent, followed by educational and then emotional neglect.

Three major changes occurred in the incidence of child abuse and neglect (using the original definitions) between 1980 and 1986. First, identified cases of child abuse and neglect increased by 47%. Second, among the abuse cases, a notable increase in the incidence of sexual abuse occurred, with this form of abuse nearly tripling in 1986 as compared to 1980. Third, neither emotional abuse nor any of the forms of neglect (educational, physical, emotional) showed significant changes (National Center on Child Abuse and Neglect, 1988a).

TABLE 2.6 Breakdown of 1993 Child Maltreatment Reports by Type

Type of Abuse	Reported (%)	Substantiated (%)
Physical abuse	30	25
Sexual abuse	11	15
Emotional abuse	2	4
Neglect	47	47
Other[a]	10	9

a. Includes cases such as abandonment, educational neglect, dependency, and other situations not specified in the data collection instrument.

NATIONAL COMMITTEE TO
PREVENT CHILD ABUSE DATA

Statistical data collected from 49 states by the National Committee to Prevent Child Abuse (NCPCA) in 1993 estimated that 3,005,000 children were reported for abuse and/or neglect. The rate of reporting was 45 children out of every 1,000 for 1992 and 1993. Based on data from 37 states, it is estimated that 1,016,000 children, or 34% of child abuse reports, were confirmed for abuse and/or neglect. Caution must be raised about unsubstantiated reports. These reports should not be considered as false reports, because the primary reason why reports are not substantiated is a lack of important information about the child, the family, or the suspected abuse. Table 2.6 presents a breakdown of all reported and substantiated cases of child maltreatment by type of abuse and neglect.

AMERICAN HUMANE ASSOCIATION DATA

The American Humane Association (1995) collected data on child abuse from states from 1976 to 1987. In subsequent years, these statistics were compiled by the NCPCA. In 1976, an estimated 669,000 children were reported to child protective services, and in 1994, as can be seen in Table 2.7, the number increased to 3,140,000. This means that approximately 47 children per 1,000 experienced maltreatment in 1994, as compared to 10.1 per 1,000 in 1976. (Except for 7 states out of 54 jurisdictions reporting, these figures duplicate reports when a child and/or family may be reported more than once in a given year.) The increase in reporting may be due in part to a

TABLE 2.7 National Estimates of Child Abuse and Neglect Reports, 1976-1994

Year	Estimated Number of Children Reported (in thousands)	Estimated Number of Children per 1,000 Population
1976	669	10.1
1977	838	12.8
1978	836	12.9
1979	988	15.4
1980	1,154	18.1
1981	1,225	19.4
1982	1,262	20.1
1983	1,477	23.6
1984	1,727	27.3
1985	1,928	30.6
1986	2,086	32.8
1987	2,178	34.0
1988	2,265	35.0
1989	2,435	38.0
1990	2,557	40.0
1991	2,723	42.0
1992	2,916	45.0
1993	3,005	45.0
1994	3,140	47.0

heightened awareness about child abuse on the part of the general public and professionals who are mandated by law to report suspected cases of child abuse. The increase also may be the result in part of universal methods of data collection being used by the various states.

❑ Differences in Various Study Data

Differences can be noted in the data reported above from the various studies. The Straus and Gelles data indicate that child abuse decreased from 1975 to 1985. The National Incidence Studies report that child maltreatment rose significantly from 1980 to 1986. Likewise, the American Humane Association data reflect an increase in child abuse and neglect reports from 1976 to 1994.

Several observations regarding this discrepancy can be noted. Data collected by the National Incidence Studies and the American Humane Association may be referred to as "treatment" or "intervention" data. These data reflect the number of cases reported to child protective services or other community agencies. Data from the Straus and Gelles studies may be closer to true incidents of child maltreatment, as parents identified violent acts they engaged in with their children. These acts, however, were not necessarily reported or known to authorities concerned with child maltreatment (Straus & Gelles, 1988).

> *The differences in the data may not be contradictory but rather complementary.*

The differences in the data—an increase shown in one set and a decrease in the other—may not be contradictory but rather complementary. As local, state, and federal organizations continue to work aggressively for the treatment and prevention of child maltreatment, as reflected in increased number of reported cases, the impact of their efforts may be reflected in the decrease in violent acts reported by parents against their children (Straus & Gelles, 1986, 1988).

❏ **Fatality Following Child Abuse**

Being a victim of child abuse places a child at risk for fatality. Between 1973 and 1986, 11,085 children born in Washington state were reported to the state child abuse registry. The fatality rate of these children was compared to a group of nonabused children matched on gender, county of birth, and year of birth. The children who had been abused had a risk of death three times as large as that of the nonabused group. The abused children were almost 20 times as likely as their nonabused counterparts to die from homicide. Those children at highest risk were the ones abused prior to 1 year of age. There were no differences between the two groups by gender (Sabotta & Davis, 1992).

Statistical data at the national level on fatalities resulting from child maltreatment indicate that in 1992, 992,617 children were confirmed victims of child abuse and neglect. It is reported that 1,068 of these children died from their maltreatment. Researchers caution, however, that this may be a conservative estimate because of potential misdiagnosis of death as a result of either sudden infant death syndrome, shaken baby syndrome, homicide, or accidents. In addition, many states have difficulty in acquiring sufficient information from the coroner's office and the judicial system about the particular circumstances surrounding a child's death to determine if abuse or neglect may have been a factor. Between 1991 and 1993, 40% of the abuse- or neglect-related fatalities that occurred were attributed to neglect, 55% to abuse, and 5% to both abuse and neglect. Of the children who died, 42% previously had been or currently were known to child protective services. Children under the age of 5 are the most vulnerable segment of this population. The NCPCA found that 86% of the children who died as a result of abuse or neglect between 1991 and 1993 were under the age of 5, and an estimated 46% were under the age of 1. Twenty-nine percent of the fatalities occurring between 1991 and 1993 involved parental drug or alcohol abuse (National Resource Center on Child Abuse and Neglect, 1995).

Interagency child death review teams have emerged in metropolitan areas across the country in response to the increasing awareness of severe violence to children resulting in death. Child death review involves a systematic, multidisciplinary, and multiagency process of coordinating data and resources from the coroner, law enforcement agencies, the courts, child protective services, and health care providers. The teams generally review all coroner cases (unattended death or questionable cause of death) for children 12 years of age and younger (Gellert, Maxwell, Durfee, & Wagner, 1995).

❏ **Summary**

Data on the scope of child maltreatment reflect a growing awareness of and sensitivity to the problem. Despite differences in interpreting findings on the extent of this problem, the number of children in American society experiencing abuse and neglect remains alarmingly high.

❏ **Suggested Reading**

Russell, D. (1986). *The secret trauma.* New York: Basic Books.

This book reports the results of Dr. Russell's San Francisco study, referred to in this chapter. Case examples describe the victims, the perpetrators, and their families.

Straus, M., & Gelles, R. (1986). Societal change and change in family violence from 1975 to 1985 as revealed by two national surveys. *Journal of Marriage and the Family, 48,* 465-479.

This article compares the rate of physical child abuse from the initial study identified below with that from a 1985 replication.

Straus, M., Gelles, R., & Steinmetz, S. (1980). *Behind closed doors: Violence in the American family.* Garden City, NY: Anchor.

Findings from the first comprehensive study of family violence in the United States are reported in this book.

3

Historical Perspective

We take for granted, today, society's obligations to protect children and ensure that they have opportunities for their optimum psychosocial development. Historically, however, these obligations have not always been widely recognized. A historical review of child maltreatment legislation and programs reveals the progress that has been made and the foundation on which future efforts can continue to build. This chapter will trace the path child abuse prevention and treatment has taken in the United States, including the development of public policy, political aspects of this process, and the formation of public and private preventive and treatment resources.

❏ Children in Early American Society

In early American society, children were viewed differently from how they are today and consequently often were victims of abuse and neglect. Several factors account for this. First, parents often did not become as emotionally invested in children as they do today because many children did not survive childhood (DeMause, 1976).

Childhood illnesses that today are no longer regarded as life threatening because of immunization took heavy tolls on the lives of children. Consequently, parents had large families so that some children would survive.

In early American society, children were viewed differently from how they are today.

Second, economic needs of families forced children to terminate their education and go to work at an early age. As had occurred in England, in colonial America children frequently were exploited for their labor. The exploitation and accompanying abuse of children were particularly prevalent during the Industrial Revolution, when very young children were put to work in factories. For example, an advertisement appeared in an 1808 Baltimore newspaper seeking boys and girls from 8 to 12 years old to work in a cotton mill. Children often were apprenticed out of their homes or orphanages to work in mills, factories, and various industries (DeMause, 1976; Giovannoni & Becerra, 1979; Kadushin & Martin, 1988).

Third, children were not provided special protection under early American law, which was modeled after English poor laws. Consequently, they frequently became victims of abuse and neglect. Physically, emotionally, and mentally handicapped children, as well as delinquent and orphaned children, were warehoused together in workhouses or on poor farms in early 19th-century America. Child maltreatment was rampant in these institutions. Indenture and apprenticeships, while providing children an exit from these institutions, in many instances set them up to be victims of further maltreatment from their masters (DeMause, 1976).

Finally, religious beliefs often reinforced stern and even abusive parental behaviors toward children. Calvinistic theology in early American society was preoccupied with the issue of infant depravity and damnation, emphasizing the inherent corrupt and sinful nature of children (Greven, 1977). This negative perception of children called for stern methods of discipline, including the use of corporal punishment, for which biblical justification was found. Corporal punishment, such as beating a child with a rod, was regarded as an appropriate and acceptable method of discipline, even though today this would be considered child abuse.

❑ A Beginning

The first efforts to combat child maltreatment often are associated with the story of Mary Ellen. Etta Wheeler, a church social worker, heard in 1874 of 9-year-old Mary Ellen, who was abused and neglected by Francis and Mary Connolly, to whom she was apprenticed. The story reports that Mrs. Wheeler, attempting to find some legal way to rescue Mary Ellen, appealed to the Society for the Prevention of Cruelty to Animals on the basis that Mary Ellen was at least a member of the animal kingdom. A court heard the case and found Mary Connolly guilty of maltreatment. She was sentenced to a year in prison. Mary Ellen was placed in a new home.

Identifying the case of Mary Ellen as the first effort to combat child maltreatment is historically incorrect. Criminal cases involving child abuse were recorded in Massachusetts as early as 1655. Also, in the early 1800s, historical documents reveal that public authorities were legally authorized to remove children from homes where parents were cruel or neglectful. In some communities, laws were in effect for the protection of children, although often they were not enforced (Watkins, 1990).

Historically, it may be more correct to say that the Mary Ellen case represents the beginning of an aggressive effort to combat child maltreatment. The Mary Ellen case prompted the founding of the New York Society for the Prevention of Cruelty to Children and similar so-

> *The Mary Ellen case represents the beginning of an aggressive effort to combat child maltreatment.*

cieties throughout the United States concerned with child maltreatment (Watkins, 1990). The societies for the prevention of cruelty to children organized in many cities across the nation frequently were divisions of already existing organizations concerned with the protection of animals (McCrea, 1910). The American Humane Association, whose mission was animal protection, in 1887 formed a bureau for coordinating the efforts of the many protective services societies. These societies soon discovered, based on their common experiences with children, that their mission could not be limited to rescuing children who were being neglected, abused, or exploited, despite the pressing demand for these efforts. Rather, laws had to be enacted and enforced to ensure protection of children from maltreatment. The various state societies for the protection of children under the auspices of the American Humane Association assumed a leadership role in advocating the enactment and enforcement of legislation protecting children.

Although these societies, as private voluntary agencies, initially assumed primary responsibility for child protective services, this pattern changed with the passage of the Social Security Act in 1935. Child welfare services, including protective services, received federal support under the Social Security Act. In those states where public child welfare services were underdeveloped, however, private child welfare agencies often continued to provide child protective services (Kamerman & Kahn, 1976).

During the initial decades of the 20th century, important legislation on behalf of children was passed. This legislation, although not focusing directly on child maltreatment, provided children with a positive environment for their physical, emotional, and social development. Such legislation included Aid to Dependent Children (ADC), now known as Aid to Families with Dependent Children (AFDC), the Fair Labor Standards Act restricting child labor, and legislation enacted by states requiring schooling for children.

Although a rapid development of protective services agencies occurred in the late 19th and early 20th centuries, concern specifically for child abuse and neglect received little emphasis between 1920 and 1960. Protective services under private agency auspices also declined as interest shifted in these agencies to the development of family counseling services. In many instances, child protective services fell to the responsibility of local departments of public welfare that were overwhelmed in meeting the financial needs of the clients they served (Kadushin & Martin, 1988).

❑ **The Movement Grows**

The development of diagnostic X-ray technology in the 1940s was a significant step forward in discovering child maltreatment. The use of X rays opened up new possibilities for determining injuries in children resulting from physical abuse. Dr. John Caffey (1946), a New York pediatrician, published an article in 1946 in a radiology journal. He shared his observations on six infants who had multiple fractures of long bones and chronic subdural hematoma. Dr. Caffey attempted to explain these observations from a medical perspective based on factors such as injury that may have occurred from convulsive seizures, scurvy, or other skeletal diseases. He ruled out these reasons for the fractures and concluded that "the fractures appear to be of traumatic origin but the traumatic episodes and the causal mechanism remain obscure" (p. 173). Dr. Caffey obviously was suspicious but seemed reluctant and fearful to admit that the injuries could have resulted from child abuse.

Other physicians began to observe children in their practice who appeared to be victims of physical abuse from their parents. Almost two decades later, Dr. C. Henry Kempe and colleagues at the University of Colorado Medical Center published an article in the *Journal of the American Medical Association* in which they labeled the phenomenon being observed—the battered children syndrome (Kempe, Silverman, Steele, Droegemueller, & Silver, 1962). This article brought to public attention a serious problem occurring in the United States, documented by authors who were physicians observing battered children on a regular basis in their offices.

John Demos (1986), a historian, comments on the impact of this article:

> Child abuse evoked an immediate and complex mix of emotions: horror, shame, fascination, disgust. Dr. Kempe and his co-authors noted that physicians themselves experienced "great difficulty . . . in believing that parents could have attacked their children" and often attempted "to obliterate such suspicions from their minds, even in the face of obvious circumstantial evidence." In a sense the problem had long been consigned to a netherworld of things felt but not seen, known but not acknowledged. The "Battered Child" essay was like a shroud torn suddenly aside. Onlookers reacted with shock, but also

perhaps with a kind of relief. The horror was in the open now, and it would not easily be shut up again. (p. 69)

Following identification of the "battered child syndrome," efforts were made to understand this problem theoretically. When the Kempe article was published and for several years following, the psychopathological functioning of the abusive parents was seen theoretically as the reason for child maltreatment. Later, when disciplines other than medicine or psychiatry began to study child maltreatment from an ecological perspective, social and cultural factors were identified as contributing significantly to this problem. Social and cultural factors included, for example, poverty, unemployment, inadequate housing, stress, and the absence of day care resources (Howze-Browne, 1988). The types of factors identified as associated etiologically with child abuse are important relative to the politics of child abuse, an issue to be discussed later in this chapter. Kempe et al. (1962) reflect this narrow theoretical understanding of child abuse in their article on the battered child:

> *Following identification of the "battered child syndrome," efforts were made to understand this problem theoretically.*

> Psychiatric factors are probably of prime importance in the pathogenesis of the disorder, but our knowledge of these factors is limited. Parents who inflict abuse on their children do not necessarily have psychopathic or sociopathic personalities or come from borderline socio-economic groups, although most published cases have been in these categories. In most cases some defect in character structure is probably present; often parents may be repeating the type of child care practiced on them in their childhood. (p. 24)

Following publication of the Kempe article on the battered child, organizations were formed in communities throughout the nation dedicated to identifying, preventing, and treating this serious social problem. In many instances, leadership in these organizations came from individuals who had been victims of child abuse.

❑ Child Abuse Legislation

Several pieces of legislation passed by Congress in recent years have had significant effects on society's response to child maltreatment.

THE CHILD ABUSE PREVENTION AND TREATMENT ACT

In January 1974, Congress passed the Child Abuse Prevention and Treatment Act, Public Law 93-247 (see Appendix A). This historic legislation has had profound effects on the identification, treatment, and prevention of child maltreatment. The passage of this legislation demonstrates how social policy can influence a nation's attempt to cope with a serious social problem at the federal, state, and local levels.

The Child Abuse Prevention and Treatment Act, originally sponsored by Sen. Walter Mondale, created stringent requirements of programs and policies that states had to implement if they wished to secure federal funding for child maltreatment programs. These included the passage of child abuse and neglect laws; procedures for reporting child abuse, including immunity from prosecution of persons doing the reporting; procedures for investigating and adjudicating reported cases; confidentiality of records; training of personnel; and appointment in judicial proceedings of guardians ad litem for children who were victims of child maltreatment. States proceeded to enact statutes in accordance with the act to become eligible for funds.

This historic legislation provided other means for combating child maltreatment. The law provided financial assistance to public and private agencies for demonstration projects that would identify, treat, and prevent child abuse and neglect. The act established the National Center on Child Abuse and Neglect. This center assumed a leadership role in coordinating research on the causes of child abuse, the extent of this social problem in the nation, and the relationship of child abuse and neglect to drug abuse. (See Appendix B for the addresses and telephone numbers of the organizations cited in this chapter and elsewhere.)

The legislation also established the Clearinghouse on Child Abuse and Neglect Information, which designs and maintains bibliographic databases, develops publications, and disseminates materials in response to requests for information. The clearinghouse became a major informational resource for professionals and concerned citizens interested in child maltreatment. It continues to function in this manner. In summary, this historic legislation laid a foundation that public and private organizations continue to build on in their battle against child abuse and neglect.

> *The goal of family-based services is to ensure that every effort is made to maintain the family.*

THE ADOPTION ASSISTANCE AND CHILD WELFARE ACT

This legislation, identified as Public Law 96-272, was passed by Congress in 1980. It prescribes that social services direct their family services to prevent unnecessary substitute placement, to offer rehabilitation and reunification services in order to restore families whose children are in substitute care, and to ensure that permanent plans are made for children who cannot be reunited with their parents.

This legislation mandated a new approach to child welfare services, namely, a family-focused or family-based approach. This approach to the delivery of social services has become known as family-based services.

The goal of family-based services is to ensure that every effort is made to maintain the family as a functioning unit. Family-based services are designed to provide maximum services to a family at a time of crisis, such as a report of child maltreatment, to prevent the breakup of the family. This service delivery approach focuses on families rather than on individuals. Services in this context are intended to strengthen and maintain the family and to prevent family dissolution through foster home placement or the termination of parental rights. This is important in child maltreatment cases, in which children historically often were removed from an abusive home rather than efforts being made to eliminate the dysfunctional behavior and retain the family unit.

❏ The Politics of Child Abuse

What factors account for the passage of federal legislation on child maltreatment when other social problems, such as rape, domestic violence, and alcoholism, do not receive this attention, especially at the federal level? Nelson (1984) comments,

> The rediscovery of child abuse occurred in an era when issues of equity and social responsibility dominated public discourse. A long period of concern with a variety of equity issues began with the civil rights movement in the mid and late 1950s. The 1962 amendments to the Social Security Act urging child welfare services in every county demonstrated that the interests of children were part of the equity cycle. The child welfare amendments were followed by the "War on Poverty," which emphasized the importance of services to children as a method of eliminating poverty. In 1967 the equity cycle was given tremendous impetus by the Supreme Court's *In re Gault* opinion, which extended Bill of Rights protection to children. Later, the months spent crafting the Comprehensive Child Development Act (ultimately vetoed by President Nixon) educated members of Congress to the centrality (and difficulty) of providing adequately for the needs of all children. (p. 12)

The way child maltreatment initially was defined and theoretically understood also contributed to the political success of this issue. The initial definition of child maltreatment focused on the physical abuse of children. Physicians who were seeing this form of child maltreatment in their medical practices proposed this definition. Later, a broader definition was developed, as reflected in the definition used in the 1974 Child Abuse Prevention and Treatment Act (see Appendix A, Section 3). This comprehensive definition included child neglect, mental injury (later to be identified as psychological maltreatment), and sexual abuse. At the same time, research findings began to present a broader theoretical understanding of factors associated with child maltreatment. Initially, the etiology of child abuse was associated with the psychological dysfunctioning of the perpetrator. As the problem of child maltreatment came under scrutiny from scholars in different disciplines, social and cultural factors, such as poverty, inadequate housing, unemployment, and other social problems, became associated with an understanding of the etiology, treatment, and prevention of child maltreatment (Nelson, 1984).

Nelson (1984), commenting on the role the narrow definition played politically in child abuse becoming a national issue, states,

> The definition of child abuse found in the Child Abuse Prevention and Treatment Act provides a more comprehensive statement of the problem than one might expect after reading the transcripts of the legislative hearings. In the public debate over the congressional legislation, comprehensive definitions were actively suppressed to enhance the noncontroversial nature of the issue.
>
> In fact, at each point when child abuse achieved a governmental agenda, the narrow definition was emphasized. The narrow definition predominated during agenda setting for three related reasons. First, agenda setting by the Children's Bureau and state legislatures occurred while the narrow definition was still quite popular. Second, physicians preferred the narrow definition because it best fit their experiences in hospital emergency rooms, and physicians, by virtue of their high status, had easy and early access to officials. Third, and most important, a narrow definition of abuse reduced conflict, particularly from right-wing critics. The use of a narrow definition thwarted a potential conservative challenge to what might be seen as governmental action against normal parental discipline.
>
> Favoring the narrow definition during agenda setting had important, long-lasting effects on the shape of child abuse policy. By ignoring neglect, the connection between poverty and maltreatment was purposely blurred. In fact, strenuous efforts were made to popularize abuse as a problem knowing no barriers of class, race, or culture. For some politicians, particularly Mondale, this was part of a conscious strategy to dissociate efforts against abuse from unpopular poverty programs. The purpose was to describe abuse as an all-American affliction, not one found solely among low-income people. While acknowledging that abuse and neglect were found in all strata of society, a number of scholars severely criticized this approach and maintained that the larger number of cases found among the poor was not only a function of reporting biases, but was present because poor people actually abused or neglected their children more. The message

of the research was not that poor people were bad people or bad parents, but that the deprivations of poverty were real and encouraged abuse. These findings were very unpopular, however, and the "myth of classlessness" promoted during agenda setting was very difficult to counter. (pp. 14-15)

Substantial evidence exists in the literature that social and cultural factors, especially poverty, are significantly related to child maltreatment (Garbarino, 1976; Gil, 1970; Hawkins & Duncan, 1985; National Center on Child Abuse and Neglect, 1988a, 1988b; Pelton, 1978). A denial of this linkage supports a myth of classlessness in child maltreatment. The myth of classlessness serves political interests in that attention is diverted away from a significant causative factor—poverty. Confronting the issue of poverty, however, represents a threat to power structures in society (Kelly & Scott, 1986).

Including child sexual abuse in the definition also would have represented a political threat to the success of passing legislation on child maltreatment. Child sexual abuse, a gender-related form of child maltreatment, represents a significant threat to traditional societal power structures that are male dominated. This threat can be seen from the way society has attempted to ignore the problem of child sexual abuse by denying its existence, minimizing its extent and impact, and even blaming the victim. The denial of intrafamilial sexual abuse, for example, can be seen historically in the writings of Sigmund Freud. Freud reacted to women reporting childhood accounts of sexual seduction by male family members as fantasy and part of the Oedipus complex in women (Masson, 1990; Russell, 1986).

Feminist theorists assert that sexual abuse stems from gender issues in society, namely, male domination and manipulation of women. These writers have pointed out that sexual abuse of females, children as well as adults, can be eradicated only if gender and status are disassociated. This must occur in the workplace, where equal payment must be made for equal work, without regard to gender; in the home, where discrimination by gender must be removed in spousal and

Feminist theorists assert that sexual abuse stems from gender issues in society.

sibling relationships; and in the political arena, where political power should no longer be equated with male gender (Driver, 1989; Van Den Bergh & Cooper, 1986; Waldby, Clancy, Emetchi, & Summerfield, 1989). Again, these issues represent a threat to traditional power structures.

The question of what factors account for the passage of federal legislation on child maltreatment, when other social problems do not receive this attention, may be answered summarily with the following statement: "Government more readily adopts issues which are constructed as social illness than causes which confront long established power arrangements" (Nelson, 1984, p. 17).

❏ Subsequent Child Abuse Legislation

Additional federal legislation relative to the treatment and prevention of child abuse and neglect has been passed since the original Child Abuse Prevention and Treatment Act (PL 93-247) of 1974. This includes Public Law 95-266, passed by Congress in 1978; Public Law 98-457, passed in 1984; and Public Law 100-294, the Child Abuse Prevention, Adoption, and Family Services Act of 1988. These laws amended the original Child Abuse Prevention and Treatment Act of 1974 and provided additional legislation relative to the welfare of children. For example, the Child Abuse Amendments, Public Law 98-457, mandated a nationwide study of the incidence and prevalence of child abuse and neglect, discussed in the previous chapter.

Although significant federal legislation has been passed relative to child maltreatment, in recent years the federal government's role in intervening in this social problem has changed. This is especially evident following President Ronald Reagan's election. In an attempt to balance the budget, responsibility for confronting social problems such as child maltreatment was shifted from the public to the private sector (Nelson, 1984). Government funds for child maltreatment programs were reduced drastically, forcing organizations to depend increasingly on voluntary support.

❑ **Voluntary Organizations Working
in Child Abuse and Neglect**

Voluntary or non-tax-supported agencies play a significant role today in combating child maltreatment. (In some instances, certain agencies may receive federal funding for specific aspects of their programs.) Parents Anonymous (PA) is an example of a voluntary organization and interventive program. Founded in 1970 by Jolly K, a parent with abuse problems, and Leonard Lieber, a licensed clinical social worker, PA was designed to meet the absence of services for families in which child abuse was a problem (Fritz, 1989). Based in part on a model provided by Alcoholics Anonymous, parents having difficulty in parenting have weekly meetings, with parent leaders and professional persons serving as sponsors. The meetings provide parents with an opportunity to share common concerns and problems in parenting and to learn effective parenting methods. The groups also provide valuable support to parents in breaking the social isolation that many abusive and neglectful parents experience. PA chapters have been established in communities throughout the United States.

The National Committee for Prevention of Child Abuse (NCPCA; later the National Committee to Prevent Child Abuse) was established in 1972 by Donna Stone. The mission of the organization focuses on the prevention of child maltreatment. Operating primarily with private or nongovernmental funds, the NCPCA has chapters in all 50 states. This organization disseminates materials on the prevention of child maltreatment that can be used by parents and schools, provides information on effective programs, and translates knowledge about child maltreatment prevention into sound policies and programs through its chapters at the community level.

Several voluntary national organizations reflect a long history of concern for child abuse and neglect. The Child Welfare League of America (CWLA) was established in 1920 as a national accrediting and standard-setting organization for child welfare agencies. This national organization, funded by dues from member agencies (both public and private) throughout the United States and Canada, has as its mission the improvement of services to children. The CWLA takes a strong role in lobbying for legislative action on issues related to child welfare, including day care, residential treatment, homemaker services, foster care, adoption, and protective services. This organization establishes standards for each of these services, conducts research, issues child welfare publications, and sponsors regional conferences. Its *Standards for Services for Abused or Neglected Children and Their Families* (1989) provides guidelines to protective services agencies for the effective provision of services.

The American Association for Protecting Children (AAPC) is the children's division of the American Humane Association. Although initially the organization provided protective services to abused and neglected children, these services largely have been assumed by public (tax-supported) child protective agencies. The American Humane Association provides comprehensive training in the fundamentals of child protective services intervention to personnel of state and local public and private child protective agencies. The association operates the National Resource Center on Child Abuse and Neglect with the goal of improving the capacity of public and private agencies to respond effectively to child maltreatment.

The American Public Welfare Association (APWA), since its founding in 1930, has been concerned with developing and advocating effective public policies directed at improving the lives of low-income individuals and families. In 1988, the APWA's National Association of Public Child Welfare Administrators published *Guidelines for a Model System of Protective Services for Abused and Neglected Children and Their Families*, which has served as a standard for states and communities in assessing child protective services.

❏ Multidisciplinary, Corporate, and International Perspectives

Concern with the prevention and treatment of child abuse has assumed, in recent years, a multidisciplinary, corporate, and international perspective. Numerous disciplines including anthropology, sociology, social work, psychology, medicine, religion, and law are studying this social problem from their unique perspectives. The American Professional Society on the Abuse of Children (APSAC) is an example of an interdisciplinary association of professionals working together in child abuse and neglect prevention and treatment. This organization supports research, education, and advocacy on behalf of abused children and concerning both the perpetrators of abuse and the societal conditions associated with abuse. Membership in the organization includes a subscription to the *Journal of Interpersonal Violence* and a quarterly newsletter titled *The Advisor*.

National professional organizations are taking active roles in educating their memberships to be sensitive to an array of issues associated with child abuse and neglect. For example, the American Academy of Pediatrics, a professional association for certified pediatricians, educates its membership in the identification, investigation, and treatment of child abuse and neglect as well as supporting legislation at the state and federal levels on the prevention and treatment of this social problem.

The American Bar Association Center on Children and the Law, formerly the National Legal Resource Center for Child Advocacy and Protection, confronts child maltreatment and related legal matters by educating attorneys, judges, and other professionals involved in court proceedings affecting children. An annual report of the American Bar Association's Center on Children and the Law (1988) describes the complex situation confronting attorneys working in child abuse and neglect and reflects this national organization's educative efforts:

> No longer can lawyers who deal with child maltreatment cases only be familiar with how to prove the "battered child syndrome." Comprehensive knowledge is required, for example, on how to establish evidence of child sexual abuse and exploitation, emotional maltreatment, and "failure to thrive" infants; how to deal with housing, drug, or mental health problems leading to child protective intervention; how to zealously advocate for children at foster care review proceedings, in termination of parental rights actions, and at special education administrative hearings; and how to work effectively with social workers, physicians, and law court-appointed advocates for the child. (p. 1)

Lawyers prosecuting child maltreatment cases can receive assistance through the National Center for Prosecution of Child Abuse. The American Prosecutors Research Institute founded this organization in 1985 in response to dramatic increases in child abuse cases reported to law enforcement. The organization's mission is to improve the investigation and prosecution of child abuse through court reform, professional specialization, and interagency cooperation. By demanding full accountability for the crime of child abuse, along with comprehensive support services for the child, the center reflects the commitment of prosecutors to a particularly vulnerable group of crime victims. The center serves prosecutors by providing expert training and technical assistance through national and regional conferences, workshops, on-site visits, and phone consultations. The center also serves as an information clearinghouse on court reforms, case law, legislative initiatives, and trial strategies; by facilitating research on reducing trauma in court for child sexual abuse victims and other child victims; and by providing a nationwide network for child abuse prosecutors. The National Center for Prosecution of Child Abuse publishes *Investigation and Prosecution of Child Abuse,* an authoritative manual used by many child abuse prosecutors.

The prevention and treatment of child maltreatment has become a concern of the corporate world as well. In recent years, many voluntary agencies working in child abuse prevention and treatment were forced to look to new sources of funding for their programs because of inflation and cutbacks in federal and state funding. Small and large corporations have become involved at local and national levels by providing financial support for child abuse prevention and treatment programs. Personnel from these corporations volunteer for an array of tasks, ranging from helping in day care centers for abused and neglected children to serving as board members.

The prevention and treatment of child maltreatment has become a concern of the corporate world.

Concern for child abuse and neglect has become global. The International Society for the Prevention of Child Abuse and Neglect was founded in 1977 with the goal of preventing cruelty to children—whether cruelty occurs in the form of abuse, neglect, or exploitation—in every nation, and thus to enable the children of the world to develop physically, mentally, and socially in a healthy and normal manner. The society's past and current boards of directors have comprised representatives from many nations, including Australia, the Netherlands, Norway, Belgium, Israel, Japan, Italy, France, Great Britain, Malaysia, Sweden, Greece, Brazil, Scotland, the Dominican Republic, and the United States. The organization annually sponsors an international conference on child abuse and neglect and publishes a multidisciplinary journal, *Child Abuse & Neglect*. An awareness is developing that the problem of child abuse and neglect is a global one, facing every nation in the world.

❏ Summary

This historical review traces society's attempt to attack a social problem that at first was ignored, then became the concern of a relatively few individuals, and eventually was the focus of important legislation at the federal level. Child maltreatment, a problem at one time considered a private family matter, has developed over the past decades into a serious problem facing American society. Combating child abuse and neglect, closely associated with other social problems such as poverty, requires the efforts of government, voluntary organizations, and concerned citizens.

❏ Suggested Reading

DeMause, L. (1976). *The history of childhood*. London: Souvenir.
Pollack, L. (1983). *Forgotten children*. Cambridge, England: Cambridge University Press.
   These two books present comprehensive and sometimes differing views of the history of childhood. DeMause writes from the perspective of a psychoanalyst. He sees the history of parental love and concern for children looking gloomier the further back one goes. Pollack, on the other

hand, submits historical evidence, from an extensive study of diaries and autobiographical works, of a deep emotional involvement of parents with their children.

Nelson, B. (1984). *Making an issue of child abuse: Political agenda setting for social problems.* Chicago: University of Chicago Press.

This book recounts the history of child abuse policy making over the past three decades and discusses political agenda setting, using the issue of child abuse as an example.

4

Factors Associated With Child Maltreatment

The opening chapter of this book introduced several case examples of child maltreatment: Mr. Roberts, who injured his 5-year-old son, Mike, when disciplining him; Paul, who sexually abused his 8-year-old niece, Melissa; and 17-year-old Linda, who neglected her 2-month-old infant, Cherise. How could a father whip a child so severely that bruises and welts result? What would prompt an uncle to sexually abuse his young niece? How could a mother endanger the life of her infant by caring for the child inadequately? People respond to these questions in a variety of ways—by minimizing the problem, by ignoring it, by blaming the victim, or by simply saying, out of frustration, "These people are sick, they're crazy."

To respond in these ways neither helps the victim nor prevents the problem from occurring again. Human service professionals faced with the responsibility of working with individuals and families in cases of child maltreatment must try to understand the problem. As you begin to understand why child abuse and neglect may occur, you can identify ways to treat the individuals involved and prevent the problem from occurring in other families. Research helps in this process by identifying factors that may contribute to the problem. This chapter will present factors associated with the various types and forms of child maltreatment.

❑ Factors Associated With Child Neglect

Three categories of factors will be identified for each of the types of child maltreatment. These categories are individual-related factors, family-related factors, and social and cultural factors.

INDIVIDUAL-RELATED FACTORS

Initial studies of factors associated with child neglect focused on the mothers' personality characteristics. In families where neglect was prevalent, the mothers were described as childlike, dependent, impulsive, unable to assume responsibility, showing poor judgment, and exhibiting ego deficits (Meier, 1964; Nurse, 1964; Young, 1964). Neglectful mothers living in the mountains of Appalachia were seen as apathetic-futile because they were passive, lacking in affective expression, and withdrawn in their behavior. They appeared to be verbally inaccessible in that they were not able to discuss feelings and attitudes with others (Polansky, Borgman, & DeSaix, 1972; Polansky, Chalmers, Buttenwieser, & Williams, 1981).

Findings from these studies, if not interpreted from an ecological perspective, inappropriately blame and label the mothers. An ecological perspective presents human behavior not as occurring in a vacuum, an impression left by early personality theorists, but rather as resulting from complex interactions of individuals and families with their social and cultural environments (Germain & Gitterman, 1980).

If these findings are interpreted from an ecological perspective, several factors may be noted. First, emphasis was placed on the intrapsychic functioning of these mothers, using psychoanalytic theory, without recognizing social and cultural constraints. Second, many of the mothers were functioning in powerless, gender-related roles in their families. They received little social and physical support from their mates and had very limited social networks. (Although African Americans were not included in the Polansky et al. samples, the variable of race, in addition to gender, has been found to be important in studies of child neglect.) Third, the mothers often were caught in an intergenerational cycle of neglect. According to the concept of modeling from social learning theory, their functioning resulted, in part, from the deprivation they experienced from their parents, which they in turn were repeating in their own lives. Fourth, the findings fail to account for the environment in which these families were living. For example, Appalachia comprised some of the poorest counties in the United States. Inadequate educational facilities, insufficient mental health and social services, and rigid social stratification characterized this geographical area (Chilman, 1973). Large corporations, interested only in profits from mining coal and having little or no regard for the residents' welfare, were ravaging the area (Caudill, 1963).

In addition to the stress factors of insufficient income and inadequate housing, mothers often were forced to assume primary parenting responsibilities. Gender-related role prescriptions were partly responsible for this; however, many husbands were not able to assist their wives because of the long hours they worked, the strenuous nature of their employment, or physical injuries (or even their absence because of death) resulting from their hazardous employment in the mines. Finally, cultural restraints operating among Appalachian families that prohibited sharing feelings and attitudes with others, especially individuals from outside the community, contributed to their verbal inaccessibility (Polansky, Borgman, DeSaix, & Sharlin, 1971; Polansky et al., 1981).

Children born to mothers who used drugs during pregnancy were at a higher risk of subsequent neglect.

More recent research shows that children born to mothers who used drugs during pregnancy were at a higher risk of subsequent neglect than were children from the general population (Jaudes, Ekwo, & Voorhis, 1995). Neglect was defined by the researchers as inadequate supervision, feeding, clothing, or provision of shelter;

medical neglect or abandonment; failure to thrive; malnutrition; and environmental neglect.

Mothers who neglect their children tend to exhibit higher rates of depression as compared to nonneglectful mothers. The neglectful mothers also experience a high degree of stress. The mothers may react to the high stress and depression by resigning from their parental role (Ethier, Lacharite, & Couture, 1995).

FAMILY-RELATED FACTORS

Absence of Father. Research identifies the absence of a father in a family to be a significant factor in child neglect (Polansky et al., 1981). A father's absence from a family generally means that the family has a markedly lower income than when the father is present. Also, when fathers are absent, mothers lack emotional support from a mate, an important factor in child neglect.

Dysfunctional Parent-Child Relationships. In families in which child neglect occurs, a predominance of negative rather than positive contacts was found among family members (Burgess & Conger, 1977; Reid, 1978). Researchers have analyzed the nature of family interactions using in-person observations in the families' homes in a sample of neglectful and abusive families and a matched control group of nonneglectful and nonabusive families (Burgess & Conger, 1977; Reid, 1978). The data revealed that in families where neglect was occurring, family members, as a whole, directed positive contacts to one another significantly less often than did their matched control families. Neglectful mothers also were found to direct more negative contacts to their children than did their matched controls. The negative contacts may reflect the mothers' poor parenting skills, which in turn contributed to the neglect found in these families.

Disengagement of Family Members. Parental failure to attend to the physical and emotional needs of a child is associated with a form of child neglect identified as nonorganic failure to thrive. Parental lack of attention, conceptualized as parental disengagement, generally is associated with stress or crises occurring in a family (Alderette &

deGraffenried, 1986). Stress or crises may include unemployment, physical illness, financial difficulties, and similar social or environmental problems. Crises of this nature require a family to rally and respond. In cases of nonorganic failure to thrive, however, the family fails to rally and respond because of factors such as the persistency of the stress and poor coping skills (Minuchin, 1974). Family members distance or detach themselves from one another, most visibly seen in communication patterns. The child's physical and emotional needs become lost in the process, and neglect may occur. In some instances, the disengagement response may represent a generational pattern of family functioning.

SOCIAL AND CULTURAL FACTORS

Poverty. Poverty is a significant factor in child neglect (Kotch et al., 1995). The National Incidence Studies, referred to earlier, identified inadequate income as a risk factor for child neglect (National Center on Child Abuse and Neglect, 1988a, 1988b).

Wolock and Horowitz (1979) found the absence of adequate financial resources to be a significant factor in a sample of maltreating families, a large portion of whom had been reported for neglect. The researchers described the world of poverty for these families as "one in which they and the communities in which they live are without many of the things most Americans regard as essential for a minimal standard of living" (Wolock & Horowitz, 1979, p. 186). Similarly, Hawkins and Duncan (1985), in studying the family characteristics of a sample of 647 adults reported for child neglect, found that 85% of the male adults were unemployed, thus creating severe financial difficulties for the family.

Giovannoni and Billingsley (1970) studied a sample of 186 families of three different ethnic backgrounds (Black, Caucasian, and Hispanic) to determine the extent to which economic factors related to child neglect in these families. Researchers rated families according to the level of child care they were providing: adequate, potentially neglectful, and neglectful. All the families were on public assistance, but the neglectful families were significantly poorer than the other two groups (Giovannoni & Billingsley, 1970).

Social Isolation. Social isolation and alienation are factors distinguishing neglectful families from other families living in poverty (Polansky et al., 1981; Wolock & Horowitz, 1979). Researchers report that mothers in families in which neglect occurs frequently do not associate with neighbors and are critical of the community in which they live. Although family members and neighbors were reasonably accessible to the mothers geographically, the mothers rarely or never visited with their siblings or made contact with neighbors. Thus, there were far fewer persons in their social networks compared to nonneglectful families of the same economic level. Their social isolation exacerbated the neglect by preventing them from utilizing resources readily available to them in their community, such as free lunch programs, that could have alleviated some of their problems (Hally, Polansky, & Polansky, 1980).

❏ Factors Associated With Physical Abuse

Three categories of factors associated with physical abuse will be discussed: individual-related, family-related, and social and cultural.

INDIVIDUAL-RELATED FACTORS

Parental Abuse as a Child. The intergenerational theory of abuse is one of the most frequently cited in association with child physical abuse. This theory suggests that children who were victims of physical abuse in turn abuse their children when they become parents. This theory is based largely on self-reports from abusive parents rather than on data from rigorous empirical studies (Baldwin & Oliver, 1975; Conger, Burgess, & Barrett, 1979; Elmer, 1960; Green, Gaines, & Sandgrund, 1974; Johnson & Morse, 1968; Nurse, 1964; Oliver & Taylor, 1971; Paulson & Chaleff, 1973; Silver, Dublin, & Lourie, 1969). Although being physically abused as a child may put one at risk for treating children in a similar way (Bagley, Wood, & Young, 1994), many circumstances mitigate against this happening. These include the influence of a mate who did not experience abuse, parents' commitment not to treat their children the way they were treated, and parental acquisition of new parenting knowledge and skills that do not support the use of physical abuse (Kaufman & Zigler, 1987; Wiehe, 1992).

Inappropriate Expectations. Parents holding unrealistic expectations of themselves and their children may resort to physical abuse when these expectations are not realized. Unrealistic parental self-expectations may be seen, for example, in assuming continuous responsibility for child care without the use of baby-sitters or day care (Hawkins & Duncan, 1985). This expectation may prevent a mother from pursuing desired career goals or assisting in the financial support of the family, thereby putting stress on the mother and family. Unrealistic expectations of children often focus on issues such as premature toilet training, cessation of crying, and achievements in school and extracurricular activities (Bavolek, 1989; Berg, 1976; Clark, 1975; Kravitz & Driscoll, 1983).

> *Parents holding unrealistic expectations of themselves and their children may resort to physical abuse.*

Stress. Inadequate financial resources, marital problems, and negative life experiences may create stress on parents that may in turn affect their parenting abilities and put them at risk to be physically abusive to a child (Burrell, Thompson, & Sexton, 1994; Chan, 1994; Hawkins & Duncan, 1985; Whipple & Webster-Stratton, 1991). Research shows, for example, that listening to long hours of infant crying can produce high levels of stress in parents (Tyson & Sobschak, 1994).

Inadequate Parenting Skills. Inadequate parental knowledge and skills are associated with the physical abuse of children. In one study, for example, poor problem-solving abilities discriminated between samples of abusive and nonabusive mothers (Azar, Robinson, Hekimian, & Twentyman, 1984). Abusive parents demonstrated a narrow or limited repertoire of responses to problems commonly encountered in their child-rearing experiences, such as in the area of discipline. Parental frustration and inability to cope effectively with child-rearing problems may result in the use of severe forms of corporal punishment as a way of maintaining control over children (Reid, Taplin, & Lorber, 1981).

Role Reversal. Reversal of parent and child roles is associated with the physical abuse of children. Role reversal occurs when children are expected to be sensitive to and responsible for the happiness and emotional well-being of the parents (Ackley, 1977; Bavolek, 1984; Steele, 1975). Parental role reversal may be associated with emotional deprivation that adults experienced early in their own life for which they attempt to compensate by turning to their children. Parenting generally requires more emotional giving to children rather than taking from them. When parents become frustrated in not having emotional needs met by their children, they may resort to physical abuse as well as psychological maltreatment.

Lack of Empathy Toward Children's Needs. Child rearing demands that parents be empathic—that is, able to identify with how a child may be feeling and to respond accordingly. Research indicates that abusive mothers are less empathic toward their children than are nonabusive mothers (LeTourneau, 1981; Wiehe, 1987). Studies identify the ability to empathize as a moderating or controlling variable for individuals in psychological experiments who were asked to administer an electrical shock to a person in another room. Those individuals scoring high on empathy measurements were not able to administer an electrical shock (Feshbach, 1964; Feshbach & Feshbach, 1969; Mehrabian & Epstein, 1972). It was as if they were saying to themselves, "How would I feel if someone were doing this to me?" Likewise, empathic parents may avoid physically abusive behavior, such as slapping a child across the face or whipping a child with a belt, because they are able to identify with how they would feel if they were the child. Similarly, research shows that empathic mothers are not provoked to anger by their infants' crying. Such crying can lead less empathic mothers to abuse infants by violently shaking them. Empathic mothers identify with their children's discomfort and attempt to meet their needs (Frodi, 1981; Frodi & Lamb, 1980).

Substance Abuse. Research shows a significant relationship between substance abuse and physical child abuse (Behling, 1979; Famularo, Kinscherff, & Fenton, 1992; Famularo, Stone, Barnum, & Wharton, 1986; Murphy et al., 1991). In a review of 190 randomly selected records from the caseload of a large juve- nile court, researchers found that 67% of the cases involved parents who could be classified as substance abusers. Alcohol abuse was related significantly to physical abuse, and cocaine abuse to sexual mal- treatment (Famularo et al., 1992).

> *Alcohol abuse was related significantly to physical abuse, and cocaine abuse to sexual maltreatment.*

A study of children born to mothers who used drugs during pregnancy showed that the children were at a higher risk of subsequent abuse than were children from the general population (Jaudes et al., 1995). Children born at an urban medical center during a 5-year period whose mothers used drugs during their pregnancy were identified using results of toxicology screens from birth and maternal records. Evidence of child maltreatment was obtained from the State Central Registry of Abuse and Neglect. One hundred fifty-five (30.2%) of the 513 children exposed in utero to drugs were reported as abused, and 102 (19.9%) of these had substantiated reports. The rate of abuse was two to three times that of children living in the same geographic, high-abuse-risk area of the city in which the research occurred.

Relationship to Child. Research shows that mothers' boyfriends are responsible for substantially more child abuse than are other non-parental caregivers, even though they perform relatively little child care. Several reasons are suggested for this finding. Mothers' boyfriends tended to use more physical coercion than other caregivers, possibly because their social role lacked legitimate authority. Violent outbursts by a boyfriend against his girlfriend's child or children appeared to be associated with either the boyfriend siding with the mother against the child or the boyfriend perceiving that the mother and child were against him (Margolin, 1992). The boyfriend also may not be bonded to or have formed a relationship with the child.

Mother's Age. Research shows that the age of the mother is a significant factor associated with the physical abuse of a child. The age of the mother at the time of the child's birth, rather than at the time the abuse occurred, was related significantly to child abuse in a sample of nearly 2,000 abusive mothers. The data suggest that abuse may be associated with the mother's young age at the time of her child's birth. Her immaturity, lack of education, and low income place her at risk for not being able to handle the stress of parenthood (Connelly & Straus, 1992).

FAMILY-RELATED FACTORS

Interaction of Parents and Children. Parents may abuse their children as a futile last effort to gain control, or at least some degree of balance, in parent-child relationships (Patterson, 1982). A major cause for such a breakdown in family equilibrium is a lack of skill by the parents in handling discipline and in teaching their children appropriate social skills. The result is that parents correctly perceive that they have lost control of the child and thus believe that the child is manipulating and controlling them. Parents experience a growing feeling of hostility toward the child and vice versa. At some point in this escalating cycle, the frustrated parent may strike out in an attempt to gain control (Lorber, Felton, & Reid, 1984; Patterson, 1982; Reid et al., 1981).

Family Composition. Gender of children, age of children, and family size are factors associated with child physical abuse. Female children experience physical abuse more often than do males. The National Incidence Studies found that the risk of death resulting from physical abuse was greatest in the youngest age groups (2 years of age and under). Older children tended to sustain moderate injury or impairment. Children from families with four or more children were more endangered and experienced more physical abuse in comparison with children from smaller families (National Center on Child Abuse and Neglect, 1988a, 1988b).

SOCIAL AND CULTURAL FACTORS

Poverty. Low income is a significant risk factor for child abuse, as was indicated earlier for child neglect. The 1985 National Incidence Study found a physical abuse rate of 8.4 of each 1,000 children from families with less than $15,000 in annual income, as compared to 2.4 for families with incomes of $15,000 or more.

Economic distress was a factor distinguishing differences in child abuse rates among several New York counties (Garbarino, 1976). This study found that economic distress frequently occurred because women were earning substantially less than men as a result of gender discrimination. Poverty limited the mothers' access to educational, recreational, and day care resources for their children. The use of these resources could have reduced stress associated with the mothers' physical abuse.

Undesirable economic change leads to increased child maltreatment. Financial difficulties resulting from high job loss in two geographic areas in California were found, over a 30-month period, to be associated with increases in child abuse (Steinberg, Catalano, & Dooley, 1981).

Social Isolation. Physical abuse of children is associated with parents not having access to supportive services and social networks. Resources such as day care or family members can provide respite to parents overwhelmed with the stress of parenting and other life stresses (Hawkins & Duncan, 1985).

Cultural and Religious Values Regarding Corporal Punishment. Cultural and religious values may support the use of corporal punishment, including severe forms involving whipping or beating a child with a rod, which may be labeled as physically abusive. Biblical texts, if taken literally, are used to advocate corporal punishment of children (Proverbs 13:24, 19:18, and 22:15; Hebrews 12:5-10). The text of Proverbs 13:14, "He who spares the rod hates his son, but he who loves him is careful to discipline," is often shortened to the proverbial form: "Spare the rod and spoil the child." Old Testament scholars point out that the biblical text is very different from the proverb. The proverb makes a causal link between the use of the rod and its effect on the child—spoiling the child. The biblical text, however, refers to the attitudes of the caregiver and makes no reference to the effect of the discipline on the child. Rather, it appeals to providing love and careful discipline. Finally, the rod probably refers to a shepherd's staff used to guide sheep, not to beat them (Carey, 1994).

Theological dogma may view children as inherently corrupt and sinful. Consequently, the deduction inappropriately may be made that children are in need of severe discipline to correct this state (Greven, 1977). These views are seen most prominently in the Bible Belt of the southern part of the United States (Flynn, 1994). In a sample of 881 members of religious denominations classified as literal or nonliteral believers in the Bible, persons who were members of churches subscribing to a literal belief in the Bible preferred the use of corporal punishment over alternate methods of discipline (Wiehe, 1990a).

❏ Factors Associated With Psychological Maltreatment

Psychological maltreatment, as defined earlier, in addition to being a distinct type of child abuse, generally is a component in all other types of child maltreatment (Hart & Brassard, 1987). Thus, factors associated with other types of maltreatment may be applicable to understanding psychological abuse. Following are factors identified from research as associated specifically with psychological maltreatment. Again, the discussion will be divided into the categories of individual-related, family-related, and social and cultural factors.

INDIVIDUAL-RELATED FACTORS

Parents who repress emotions (pain, sadness, joy, anger) may encourage similar behavior in children and thus be unresponsive to children's emotional needs (Brassard & Gelardo, 1987; Miller, 1983). Cultural factors may reinforce such parental behavior. Children may respond to parental denial of emotions by feeling unloved and unwanted. This parental behavior may be identified as psychological abuse.

FAMILY-RELATED FACTORS

Parental Scapegoating. Children can become the scapegoats for problems occurring in the marital relationship: Parents may attribute their own problems to their children. This may occur through parents blaming children for marital conflicts, through attributing family financial problems to expenses associated with raising children, and through projecting personal dislikes and frustrations on a child who resembles a spouse (Garbarino & Vondra, 1987). This behavior is emotionally abusive for children because they unjustly are made to feel responsible for their parents' problems or that it would be better if they did not exist.

Parent-Child Communication Patterns. Psychological maltreatment may be seen in parental communication consisting primarily of aversive exchanges (emphasizing what children are doing wrong) and the absence of prosocial communication (verbally rewarding children for good behavior). Parental communication consisting primarily of aversive exchanges may reinforce negative behaviors in the child (whining, pestering, misbehaving) as a way of gaining parental attention even though, in a cyclical fashion, the attention prompts further emotional abuse. The aversive nature of the parents' communication with the child negatively affects the child's self-esteem and self-worth (Patterson, 1982).

Inappropriate Expectations. A child's failure to meet parental expectations that may be unreasonably high or inappropriate to a child's abilities affects the child's self-concept, self-esteem, and self-confidence (Bateson, 1972; Bavolek, 1984; Garbarino & Vondra, 1987). Inappropriate expectations frequently are created when parents compare a child with siblings who have different abilities and talents. Unrealistic and inappropriate expectations also may result when parents lack knowledge of child developmental stages and accompanying cognitive and social skills. Parents may resort to psychological pressures that can be emotionally abusive in an attempt to coerce children to meet inappropriate expectations (Burgess & Conger, 1977; Patterson, 1979).

SOCIAL AND CULTURAL FACTORS

Stress. Parents may be so overwhelmed with problems and stresses in their own lives that they fail to be sensitive to and meet the emotional needs of their children. This may result in children feeling rejected and unwanted. Stress factors associated with this form of emotional abuse may include too large a family, inadequate financial resources, and parental drug and alcohol abuse, as well as a general climate in the family in which there is an absence of emotional support among family members (Garbarino & Vondra, 1987).

Sex-Role Stereotyping. Treating children differently on the basis of gender may result in psychological maltreatment. Parental beliefs and expectations about gender-appropriate behavior may influence the way parents treat children, with the result that children are not allowed to develop to their full potential (Telzrow, 1987). Parents may be reinforced in these beliefs and practices by religious and cultural values, as well as by the differential way in which genders are portrayed in the public media (Downs & Gowan, 1980; Mamay & Simpson, 1981).

❏ Factors Associated With Child Sexual Abuse

Prior to discussing factors identified in research as associated with child sexual abuse, four aspects important for understanding this social problem will be discussed: the context in which sexual abuse occurs, adults' belief of children's reports of sexual abuse, the sexual and nonsexual components of sexual abuse, and the psychopathology of perpetrators.

THE CONTEXT IN WHICH
SEXUAL ABUSE OCCURS

The media frequently portray child sexual abuse as occurring in the context of a child being lured away from its parents, for example on a playground or in a supermarket, and subsequently being molested by a stranger. Sexual abuse by strangers occurs far less frequently than abuse by relatives and acquaintances. Studies report that 75% to 80% of offenders are related to or known to the victim (Finkelhor, 1979; Finkelhor et al., 1990; MacFarlane et al., 1986; Tsai & Wagner, 1978). The perpetrator may be the father, a stepparent, a boyfriend, a grandfather, an uncle, a brother, a neighbor, a teacher, or a scout leader, or even a member of the clergy. The perpetrator will be referred to as masculine in gender because research tends to present men predominantly as the abusers of girls and boys (Finkelhor, 1984a). This is not meant to imply, however, that sexual abuse perpetrators are always male. An underreporting of female sexual offenders occurs because male victims are less likely than female victims to disclose sexual abuse (Rudin, Zalewski, & Bodmer-Turner, 1995). Victimization by a female perpetrator can have results as devastating as victimization by a male perpetrator, even though the former may not have been reported to mental health, social service, or criminal justice agencies (Johnson & Shrier, 1987).

> *Sexual abuse by strangers occurs far less frequently than abuse by relatives and acquaintances.*

Because most perpetrators of sexual abuse are known to the victim, the context in which sexual abuse occurs involves the victim implicitly trusting the perpetrator because of the loving relationship between the two persons, such as a grandfather and his granddaughter, or because of the authority role of the perpetrator, such as the scout leader and a scout. This violation of trust significantly affects the victim's ability to trust others in the future (Agosta & Loring, 1988).

Sexual abuse also occurs in the context of enticement and subsequent entrapment. The perpetrator may entice and then entrap the victim by indicating that the latter is someone special and that the sexual activity will be a mutually held secret between the two of them. This context may be reinforced by the offender giving the victim gifts, such as candy, special favors, or privileges. In other instances, as frequently occurs in sexual abuse between siblings, threat of physical injury is used by the perpetrator to force the victim to comply with his wishes (Wiehe, 1990b). The victim becomes entrapped in the desire to please the perpetrator, whom the victim trusts and respects, or the victim feels that she must comply for the sake of her or his own safety (Summit, 1983). The outcome of this scenario, as frequently seen in adults who were sexually abused as children, is self-blame for allowing oneself to become entrapped. In reality, however, the victim may have had no choice but to comply because she or he did not understand what was happening or was operating under a threat.

BELIEF IN REPORTS OF SEXUAL ABUSE

Another important aspect of child sexual abuse is the disbelief and blame children often experience when reporting their sexual victimization to a parent or another adult. When sexual abuse occurs from an offender the victim knows, a tendency exists for adults receiving the report to disbelieve it. A mother's denial of a child's report of sexual victimization may be linked to her own past victimization that she continues to defend against and deny.

Although popular media at times give the impression that a large percentage of child abuse reports are unfounded, clinical observations (Goodwin, Sahd, & Rada, 1982; Peters, 1976; Sorensen & Snow, 1991) and empirical data do not support this impression. Jones and McGraw (1987) studied 576 child sexual abuse reports made to the Denver Department of Social Services. Seventy percent of these reports were reliable, 22% were considered suspicious but unsubstantiated, and 8% were fictitious. Fictitious reports were examined in detail from a clinical perspective. No distinctive feature clearly distinguished fictitious from reliable reports. For example, an absence of emotion in describing an abusive incident, at times taken as an indicator of fictitious reporting, was found to be indicative of earlier abuse the victim had experienced and the victim's repression of emotional reactions to her earlier victimization. The authors concluded that fictitious allegations are unusual and that sexual abuse reports, even when appearing on the surface as suspicious, should be investigated carefully.

Only 56% of the mothers believed the reports if the offender was a stepfather or live-in partner.

Sirles and Franke (1989), in a study of children's disclosure of intrafamilial sexual abuse, found that mothers were most likely to believe the report of sexual abuse if the offender was a member of the extended family, such as a grandfather, an uncle, or a cousin. Mothers believed their children in 92% of these situations. Their belief of their children's sexual abuse reports decreased to 85% if the offender was a biological father. Only 56% of the mothers believed the reports if the offender was a stepfather or live-in partner. Several reasons may account for the latter. As occurs in blended families, or where the mother is bringing a boyfriend into the home, the children may not accept the new individual. The mother senses the resentment and assumes that the sexual abuse report is the child's attempt to get rid of the stepfather or friend. In addition, after an earlier failed marriage or relationship, the emotional investment a mother has in a relationship with a new husband or live-in partner may account for her unwillingness to believe a child's report of sexual abuse by such an individual.

In this study, the age of the child was an important factor in whether the report of abuse would be believed. If the child was of preschool age (2 to 5), 95% of the mothers believed the child's report of abuse. For children of latency age (6 to 11), 82% of their mothers believed them. If the child was a teenager (12 to 17), belief occurred in only 64% of the cases (Sirles & Franke, 1989). Several reasons may exist for the age factor. Mothers may tend to believe sexual abuse reports from very young children because they lack sexual experience and the ability to make up details about sexual exploitation. Younger children also are more attached to their mothers, and the latter consequently may be more willing to believe them than to believe older children. Conversely, teenagers are less attached to their mothers, possess sexual information enabling them to falsify a sexual abuse report, and may even be known by the parents to be sexually active (Sirles & Franke, 1989).

Research also shows that the attitude of a child's caretaker is an important factor in a child disclosing sexual abuse. Children with caretakers willing to even consider the possibility of abuse were more than 3.5 times as likely to disclose than those whose caretakers did not take such an open stance (Lawson & Chaffin, 1992).

Similarly, Benward and Densen-Gerber (1975), in a study of sub-stance abusing women who had been sexually abused as children, found that in those cases in which the victim had consented pas-sively, the mother gave her daughter little emotional support or did not protect her from future abuse. The more typical reaction was for the mother not to believe the daughter, to become angry with her, and to blame her.

Parental disbelief of reports of sexual abuse may affect a child in various ways. Summit (1983) categorized the typical ways in which female children who are victims of sexual assault by adults known to them respond to their abuse. He identifies these responses as the "child sexual abuse accommodation syndrome." Five components compose this syndrome: secrecy; helplessness; entrapment and ac-commodation; delayed, unconvincing disclosure; and retraction. The first two components describe the victim's vulnerable position. As indicated earlier, the perpetrator approaches the victim in the context of secrecy. Frequently, the young victim is helpless. The child may have been instructed to obey adults, may have been threatened by the perpetrator, and may not have been taught how she can attempt to prevent her victimization. The next three components describe a sequential process occurring for the victim. Following entrapment and submitting to the sexual abuse, the child may wait a while before telling anyone. For example, a young girl reported her sexual victimi-zation by a visiting uncle from a distant city a year later, when her parents announced that he was returning for another visit. When disclosure is made, it may not be convincing, and individuals close to the victim may disbelieve or blame the victim. The perpetrator responds to confrontations about the alleged abuse by engaging in excessive denial or attempting to shift responsibility for the sexual misconduct to the victim or to someone else. The victim accommo-

dates to the pressures and consequences experienced in the disclosure process, and as a way of retreating, denies that the abuse really
did occur.

Sorensen and Snow (1991), studying 630 cases of alleged child
sexual abuse, concluded that disclosure is a process, not an event.
The authors believed that their data did not support the common
presumption that most abused children are capable of immediate
active disclosure of their sexual victimization. Children composing
the research sample were not able to provide a coherent, detailed
account of their sexual victimization in an initial investigative interview. In some instances, children disclosed the sexual abuse in a very
tentative manner, subsequently recanted the disclosure, and only
later reaffirmed the original report of their victimization (Gonzalez,
Waterman, Kelly, McCord, & Oliveri, 1993).

SEXUAL AND NONSEXUAL
COMPONENTS OF SEXUAL ABUSE

Another important aspect of child sexual abuse is that the offender's behavior has both sexual and nonsexual components. The
sexual component, seen in the touching, caressing, sexual arousal,
and orgasm experienced by the perpetrator, may be a primary or
secondary factor in the abuse. The nonsexual component may include power, control, an expression of anger, dominance over the
victim, or fulfillment of identification and affiliation needs (Groth,
1979). Both sexual and nonsexual components must be considered in
understanding child sexual abuse.

THE PSYCHOPATHOLOGY OF PERPETRATORS

Historically, theories about child sexual abuse have focused on the
offender's psychopathology, namely, that perpetrators of child sexual abuse were a small group of highly deviant individuals and that
their psychopathology was the cause of the abuse. This view of
sexual abuse perpetrators has been based on the type of samples
studied, namely, incarcerated perpetrators (Finkelhor, 1984a). Incarcerated perpetrators, however, represent only a small fraction of
individuals engaging in child sexual abuse. Those incarcerated may

not be representative of adults engaging in this behavior who otherwise are functioning normally in society.

Two studies cited earlier demonstrate the small number of perpetrators ever brought to court for their offense (Finkelhor et al., 1990; Russell, 1986). In the Finkelhor et al. (1990) study, the researchers found in a national sample of adult men and women that 27% of the women and 16% of the men reported a history of childhood sexual abuse. Nearly half of these men and a third of the women never disclosed their abuse to anyone. Thus, it is likely that only a very small percentage of the perpetrators were ever prosecuted.

> *Sexual interest in children may be far more common than generally thought.*

Russell (1986), in a survey of 930 women in the San Francisco area, found 648 cases of child sexual abuse before the age of 18. Only 5% percent, or 30 cases (4 cases of incestuous abuse and 26 cases of extrafamilial child sexual abuse), were ever reported to the police. Only 7 of these 30 cases were known to result in convictions.

Thus, sexual abuse may not involve a small, extremely deviant subgroup of the population. Rather, sexual interest in children may be far more common than generally thought in our culture. In a survey of 193 male undergraduate students regarding their sexual interest in children, 21% of the respondents reported sexual attraction to some small children. Of these, 9% described having sexual fantasies involving children, 5% admitted to having masturbated to such fantasies, and 7% indicated some inclination to have sex with a child if they could avoid being caught (Briere & Runtz, 1989). Adult sexual interest in children, in part, may be stimulated by child pornography and the sexualization of children as seen in films and advertising, in which children assume roles of miniature adults (Finkelhor, 1984a).

FOUR PRECONDITIONS OF SEXUAL ABUSE

Factors in understanding child neglect, physical abuse, and psychological maltreatment have been organized according to individual, family, and social and cultural categories. Finkelhor (1984a) integrates these categories into a comprehensive theoretical model for understanding child sexual abuse, identified as the Four Preconditions of Sexual Abuse.

Finkelhor argues for a multifactor theoretical model for understanding child sexual abuse because of the complexity of the problem. This model places earlier theories on the subject (Lukianowicz, 1972; Lystad, 1975; Tierney & Corwin, 1983) into an organizing framework. Finkelhor (1984a) states,

> Most approaches (theories) have tended to emphasize a few factors such as deviant patterns of sexual arousal or psychosexual immaturity. However, there is a large range of behaviors that needs to be explained. It includes the man who spends his whole life fixated on ten-year-old boys, or the man who after many years of heterosexual fidelity to his wife is possessed by a strong impulse to caress his granddaughter's genitals, or the man who persuades his girlfriend to help bring a child into their bed to "experience something new," or the adolescent, preoccupied with his lack of sexual experience, who forces his younger sister to have sex with him, or the father who promiscuously fondles all his daughters and all the friends they bring home. To explain all this diversity, a multifactor model that matches a variety of explanations to a variety of different kinds of abusers is needed. (p. 36)

Finkelhor's model for understanding child sexual abuse is based on four preconditions that must be met before abuse can occur. The model can be generalized to different types of sexual abuse within the context of intra- and extrafamilial abuse. The model incorporates both psychological and sociological factors. The preconditions include the following:

I. The potential perpetrator must have some motivation for sexually abusing a child.

II. The potential perpetrator must overcome internal inhibitions against following through on this motivation.

III. The potential perpetrator must overcome external barriers to following through on his motivation.

IV. The potential perpetrator or some other factor must influence, undermine, or overcome a child's possible resistance to the sexual abuse (Finkelhor, 1984a, p. 54).

BOX 4.1

Preconditions for Sexual Abuse

| | *Level of Explanation* | |
	Individual	*Social/Cultural*
Precondition I: **Factors related to motivation to sexually abuse**		
Emotional congruence	Arrested emotional development Need to feel powerful and controlling Reenactment of childhood trauma to undo the hurt Narcissistic identification with self as a young child	Masculine requirement to be dominant and powerful in sexual relationships
Sexual arousal	Childhood sexual experience that was traumatic or strongly conditioning Modeling of sexual interest in children by someone else Misattribution of arousal cues Biologic abnormality	Child pornography Erotic portrayal of children in advertising Male tendency to sexualize all emotional needs
Blockage	Oedipal conflict Castration anxiety Fear of adult females Traumatic sexual experience with adult Inadequate social skills Marital problems	Repressive norms about masturbation and extramarital sex
Precondition II: **Factors predisposing to overcoming internal inhibitors**	Alcohol Psychosis Impulse disorder Senility Failure of incest inhibition in family dynamics	Social toleration of sexual interest in children Weak criminal sanctions against offenders

BOX 4.1

Continued

	Level of Explanation	
	Individual	*Social/Cultural*
		Ideology of patriarchal prerogatives for fathers
		Social tolerance for deviance committed while intoxicated
		Child pornography
		Male inability to identify with needs of children
Precondition III: **Factors** **predisposing to** **overcoming** **external** **inhibitors**	Mother who is absent or ill	Lack of social supports
	Mother who is not close to or protective of child	Barriers to women's equality
	Mother who is dominated or abused by father	Erosion of social networks
	Social isolation of family	Ideology of family sanctity
	Unusual opportunities to be alone with child	
	Lack of supervision of child	
	Unusual sleeping or rooming conditions	
Precondition IV: **Factors** **predisposing to** **overcoming** **child's** **resistance**	Child who is emotionally insecure or deprived	Unavailability of sex education for children
	Child who lacks knowledge about sexual abuse	Social powerlessness of children
	Situation of unusual trust between child and offender	
	Coercion	

SOURCE: Adapted from *Child Sexual Abuse: New Theory and Research,* Finkelhor, © copyright 1984 by David Finkelhor. Reprinted with permission of The Free Press, a division of Simon & Schuster.

Precondition I: Motivation to Sexually Abuse. Precondition I suggests that there are reasons for adults being sexually interested in
children. Three reasons are identified: emotional congruence, sexual
arousal, and blockage (Finkelhor, 1984a).

Emotional congruence suggests that an adult may find relating to
a child emotionally gratifying. The emphasis is on emotional rather
than sexual gratification. As stated earlier, child sexual abuse may
involve sexual as well as nonsexual components. Some adults are
more comfortable, emotionally, relating to a child than to peers
because of their poor self-esteem, poor self-worth, or arrested psychological development (Groth, Hobson, & Gary, 1982). Sexual involvement with a child may meet other emotional needs by providing the perpetrator with a sense of power, control, and security that
he cannot achieve with peers (Finkelhor, 1984a). The source of this
need for power and control, according to feminist perspectives of
psychosocial development, stems from male socialization. Men are
socialized to be dominant and in control, and women to be submis-
sive and passive (Russell, 1986).

The second motivation for an adult to sexually abuse a child is the
adult's sexual arousal from children. Some adults not only find
fulfillment of emotional needs from children but physiologically are
aroused by children. Briere and Runtz's (1989) research, cited earlier,
suggests that adult male sexual interest in children may be more
widespread than generally thought. Why this arousal is evident or
stronger in some adults as compared to others remains largely unex-
plained. Possible reasons include the sexualization of small children
in the media, an offender's history of sexual traumatization as a child,
and biological factors such as hormonal levels or chromosomal composition (Finkelhor, 1984a).

Blockage refers to adults' inability to have emotional and sexual
needs met in relationships with other adults. Blockage may result
from earlier unsuccessful attempts at sexual gratification with adults.
For example, a male may experience impotence in an adult sexual
relationship or rejection from a mate, with the result that sexual
activity with another adult represents discomfort and frustration.
Consequently, the adult male may turn to a child with whom he can
be in control and can be assured of sexual success. Blockage also may
result when a marital relationship is unsatisfactory and sexual grati-

fication is sought from an easily accessible individual such as a daughter (Finkelhor, 1984a; Meiselman, 1978). Feminist theory, however, is critical of the latter explanation because it assumes a role of sexual subservience on the part of women. An underlying assumption in this explanation is that a woman is expected to meet her mate's sexual demands without regard for her own wishes. If she fails to do so, the consequence is that her mate may transfer his sexual interests to a daughter (Driver, 1989).

Precondition II: Overcoming Internal Inhibitors. Internal inhibitions may be absent or must be overcome by the perpetrator in order for child sexual abuse to occur. Factors cited for a breakdown in inhibition include substance abuse, found in a large number of child sexual abuse cases (Rada, 1976); psychosis, found relatively rarely (Marshall & Norgard, 1983); and poor impulse control (Groth et al., 1982).

Feminist theories add that inhibitions against sexual abuse are lowered when society blames the victim rather than the perpetrator. Blaming the victim provides offenders justification for their behavior (Rush, 1980). The view that the home is a man's private domain in which he has the privilege of doing as he wishes may be interpreted by some males as including intrafamilial sexual abuse (Rush, 1980; Finkelhor, 1984a).

Precondition III: Overcoming External Inhibitors. Whereas Preconditions I and II focus on the perpetrator's behavior, Preconditions III and IV focus on the setting or social and cultural environment in which sexual abuse occurs, as well as on the victim. Precondition III suggests that external inhibitors outside the perpetrator and child victim must be overcome in order for sexual abuse to occur (Finkelhor, 1984a). Parents are expected to provide a child with protection from sexual victimization. When parents are physically or psychologically absent, such as through death, divorce, or illness, the likelihood of sexual abuse occurring increases (Kaufman, Peck, & Tagiuri, 1954; Maisch, 1973). A study of sibling sexual abuse revealed that older brothers often took sexual advantage of their younger sisters when they were baby-sitting their sisters after school before the parents returned home from work or in the evening when the parents were away (Wiehe, 1990b). Social and physical isolation of families, as well as the absence of privacy in sleeping arrangements, may also increase a victim's vulnerability (Summit & Kryso, 1978; Wiehe, 1990b).

Precondition IV: Overcoming the Resistance of the Child Victim. The potential perpetrator must in some way influence, undermine, or overcome a child's possible resistance to the sexual abuse. A child's emotional insecurity or affectional deprivation, possibly stemming from psychological maltreatment, may make the child vulnerable to attention and affection from a potential perpetrator. Lack of sexual information also may increase a child's likelihood of succumbing to a perpetrator's sexual advances. The trust and respect a victim has for the perpetrator—such as the trust a child holds for a close family member or the respect a student has for a teacher—also may undermine a child's resistance to sexual abuse. Finally, threats of physical harm from the perpetrator may break down a child's resistance to sexual victimization (Finkelhor, 1984a; Summit, 1983; Wiehe, 1990b).

❏ Feminist Perspectives on Child Sexual Abuse

Feminist literature criticizes the association often made between the dysfunctional family and child sexual abuse. Emphasizing the role of the dysfunctional family as a causative factor in child sexual abuse supports the traditional family hierarchy, in which males control and dominate females. The dysfunctional family theory implies that sexual abuse may occur when family members do not assume expected, traditional roles. For example, as stated earlier, a wife may be blamed unjustly, for not fulfilling an expected role of providing her husband with sexual gratification, when he turns to the daughter for fulfillment of this need. An emphasis on the dysfunctional family also may shift the therapeutic focus from incest as the primary issue to dysfunctional family relationships. This shift in treatment is dangerous because the restoration of traditionally expected family roles becomes the primary focus of treatment and the sexual abuse becomes a secondary issue. The restoration of traditionally expected family roles may include reinforcing male domination and manipulation of females rather than redistributing power among family members irrespective of gender (Driver, 1989; Waldby, Clancy, Emetchi, & Summerfield, 1989).

Feminist theoretical perspectives on child sexual abuse focus on the concepts of structural and personal power (Waldby et al., 1989). Structural or institutionalized power is defined as the power granted by society to individuals and groups. Individuals and groups use structural power to dominate others through variables such as gender, race, income, and religion. For example, men control women, whites dominate African Americans, and the rich control the poor. Groups of persons with little or no structural power, such as women, African Americans, and the poor, are victims of the misuse of this power through exploitation and aggression by those holding structural power—men, whites, and the wealthy. The misuse of structural power can be seen in sexual abuse. Waldby et al. (1989) state,

> Child abuse represents a misuse of the power that society "legitimately" accords to males and to adults. As this structural power of males and adults exists, there also exists the *potential* for every man to misuse his power over women (e.g. rape) and for every adult to misuse his/her power over children (e.g. sexual assault). As well as this potential, there exists the *option* for abuse, as society actually legitimizes the misuse of power. The legitimizing of the abuse of power is child sexual abuse. It occurs on several fronts. For example, the child who disclosed to adults, who she hopes will protect her from abuse, is often not believed. Society reinforces this situation by perpetuating some of the myths about child sexual abuse. Secondly, the legal system allows for relative ease of removal of the child survivor from the family, yet poses difficulty in removing the offender, thus reinforcing the blame on the child and granting the right to continue offending on the male/adult. Thirdly, society provides limited punishments for sex offenders; imprisonment for those even fewer offenders who are found guilty by the criminal justice system; and the public shaming for those even fewer offenders who become newsworthy for a day. On the whole, most offenders are not punished by society. (pp. 102-103)

This abuse of structural power can be checked through the enhancement of personal power. Personal power is defined as inner strength, the desire and drive within individuals to attain mastery of their lives and to achieve desired goals. The abuse of personal power can be seen in the control of others for personal gain, with little thought to their physical or emotional needs. Sexual abuse represents a violation of personal power. Adults thwart children from reaching their full human potential by sexually victimizing them and by creating problems in living resulting from this victimization that may persist into adulthood. A proper use of personal power should assure all individuals the right to develop to their full human potential. Individual family members must guard, nourish, and develop the personal power of other family members.

Feminist perspectives on sexual abuse have implications for understanding, preventing, and treating this social problem as well as fostering sociopolitical change. An understanding of child sexual abuse must include the association between certain classes' and groups' abuse of power and sexual victimization. Prevention of sexual victimization must encompass the empowerment of females, both children and adults, against abuse and support ownership of their bodies. Therapy with individuals and families should focus on the goal of enhancing each individual's personal power. Public policy must prevent the abuse of structural and personal power to the advantage of certain individuals and groups but to the detriment and destruction of others (Waldby et al., 1989).

❏ **Application to Practice**

Protective services agencies vary in the way they require workers to record data acquired in the assessment of child maltreatment reports. At some point in time, however, the social worker must prepare a diagnostic summary that assimilates into a coherent, meaningful, and useful statement the wealth of information acquired during the assessment phase of the problem-solving process. The worker's understanding of factors associated with the various types of child maltreatment will serve as a basis for accomplishing this task.

Factors associated with child maltreatment, presented in this chapter, will now be used to analyze examples of physical and sexual abuse. A brief summary of each case will be presented, culminating in a diagnostic summary and treatment plan. The diagnostic summary organizes the information acquired by the social worker during the assessment phase. The treatment plan identifies specific goals to be accomplished in treatment. Goals identified in the treatment plan will be used to evaluate treatment effectiveness, the subject of a later chapter.

THE ROBERTS FAMILY

In Chapter 1, the Roberts family was presented as an example of physical abuse. Mrs. Roberts and her sister took 5-year-old Mike to an emergency room for injuries supposedly sustained from having fallen off his bicycle. Further investigation revealed that his injuries appeared to be the result of a beating.

Following a report of the abuse to child protective services, a protective services worker conducted an assessment. During an individual interview, Mrs. Roberts described her husband as a "hothead." Mr. Roberts recently was fired from his job as a welder because he had threatened to "punch out the boss" when the latter criticized his poor work performance. On another occasion, Mr. Roberts had been jailed after becoming involved in a neighborhood fight.

Mrs. Roberts was sensitive to her husband's anger, which erupted periodically. She attempted to maintain an equilibrium in the family by avoiding situations that might provoke him. When questioned if Mr. Roberts had been physically abusive to her, she stated that he had hit her in the past. He had not physically abused her, however, after she threatened to take the children and leave him. She appears to accept his violent outbursts through rationalization by saying, "That's just the way he is, although sometimes he can be hell." (This is an individual-personality factor.)

Mike has an older sister, Marie, age 7. Mr. and Mrs. Roberts described at great length the differences in behavior between Marie and Mike. Marie is a very compliant, obedient child who responds to her parents' wishes with a minimal need for discipline. Mike, on the other hand, was described by Mr. Roberts as "bullheaded" and "having a will of his own." Mr. and Mrs. Roberts characterized Mike as being restless and charged with energy from the day they brought him home from the hospital, whereas Marie was exactly the opposite—calm and quiet. The social worker concluded from this discussion that a battle of wills had developed, especially between Mr. Roberts and Mike, with Mr. Roberts resorting to increasingly stronger disciplinary methods when Mike would not comply with his demands. The injuries Mike received apparently were inflicted the previous evening, when Mike would not eat his dinner and his father, according to Mrs. Roberts, "blew up at Mike." (This is a family-related factor: parent-child interaction.)

Mr. Roberts discussed with the social worker his views of discipline, which focused primarily on a use of corporal punishment, including a belt or rod. Mr. Roberts justified this form of discipline on two bases. First, he had been disciplined this way by his parents, and, as he verbalized, "My parents whipped me and I turned out all right." Second, the preacher at their church recently had spoken about how kids would not be in so much trouble today if their parents had "not given up on taking them behind the woodshed." (These are both social and cultural factors.)

Diagnostic Summary and
Treatment Plan for the Roberts Family

Referral. Mr. and Mrs. Roberts were reported for possible child physical abuse by Social Services at Mercy Hospital after Mrs. Roberts and her sister appeared at the emergency room with Mrs. Roberts's 5-year-old son, Mike. Although the mother reported that Mike had "fallen off his bicycle," an examination revealed that Mike's injuries—consisting of bruises on his back, a large welt on his buttocks, and a sprained arm—were more likely to have occurred as a result of a beating. Subsequent information from Mr. and Mrs. Roberts confirmed the use of corporal punishment (whipping and hitting) in disciplining Mike.

Diagnostic Summary. Assessment interviews with Mr. and Mrs. Roberts revealed the following.

1. Mr. Roberts exhibits problems with anger control. Mr. Roberts recently was dismissed from his job following an altercation with his boss. There is some evidence that in the past he has been physically abusive to his wife and may continue to abuse her verbally. Mr. Roberts has been physically abusive to Mike.

2. Mr. and Mrs. Roberts's interaction with Mike, and vice versa, consists largely of aversive behaviors. Mr. and Mrs. Roberts are having problems in handling Mike, an assertive and aggressive child, compared to an older sister (age 7) who is described as compliant and obedient. Mr. Roberts's frustration and inability to control Mike, in addition to differences of opinion between Mr. and Mrs. Roberts regarding how to handle Mike, are expressed in Mr. Roberts's angry outbursts and physically abusive behavior toward Mike.

3. Mr. and Mrs. Roberts's parenting knowledge and behavior, reinforced by the way in which Mr. Roberts was disciplined as a child and the couple's religious values, are ineffective in handling Mike. Mr. Roberts is escalating his use of corporal punishment in an attempt to maintain control of Mike. Although Mrs. Roberts disapproves of her husband's severe methods of punishment, she is fearful of confronting him about this because of his problem with anger control.

Treatment Plan. The following treatment goals have been identified with Mr. and Mrs. Roberts.

1. Relative to Mr. Roberts's problem with anger control, he will attend a weekly therapy group for men sponsored by Middletown Family Services.

2. To gain new parenting knowledge and skill, especially relevant to discipline, Mr. and Mrs. Roberts will enroll in the parent education course, The Nurturing Program, to be sponsored by this agency beginning May 15.

3. Mr. and Mrs. Roberts will attend weekly Parents Anonymous meetings beginning May 1 for a minimum of 6 months.

MELISSA

Eight-year-old Melissa was sexually abused by her uncle, Paul. Melissa's mother was employed during the day as a waitress. Paul, a former miner who was on total disability because of black lung disease, took care of Melissa in the afternoon when she arrived home from school. On several occasions, Paul fondled Melissa while he masturbated when the two of them were sitting on Paul's bed watching television. Although initially he denied the sexual abuse, later, when he became aware of the legal implications of his behavior, he admitted having "touched Melissa a couple of times." He defended his behavior by saying that Melissa really did not seem to mind him doing so.

A protective services worker conducted several interviews individually with Melissa, her mother, and Paul, in addition to several joint interviews with Melissa and her mother. The worker used Finkelhor's (1984a) Four Preconditions for Sexual Abuse as a guide for gathering information, understanding the sexual abuse, and compiling the information into a formal diagnostic statement for the agency and the court.

Emotional congruence, a component of Precondition I, was a significant factor in Paul's abuse of Melissa. Paul had never married and had lived with his parents until their death. At that time, he moved in with his sister, who was recently divorced. Melissa's mother welcomed this move. She needed her brother's financial help in the form of room and board payments because she could not depend on Melissa's father to make regular child support payments. In addition, Paul could supervise Melissa when she was not in school. The mother's description of her brother indicated that he had no significant adult relationships. When he was living with his parents, Paul would go to work and return to his parents' home. At times, he would play ball with several of the neighborhood children, who called him "Uncle"; however, there was no evidence that sexual abuse occurred in these relationships. Melissa's mother described Paul and Melissa as "best friends." On several occasions, they had gone to a movie when Melissa's mother had to work in the evening. The protective services worker concluded that Paul related to Melissa as if she were a peer. Congruence existed between Melissa's isolation from peers, because of the geographical isolation of the family, and Paul's need for social contacts.

Inhibitions against sexual contacts with a child, a component of Precondition II, may have been overcome through Paul's occasional abuse of alcohol. Melissa's mother reported that on several occasions, upon returning home from work, she found that Paul had been drinking. She was not able to associate these incidents with the sexual abuse because the exact dates of previous abusive incidents were not available.

The social setting in which the abuse occurred, with Paul being alone and responsible for Melissa when Melissa's mother was away from the home, was conducive to the abuse (Precondition III). Economic pressures on Melissa's mother supported her use of Paul as a baby-sitter rather than use of a day care center in the community nearest to where they lived. Living in a rural, isolated area prohibited Melissa from playing with neighborhood peers after school and left her relying primarily on watching television, an activity in which Paul engaged extensively.

Finally, Melissa had little sexual information and no training in the prevention of child sexual abuse, variables in Precondition IV. Although Melissa's mother stated that she had talked with Melissa about sex, the extent of Melissa's age-appropriate sexual information was difficult to ascertain because of the mother's extreme discomfort with the subject and reluctance to discuss this area. The protective services worker's interview with Melissa's teacher revealed that no sexual prevention programs had been conducted in the school. Although the issue had been discussed in a teachers' meeting, the school principal had never followed through on arranging for training through the local child abuse council. Fundamentalist religious values permeating the community where the family lived reinforced taboos against sexual education in the schools.

Diagnostic Summary and Treatment
Plan for Mrs. Bell and Melissa Bell

Referral. Eight-year-old Melissa Bell was referred by the school counselor and principal at Broadview Elementary School because of an uncle's sexual abuse. The school counselor learned about the abuse following interviews with Melissa relative to withdrawn behavior she was demonstrating in the classroom.

Diagnostic Summary. Assessment interviews with Mrs. Bell, Melissa, and Paul revealed the following.

1. Melissa and her mother are isolated geographically and, consequently, socially. They live in a remote rural area consisting largely of abandoned mines. Their geographical isolation prohibits Melissa from playing with peers and participating in after-school activities at the school, setting up a situation in which the perpetrator, Mrs. Bell's brother, acts as a baby-sitter for Melissa after school.

2. Mrs. Bell has difficulty providing financially for herself and her daughter. Their financial situation has made it necessary for Mrs. Bell to share her home with her brother, a situation she describes as "not a good arrangement."

3. Mrs. Bell is a passive, nonassertive individual. Her current financial dilemma may be due, in part, to her lack of assertiveness in using the courts to enforce child support payments from her ex-husband.

4. Melissa has little or no sexual information appropriate to her age. She lacks empowerment against future sexual abuse from peers and adults.

5. The perpetrator, Paul, abuses alcohol at times and has received no treatment for this problem. His geographical and social isolation as well as child-care responsibilities inappropriately place him in close contact with his 8-year-old niece, whom he has sexually molested.

Treatment Plan. The following treatment goals were identified.

1. The social worker will begin working immediately with Mrs. Bell, with the goal of finding housing for Mrs. Bell and Melissa in the community where Mrs. Bell works as well as after-school care (latch-key program) for Melissa.

2. The worker will assist Mrs. Bell in contacting proper authorities for enforcing her husband's court requirement to pay child support.

3. The worker will provide materials to Mrs. Bell to assist her in giving Melissa age-appropriate sexual information.

4. Melissa will continue to meet weekly with the school counselor, who discovered the sexual abuse, relative to the abuse's impact on her life.

5. Paul will enter a sexual offender treatment program mandated by the court.

❏ Summary

Research identifies factors contributing to the various child maltreatment types and forms. These factors may be classified as individual-related, family-related, and social and cultural. When working with child abuse and neglect, knowledge of these factors will assist social workers in formulating a diagnostic summary, bringing together in a meaningful statement information acquired in assessing the maltreatment report. This diagnostic summary, in turn, serves as the basis for identifying goals to be accomplished in treatment, known as the treatment plan. These goals also will be used in evaluating the effectiveness of these interventions.

❑ Suggested Reading

THEORY

Compton, B., & Galaway, B. (1979). *Social work processes*. Homewood, IL: Dorsey.

Chapter 3, "Useful Theoretical Perspectives," presents an array of theoretical perspectives that a mental health professional can use to understand and intervene in various social problems, including child abuse and neglect.

Polansky, N. (1986). "There is nothing so practical as a good theory." *Child Welfare, 65*, 3-15.

This article discusses factors influencing a good theory and the use of theory in understanding and helping others.

CHILD NEGLECT

Polansky, N., Borgman, R., & DeSaix, C. (1972). *Roots of futility*. San Francisco: Jossey-Bass.

Polansky, N., Chalmers, M., Buttenwieser, E., & Williams, D. (1981). *Damaged parents: An anatomy of child neglect*. Chicago: University of Chicago Press.

These books present studies of child neglect in the settings of rural Appalachia and urban Philadelphia, Pennsylvania. Practical application of the data is made to working with neglectful families. The findings relative to personality characteristics of neglectful mothers, however, must be interpreted in the light of an ecological theory of child maltreatment, as discussed in this chapter.

PHYSICAL ABUSE

Parke, R., & Collmer, C. (1975). Child abuse: An interdisciplinary analysis. In E. Hetherington (Ed.), *Review of child development research* (pp. 509-590). Chicago: University of Chicago Press.

This book presents an extensive analysis of child maltreatment from several theoretical perspectives. Literature subsequent to its publication can be added by the reader.

PSYCHOLOGICAL MALTREATMENT

Garbarino, J., Guttman, E., & Seeley, J. (1986). *The psychologically battered child*. San Francisco: Jossey-Bass.

Brassard, M., Germain, R., & Hart, S. (Eds.). (1987). *Psychological maltreatment of children and youth*. Elmsford, NY: Pergamon.

These books present a comprehensive analysis regarding psychological maltreatment of children.

SEXUAL ABUSE

Finkelhor, D. (1984). *Child sexual abuse: New theory and research*. New York: Free Press.

As the title implies, this book summarizes the research on understanding child sexual abuse. The Four Preconditions model for understanding child sexual abuse is discussed in the book. A chapter also focuses on the effects of childhood sexual abuse on the victim.

FEMINIST THEORY

Driver, E., & Droisen, A. (Eds.). (1989). *Child sexual abuse: A feminist reader*. New York: New York University Press.

This book is a feminist reader on child sexual abuse.

5

The Path of Intervention

Previous chapters have provided information on the types and forms of child maltreatment, its history, the extent of abuse and neglect in American society, and factors associated with the problem that help to understand it and provide ways to intervene. Appropriate questions to ask at this time include the following: "How do cases of child maltreatment become known?" and "What happens when a family is reported for abuse or neglect?"

Reports of alleged child maltreatment are filed with a child protective services agency. The agency then follows a path of intervention. This chapter will describe this path, beginning with the initial report, which is followed by an investigation and, if maltreatment is substantiated, a treatment phase (see Figure 5.1). Depending on the nature of and circumstances surrounding the maltreatment, a criminal investigation may occur, involving the civil and/or criminal court systems.

Differences across states in the ways that courts and social services are organized may change the path a protective services worker

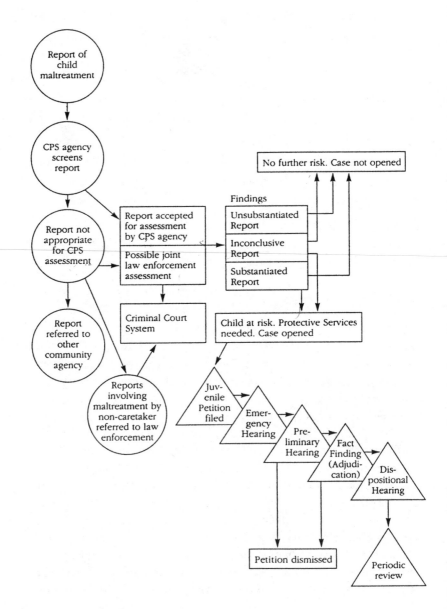

Figure 5.1. The Path of Intervention

follows in working with child abuse and neglect. Individuals working with child abuse and neglect therefore must be familiar with the way legal and social services are organized in their state, so that they can make the necessary changes in the information presented.

❏ The Report

Intervention begins when an allegation of child maltreatment is reported to a child protective services agency. Child protective services usually are administered as part of a larger public social service agency generally referred to as the Department of Human Services, the Department for Social Services, or Child and Youth Services. Different titles are used in different states. The opening pages of telephone directories usually include a section with a title such as "Community Services Guide" that informs the public of mental health and social services available in that community. Included in this listing under the category of Child Abuse are telephone numbers for reporting child maltreatment. Many states maintain a 24-hour toll-free hotline for reporting child maltreatment. A national hotline also is available, operated by Childhelp USA (1-800-4-A-CHILD). Counselors staffing this line provide information and referrals for reporting child maltreatment in the caller's geographical area.

The provision of child protective services is mandated by law in every state, a movement that began with the passage of the Child Abuse Prevention and Treatment Act, Public Law 93-247. (See Chapter 3 for a discussion of this law and Appendix A for its text.) Public Law 93-247 requires that states receiving federal funds for child protection programming meet certain provisions. One of these provisions is that states have in effect a mandatory child abuse and neglect reporting statute that provides civil and criminal immunity for persons making a "good faith" report. Compliance with this statute began in the 1970s, and by the end of the decade all states had enacted mandatory reporting laws.

The provision of child protective services is mandated by law in every state.

Public Law 93-247 also mandates that certain other standards be maintained by states in their protective services programming. For example, state statutes identify certain professionals as mandated reporters of child maltreatment. Generally, mandated reporters include physicians, nurses and other allied health professionals, social workers, teachers, and law enforcement officials. Two exceptions to professionals mandated to report are attorneys who have client privilege and clergy with penitent privilege.

In addition to describing who shall report child maltreatment, state statutes also describe the time frames for reporting, identify grounds for reporting, and clarify the conditions under which the law applies. In terms of time frames, state statutes generally require "prompt" or "immediate" reporting by mandated reporters. The grounds for making the report are usually based on a caller having "reasonable cause to believe" or "reasonable suspicion" that a child is being abused or neglected. Conditions under which the law applies include situations in which a minor (a person under 18 years of age) is abused or neglected by a parent or other caretaker. For example, if a child was mistreated by a person not in a caretaker role, then this report would be referred to the police for criminal investigation. If the maltreatment is occurring as a result of parental neglect or failure to protect, however, then a protective services agency would become involved.

❑ Intake

Intake is the first phase in the path that child maltreatment reports follow at which a reporting source can express to a protective services agency concerns regarding a child maltreatment situation. Not all calls that the child protective services agency receives in the intake phase are appropriate for investigation. On receipt of a call alleging child maltreatment, the protective services agency will determine if the report falls within the legislatively mandated mission of the agency. This process has become known as "screening" (Wells, Stein, Fluke, & Downing, 1989). Following are case vignettes exemplifying the screening process.

Case Example

Ms. Mary Smith telephoned her local child protective services agency and reported that a man had exposed himself and tried to fondle her 10-year-old daughter while she was playing at the park across the street from where the Smiths lived. There was no indication that Ms. Smith had been neglectful or failed to protect the child. The alleged perpetrator was not in a caretaking role, so this incident was referred to the local law enforcement agency for investigation.

Case Example

Gladys Thompson called the local child protective services hotline to report her concerns regarding the children of a migrant family that recently began attending the Sunday school class she taught at her church. The children reported that their father had accepted full-time employment in the community and that the family no longer would be following the crops. Ms. Thompson stated that the children appeared clean and healthy, but she thought that perhaps the family could benefit from some services to help them assimilate into the community. The intake worker determined that there were no allegations of abuse or neglect. Ms. Thompson was referred to a local community action center that offered assistance to neighborhood families.

Case Example

A medical social worker from a local hospital telephoned the local child protective services agency to report concerns regarding a 9-month-old infant recently admitted for severe head injury. The child was being treated for subdural hematoma, skull fracture, and elevated cranial pressure. The child's mother claimed that the child had fallen off the bed, striking his head on the floor. The attending physician questioned the mother's explanation because the severity of the injuries was inconsistent with the mother's explanation. In this situation, the caller had reasonable cause to believe that the child was abused or neglected while under the care of his mother. The report was accepted by the protective services agency for investigation.

Each of these examples demonstrates the intake process, in that a protective services intake worker receives a maltreatment report and then screens the report for appropriate action. If the report is not appropriate for a child protective services investigation or assessment, the caller may be referred to other appropriate resources.

❏ Assessment

If, as a result of the intake process, a report is determined appropriate for child protective services intervention, an initial assessment will occur. (This initial assessment is distinguished from a subsequent assessment known as a diagnostic assessment, which frequently occurs at the time treatment is begun with a family.) This phase of the path of intervention often is referred to as the "investigation." The term "assessment" is preferred, however, because it reflects that the social worker's gathering of information occurs in an orderly fashion, flowing from the worker's knowledge of factors associated with child maltreatment. The purpose of this initial assessment is to determine if child maltreatment has occurred and, if so, the likelihood that this might happen again; who maltreated the child; and what action should occur as a result (American Humane Association, 1980). The assessment should include a holistic view of family functioning, including both strengths and weaknesses. By contrast, an investigation may be more "incident driven" and reach only a narrow conclusion regarding a particular abusive act or, in instances of neglect, the omission of expected child care behaviors.

Law enforcement agencies may be involved in the assessment. Their involvement generally focuses on child maltreatment cases involving sexual abuse or abuse resulting in serious injury. Law enforcement's primary role is to conduct a criminal investigation.

Many states are establishing protocols that encourage more cooperation among law enforcement, child protective services, and the prosecuting attorney's office in cases of sexual abuse or in which there has been serious physical harm. The goal of these protocols is to provide maltreatment victims and their families with coordinated protective services. This cooperative effort aids in avoiding the duplication of services typically associated with multiagency involvement.

Child advocacy centers, now becoming increasingly prominent nationwide, represent the ideal in multiagency involvement both in this initial assessment phase and, subsequently, in treatment. These centers provide a regional location where representatives from child protective services, law enforcement, and the state attorney's office can come together to conduct the assessment. The greatest strength of this multidisciplinary approach is the benefit offered to the child and family. Trauma to the child is reduced by providing for a single interview in a joint session rather than conducting separate interviews to meet each discipline's needs. Workers from each discipline inform a lead interviewer of specific information needed. For example, law enforcement may be concerned primarily with evidentiary issues related to proving the occurrence of a crime, whereas the child protection worker will be concerned with protection issues such as the nonoffending parent's ability to protect the child. The advocacy center also provides a safe, family-oriented environment in which to conduct the investigation and provide family-oriented treatment. A few jurisdictions have developed formal centers, and others are beginning the process with the development of multidisciplinary team reviews, informal networking, and formalized protocols. These local multidisciplinary teams provide many of the benefits associated with advocacy centers. Many states now mandate by law joint investigation of child sexual abuse cases and some forms of child abuse and neglect.

Whether the assessment is conducted individually or with another agency, it will be initiated by a child protective services worker. The first step in the assessment will be a search of records to determine if the protective services agency has had previous involvement with the family in question.

The next step in the assessment is an interview with the alleged victim. Generally, the social worker will attempt to interview the victim in some neutral location, such as at school or in day care. If such options are unavailable, attempts will be made to interview the child victim in the home, but away from the alleged perpetrator. This will allow the child to speak freely without fear of retribution from the perpetrator or other adults who may have been involved in the child's maltreatment.

The social worker also will interview parents and other appropriate individuals in the family, such as the mother's boyfriend, a grandparent who resides with the family, or a boarder living in the family's home. These interviews also generally are conducted in the family home. There are several reasons for meeting in the family's home. First, allegations frequently involve the adequacy of home conditions. Interviewing in the home allows the worker to observe the home and to assess the possible effects of home conditions on the child. Second, observation of the home may provide information necessary to substantiate the allegation. For example, observation of the home may lend credibility to a parent's explanation of a suspicious injury. Third, as part of the assessment, the social worker will need to determine the family's general functioning. This may best be done in the family's natural setting, the home. Finally, because of the involuntary nature of the family's involvement and the hostility that often is generated by being the subject of a maltreatment investigation, motivating the family to attend an office appointment may be difficult.

As part of the assessment phase, the child protective services worker may contact key individuals who can provide additional information regarding the alleged maltreatment. Individuals such as teachers, day care providers, school counselors, and neighbors can provide valuable information on the child's condition. This may include information regarding daily hygiene, supervision of the child, and the presence of injuries not previously associated with maltreatment. Collateral sources can also assist the worker in assessing the general psychosocial functioning of the child and other family members, as well as the functioning of the family as a social system.

Physicians and allied health professionals often are important in detecting or substantiating child maltreatment. In investigating the validity of an allegation of medical neglect, for example, allied health personnel would be an obvious source to contact. The physician's training and expertise also is necessary for the detection and substantiation of certain types of physical abuse. Spiral fractures, joint separations, and swelling may be indicative of abrupt grasping, shaking, and twisting of extremities. Fractures of long bones may result from extremities having been hit or rapped. Skull fractures that supposedly occurred from a low-level fall, such as from a bed or a couch, and rib fractures frequently are indicative of abusive neglectful parental actions (Fontana, 1968; Kottmeier, 1987; Shubin, 1984). Other types of injuries frequently associated with maltreatment may also require medical assistance in diagnosis. For example, a shaken child may have injuries associated specifically with shaking that medical personnel may be able to detect. Medical staff may render an expert opinion as to whether a burn was accidental or a result of maltreatment. The opinion of a medical professional also will be important in determining when the injury occurred.

When assessing sexual abuse allegations, a medical examination will be an important resource. A physical exam will determine if there is physical injury or the presence of venereal disease. If penetration is alleged to have occurred, a doctor may be able to detect some physical signs of trauma. With the assistance of a process called colposcopy, the physician may be able to photograph and preserve medical evidence (Berkowitz, 1987; McCann, Voris, Simon, & Wells, 1990; Woodling & Heger, 1986). Some jurisdictions are now developing a protocol for conducting sexual trauma examinations that provides guidelines to physicians performing these examinations. Equally important to their role in assisting to substantiate a report of child sexual abuse, physicians can ensure the sexual abuse victim's physical well-being. It should be noted that frequently no physical evidence is detected on medical examination. This is partially attributable to the propensity for genital membranes to heal quickly and to child sexual abuse frequently being a nonviolent offense, so that no damage to the tissues is seen.

In conducting the assessment, social workers must be sensitive to the issue of client confidentiality. Most states have specific guidelines regarding the release of information acquired as a result of an investigation; for example, whether information on the investigation's outcome can be released to the individual reporting the maltreatment. The child protective services worker must be knowledgeable about laws and procedures relative to the confidential handling of client information.

As part of the assessment process, the protective services worker must be aware of and document physical and behavioral indicators of maltreatment. Although publications on child abuse and neglect frequently feature charts showing indicators of maltreatment, these charts can be misleading if indicators are not viewed in the light of the total functioning of the child in the family system. For example, behavioral indicators such as withdrawn or antisocial behavior, although often associated with victims of maltreatment, may also be indicative of other problems not associated with physical, emotional, or sexual abuse. Thus, specific emotional and behavioral indicators of child maltreatment must be viewed in the complete context of the client's functioning, including individual, family, and social and cultural factors.

A child maltreatment assessment may result in three possible outcomes: a substantiated report of child maltreatment, an inconclusive report, or an unsubstantiated report (see Figure 5.1). The following definitions reflect the worker's conclusion following the assessment process.

1. *Unsubstantiated report:* There is no indication that maltreatment has occurred, either from behavioral indicators or statements from victims, caretakers, or others.
2. *Inconclusive report:* Some indicators that maltreatment has occurred are present, such as behavioral indicators or noncorroborated statements.
3. *Substantiated report:* The allegation of maltreatment is admitted by the caretaker or, in the absence of a parental admission, there is strong evidence of maltreatment, such as the child's statements or medical evidence.

The protective services worker's assessment is summarized in the diagnostic summary (see Chapter 4). This statement reflects the worker's theoretical understanding of the case and suggests areas to which interventions will be directed. The treatment plan identifies goals to be accomplished in treatment. The child protective services agency may provide treatment services to the family, or referral may be made to other community mental health and social services agencies. An important factor relative to the provision of ongoing services, regardless of who provides the services, is the presence of further risk of harm to the child.

❏ **Engaging the Criminal or Civil Court System**

To understand how a child maltreatment case moves through the legal system, one must understand the distinction between the criminal and civil courts. (For the purposes of this chapter, the civil court is referred to as the juvenile court.) The basic distinction between the two court systems relates to their purpose for involvement in a case. A criminal court becomes involved when a criminal charge is filed alleging that a crime has been committed. The criminal court's purpose is to determine the alleged perpetrator's guilt or innocence. Juvenile court action in an alleged child maltreatment case is not intended to determine guilt or innocence but instead to make a determination as to whether a child has been abused or neglected. This determination generally is referred to as a "finding of dependency." When the court makes such a finding, the child is brought under the court's jurisdiction and orders can be issued to protect the child.

More subtle differences also exist between the juvenile and criminal courts. Juvenile court generally is less formal than criminal court. This informality refers mostly to the lesser standard of proof required in a juvenile court action. For example, before a person can be found guilty of a crime in a criminal court, the prosecution must provide evidence of guilt that is "beyond a reasonable doubt." In contrast, juvenile court usually requires only a "preponderance of evidence" that a child has been abused or neglected. Another area of informality in the juvenile court relates to the court's willingness to be more sensitive to a child's developmental needs. The latter, however, often is more a result of the judge's experience and sensitivity than of a specific rule or procedure.

As the number of families being brought before juvenile court increases, the skill level of involved attorneys also has increased. As a result, juvenile proceedings have become more sophisticated and complex. For this reason, a social worker must be knowledgeable of state statutes, case law, court rules, and other matters pertaining to the operation of the juvenile court.

A social worker must be knowledgeable of matters pertaining to the operation of the juvenile court.

All parties in a juvenile hearing are entitled to due process rights. In the same way that the accused in a criminal trial has basic rights, so also those rights must be afforded to the victim, family, and alleged perpetrator in a juvenile hearing. These rights include the following:

1. the right to formal notice of the hearing,
2. the right to legal counsel,
3. a right to a hearing in which evidence is presented, and
4. the right to present a defense and cross-examine witnesses.

The child protective services worker will be involved extensively in juvenile court proceedings. For this reason, this chapter will focus on juvenile court proceedings. The law enforcement agency has primary responsibility for the criminal action, and the child protective services worker may have a limited role in a criminal proceeding.

❏ **The Path of a Case
Through Juvenile Court**

Based on Figure 5.1, so far in this chapter a case has gone through the following steps:

1. Receipt of a report by a child protective services agency
2. Screening the report to determine appropriateness for investigation by the agency
3. Assessment of the report and determination of an outcome
4. Determination of services to be provided either by protective services or a community mental health/social services agency

In the following pages, the points at which a case may be brought to the juvenile court's attention and the path a case may follow as it goes through the court system will be discussed.

As shown in Figure 5.1, the juvenile court system generally is engaged after the report has been investigated and the need for ongoing services has been identified. A protective services worker may petition the juvenile court at this point if the family is resistant to participating in the treatment plan. The court then may order the family into compliance with the plan. Without this order, the provision of services to the family is voluntary. The point at which the juvenile court will be involved will vary, depending on the severity of the abuse and the goals of the case. Consider, for example, the following scenarios.

Case Example

The report of a 9-month-old infant with severe head injuries had been under assessment for several days. Based on medical evidence, physical abuse was substantiated, and the decision was made to provide ongoing protective services. The child had been in the hospital for the duration of the assessment and thus was not at immediate risk for further abuse. The treating physician indicated the child would be ready for discharge within a week. Because of the seriousness of the injury to this infant, the protective services worker brought the matter before the court prior to the child's scheduled discharge from the hospital, to ensure a safe environment for the child.

Case Example

A teenage mother of two children, ages 4 and 18 months, was reported to the protective services agency for neglect. The assessment revealed that the mother had been leaving the children alone at home, sometimes for several hours at a time. Housing conditions were unsanitary. The children frequently were observed in dirty, urine-soaked clothing, and the house was cluttered with dirty diapers, rancid baby bottles, garbage, and overflowing ashtrays. Neglect was substantiated, and the case was referred for ongoing protective services. The teenage mother initially was cooperative with the treatment plan, which included day care, supportive services from an agency specializing in programs for teen mothers, and a referral for employment services. After several months, however, the mother began missing appointments, and eventually she stopped sending the children to day care. The mother became hostile toward the worker, and the home conditions deteriorated. At this point, the worker petitioned the court to seek court-ordered services.

In both of these case vignettes, the child protective services worker had completed the investigation before seeking the support of the court. The point at which court assistance was sought differed, based on the case dynamics and the fact that at the time of the assessment neither case represented an emergency. Certain situations, however, may require an immediate decision to involve the court system. This decision is based on a child being at imminent risk of harm and any need to remove the child to prevent further harm.

The decision to remove a child always is reviewed by the court system, but some states allow the child to be removed before court review. For example, some state statutes allow law enforcement personnel to remove the child and then petition the court within a specific number of hours. Similarly, some states allow a physician to hold a child in a hospital for a limited number of hours in situations of imminent danger. In the majority of states, however, the child protective services worker must seek approval of the court before a child can be removed from the home.

This prior approval generally is sought in the form of an *ex parte* emergency order. The Latin phrase *ex parte* refers to an order being issued based only on the statement of the petitioner and apart from the parties involved in the case. The following case vignette demonstrates a situation in which such an order would be appropriate.

Case Example

Joey, age 6, was reported by his teacher to have massive bruising on his lower back, buttocks, and legs. The teacher became aware of the injuries when she noticed that the child was having difficulty sitting. A child protective services worker interviewed Joey and discovered that the bruises were the result of several whippings over the past several days. The worker noticed linear bruising in several different stages of healing and some areas where the skin was broken. The child stated that he usually was whipped with a belt or a switch while wearing nothing but his underwear. The most recent whipping apparently occurred over problems such as forgetting to take out the garbage. Joey was very fearful during the interview, stating that his father had forbidden him to discuss the whippings with anyone.

Immediately after interviewing the child, the worker visited Joey's home. Joey's father appeared to be intoxicated and refused the worker entry into the home. When the worker explained the purpose of the visit, the father became hostile and verbally abusive, stating that no one would tell him how to raise his child. The father also stated that he would "whip" his son for talking to the social worker at school.

Based on the seriousness of the previous incidents and the risk of further harm, the worker sought and was granted an emergency custody order.

Because an *ex parte* emergency custody order is issued without a hearing, most state statutes require a hearing within a few days of the order's issuance. This hearing, called the emergency or protective custody hearing, gives due process to the parties involved. In this hearing, the court will hear testimony to determine if probable cause exists to continue the child's emergency placement. This hearing also may serve as the preliminary hearing.

The preliminary hearing is the first step in the juvenile hearing process, resulting from an emergency custody order or a juvenile court petition. At this hearing, all parties are advised of their rights. If the allegations in the petition are sufficient, the case will be set over for an adjudicatory hearing (see Figure 5.1).

As previously stated, one of the rights afforded to parties in a juvenile action is the right to legal counsel or the right to be represented by an attorney. This right also is extended to the child named in the petition. The attorney representing the child, known as the guardian ad litem, is required by federal mandate. The guardian ad litem is intended to represent the best interests of the child. The need for the guardian ad litem is based on the adversarial roles of the other attorneys involved in a case. For example, a petition generally is filed at the request of the child protective services worker who has alleged child maltreatment by the caretaker. Generally, the petitioner's interests will be represented by a state or county attorney, operating in a quasi-prosecutorial role, who will provide proof of the allegation rather than serve as an independent representative of the child (U.S. Department of Health and Human Services, 1980). The family also may be represented by independent counsel, operating in a defense attorney capacity. The guardian ad litem's role is to act independently of the other attorneys and represent what is perceived as the best interests of the child. In this role, the guardian ad litem may review agency records, interview the child, call and cross-examine witnesses, and make recommendations to the court.

Children also may be assisted in juvenile court by individuals who are not attorneys but are trained lay volunteers known as CASA volunteers (court-appointed special advocates). The role of these volunteers varies from community to community. Their duties may include working closely with the guardian ad litem; for example, by gathering information by interviewing the child and child's family in the home so that the best interests of the child are represented and assisting the family with transportation and other needs as the case moves through the court system. The CASA volunteer also may monitor the home following an assessment and prior to periodic reviews (Duquette & Ramsey, 1986).

Following the preliminary hearing, the next step is the adjudication. Different jurisdictions refer to this step with various names. The most common names are adjudicatory hearing, fact-finding hearing, and evidentiary hearing. As implied by the various names given to this phase of the court process, the purpose of this hearing is for the state to provide evidence to prove the facts of the petition. In this hearing, the petitioner or state bears the "burden of proof" in providing evidence that the child has been maltreated. Evidence must be submitted to prove the maltreatment allegations. Although the attorney is responsible for presenting the case, the child protective services worker is viewed by the court and allied personnel (attorneys, judge, witnesses, guardian ad litem) as a knowledgeable professional who is working in the best interests of the child. To fulfill this role, the social worker must demonstrate professionalism and competency in assessing the case, in formulating a diagnostic summary and treatment plan, and in presenting testimony (evidence) in court.

Although impressions and feelings the worker may have about a case, informal diagnostic labels, and uncorroborated allegations may be acceptable in intra-agency case conferences, there is little tolerance for these in a court of law. Thus, a social worker must prepare carefully for a court appearance and must demonstrate skill in presenting evidence to justify his or her recommendations. The social worker must be clear about the type of evidence admissible in a court of law when assessing a suspected case of child maltreatment and later when testifying in court. Understanding the type of evidence required by the court will assist the worker, in the data-gathering phase of the assessment, in seeking information that will be admissible in court rather than being satisfied with informal diagnostic impressions, unwarranted inferences, and aimless descriptions (Barth & Sullivan, 1985; Bell & Mylniec, 1974). Box 5.1 summarizes the basic civil rules of evidence.

Two different outcomes may result from an adjudicatory hearing (see Figure 5.1). If there is inadequate evidence to support the petition, then the case will be dismissed. This dismissal likely will result in closure of the ongoing child protective services case, because there

BOX 5.1

Civil Rules of Evidence

A. Four types of evidence conform to the rules of evidence and are, therefore, considered competent. Competent types of evidence are as follow.

1. **Direct evidence** provides factual information that requires no further proof of fact. This type of evidence would include testimony of a witness having firsthand knowledge of a situation—for example, observation of an incident.

2. **Real evidence** refers to actual proof that can be viewed in court, such as the injured child in court or X rays or photographs of the injury.

3. **Circumstantial evidence** refers to direct observations that are used to support another fact. For example, an extension cord found in the family's home may connect the parent to the uniquely shaped injuries on the child.

4. **Expert evidence** is provided by a witness who has special expertise, training, or knowledge in a specific field. For example, a physician may offer testimony as to how or when a specific injury occurred, or a licensed psychologist may testify to the presence of an emotional injury caused by an act or omission by the caretaker.

B. Rules of evidence also cover the following types of evidence.

1. **Hearsay evidence** is secondhand knowledge and is usually not admissible because the party with firsthand knowledge is not available for cross-examination. There are, however, specific exceptions to this rule.

2. **The book-entry rule** provides for the admission of records of an organization if they are completed within the normal course of business. This rule represents one exception to the hearsay rule and underscores the need for accurate and timely record keeping.

3. **Admissions** essentially are confessions on the part of one of the parties involved in an action.

4. **The opinion evidence rule** provides that an ordinary witness can give an opinion regarding matters of common knowledge, such as the temperature of a room or the witness's belief regarding the emotional state of a party.

SOURCE: Adapted from *Helping in Child Protective Services*, the American Humane Association, © copyright 1980 by the American Humane Association; and *Child Protective Services: A Guide for Workers*, by Jenkins, Salus, and Schultze (1979). Reprinted with permission.

would be no legal grounds to continue the case. If the evidence supports the petition, then the court will issue a finding.

If a finding is issued, the court will move to the dispositional phase of the process. This phase can be held as part of the adjudicatory hearing, but in some states, a separate hearing is required. When the adjudicatory and dispositional phases are held as two separate hearings, they are referred to as "bifurcated."

The dispositional hearing represents the court's efforts to resolve a case after issuing a finding. The court will attempt to provide interventions or treatment that will ensure the child's safety from further maltreatment while strengthening the family unit. Dispositional options for the family may include ordering the family to comply with specific treatment recommendations in the worker's diagnostic summary, removing the perpetrator from the home, or ordering the child's removal. The decision for removal is the most serious dispositional option.

The next phase in the path of intervention is the periodic review. As implied by the name, these reviews are scheduled periodically to assess the family's progress. During the reviews, modification in orders may be made depending on the family's progress. For example, if the court had ordered the child to have no contact with a physically abusive parent, that order may be amended to allow supervised visits as the parent progresses in treatment. If a family fulfills the goals identified in the treatment plan and the child appears to be in no further danger of maltreatment, the case may be closed.

❏   The Decision to Remove a Child

As previously stated, the decision to remove a child is the most serious dispositional option available to the court. Although the court rarely makes this decision based solely on the opinion of the child protective services worker, the worker will have considerable influence on the decision. For this reason, the protective services worker must be aware of the legal and emotional consequences of this action. Legally, the family has a constitutional right to privacy and integrity. Based on this right, danger to the child warranting this level of intrusion into the family must be demonstrated to the court. The worker also must be aware of the emotional cost of removing a child from his or her home and parents, albeit an abusive situation, to the home of relatives or even strangers. Again, an important factor for the worker in making an assessment relative to a decision of removal is the potential risk of further emotional harm to the child caused by the family disruption.

> *The seriousness of removing a child from the home is reflected in federal legislation.*

The seriousness of removing a child from the home is reflected in federal legislation passed by Congress in 1980, namely, Public Law 96-272, the Adoption Assistance and Child Welfare Act. This law mandates that if states want federal supplementary funds for child welfare services and foster care maintenance, they must have a federally approved comprehensive plan for the substitute care of children. States responded quickly, passing their own laws or issuing regulations to enforce the requirements of the federal Adoption Assistance and Child Welfare Act (Edna McConnell Clark Foundation, 1985). The law also stipulated that states had to show that in each case of children being removed from their homes, "reasonable efforts" had been made to prevent or eliminate the need for the child's removal and that every effort was being made to allow for the child's possible return to the home. This aspect of the law is enforced through federal audits of state social services agencies. Cases of children having been removed from their homes are audited periodically, thereby necessitating that agencies carefully document their efforts at family reunification.

The Adoption Assistance and Child Welfare Act also regulates "permanency planning" for children. The concept of permanency refers to the agency's plan for finding a permanent and stable home for a child. The need for permanency planning arose from an awareness in the 1970s that children, after being removed from the home, were allowed to linger indefinitely in temporary foster care placements. The tentative nature of these placements often created problems for the child's healthy psychosocial development (Katz, 1990). To ensure adequate permanency planning, federal law requires that the agency review case plans regularly (at 6-month intervals) and that the court hold dispositional reviews every 12 months. These reviews are identified as periodic reviews in Figure 5.1. The purpose of these reviews is to ensure that the appropriateness of the child's permanency plan is reviewed regularly, to prevent unnecessary delays in achieving a permanent placement.

Several options are available to the agency in terms of permanency planning. Returning the child to the home (family reunification) will remain the plan as long as it appears that the family is amenable to and capable of successful completion of the treatment plan. If the child is in late adolescence and reunification is not possible, then the plan may be to keep the child in permanent substitute care and to assist in the development of independent living skills. Placement with a relative also may be an option. If relative placement is not available and the family is unable to provide a safe home, then an adoptive placement may be considered.

Before an adoption can occur, all persons with parental rights to the child must have those rights terminated. This action, referred to as termination of parental rights, will involve the initiation of a new court action. Depending on the state judicial structure, the hearing on termination of parental rights may occur in a circuit or superior court or in a family court system that hears all matters pertaining to children and families.

The decision to terminate parental rights is based on several legal grounds that vary from state to state. Most states require one of the following grounds: that the child was abused or neglected, that the child protective services agency provided reasonable efforts toward reunification, or that additional services to the family would not, within a reasonable period of time, enable it to meet the child's needs.

❏ The Child Protective Services Worker as Witness

As stated earlier, the child protective services worker plays an important role in the path that a child maltreatment case follows through the court system. The worker's involvement will be most intensive in child abuse and neglect or termination hearings; however, the worker also may be called as a witness in criminal court actions. To assume this role successfully, the worker must prepare for hearings thoroughly and demonstrate skill in presenting evidence. Box 5.2 provides suggestions for the worker when appearing in court.

Social workers appearing in court must differentiate between the helping orientation role in which they usually function and the adversarial relationship that characterizes court proceedings. A social worker's education and training focus on humanitarian concerns for the client. The court, although concerned with the child's best interests, is designed primarily for the dispensation of justice. Thus, a social worker may confront a value conflict when appearing in court. Workers may experience frustration, anxiety, disappointment, and even hostility when their credentials are questioned by an attorney or when the worker's opinions and recommendations are not accepted by the court. Client/worker confidentiality may be compromised when private information is discussed openly in the courtroom. A professional stance, preparation for testimony, and supervisory and peer support are important elements in avoiding the interpretation of interactions occurring in the court as personal attacks (Kadushin & Martin, 1988).

❏ Summary

An understanding of the path that a suspected case of child maltreatment follows is essential in working with child abuse and neglect. Knowledge of the child protective services and court systems also is important to human services professionals in other settings where child maltreatment may become an issue. This chapter has presented this path in a general way, and there will be differences across jurisdictions. Human services professionals must familiarize themselves with the complexities of the social services and legal systems in their own jurisdictions.

BOX 5.2

Suggestions for Effective Testimony

Appearances are important

- The child protective services worker should present a professional appearance and attitude. A witness's dress, tone of voice, and expression contribute to the judge's perception of the testimony.
- Know the expectations of the court in terms of dress code, and comply with them.
- Be polite and avoid sarcastic or antagonistic responses.
- Speak clearly and confidently and avoid professional terms or jargon.

Be prepared

- The worker should be prepared thoroughly for testimony.
- Review the case record. It is appropriate to bring the case record with you, with significant facts marked for easy reference.
- Speak with your attorney before the hearing to be aware of what issues will be covered by your testimony.
- Be specific about details whenever appropriate. For example, specify dates and times, such as "Wednesday at 4:00 p.m." as opposed to "One afternoon last week." Describe a scene accurately—for example, "There was garbage and broken glass throughout the kitchen" rather than "The house was filthy."

Know the rules

- The effective witness should be aware of the rules of evidence (Box 5.1).
- If an objection is raised, stop immediately and wait for the judge to rule before continuing testimony.
- If you are confused or do not understand a question, stop and ask for clarification.
- Answer only the question asked and avoid providing additional information. Remember, a good attorney rarely asks a question to which he or she is not already aware of the answer.

Be prepared for cross-examination

- Cross-examination is often the most difficult part of testifying. During cross-examination, an attorney may try to discredit or confuse the witness. Be prepared for these tactics.

BOX 5.2

Continued

- The witness's objectivity and/or qualifications may be questioned to make the testimony appear inaccurate or biased. Remain calm and polite while facing these types of questions.
- Remain calm and in control. Becoming flustered or angry may lead to presentation of inaccurate or misleading information.

SOURCE: Adapted from *Helping in Child Protective Services*, The American Humane Association, © copyright 1980 by the American Humane Association; and *Child Protective Services: A Guide for Workers*, by Jenkins, Salus, and Schultze (1979). Reprinted with permission.

❏ **Suggested Reading**

American Humane Association. (1992). *Helping in child protective services: A competency based casework handbook.* Englewood, CO: Author.

    This book is an excellent, comprehensive, and easy to read guide to the child protective services system, from the receipt of a report through completion of services.

Caulfield, B., & Horowitz, R. (1987). *Child abuse and the law: A legal primer for social workers.* Chicago: National Committee for Prevention of Child Abuse.

    This booklet is an excellent introductory guide to the legal system, intended for social workers. Information is provided that will help a worker understand the court system and the worker's role in that system when working with child abuse and neglect.

Landau, H., Salus, M., Stiffarm, T., & Kalb, N. (1980). *Child protection: The role of the courts* (DHHS Publication No. OHDS 80-30256). Washington, DC: Government Printing Office.

    As the title implies, this manual focuses in depth on the role of juvenile and criminal courts in the adjudication of child abuse and neglect cases. The manual provides valuable information for human services professionals who must interact with the court system.

U.S. Department of Health and Human Services. (1980). *Representation for the abused and neglected child: The guardian ad litem and legal counsel* (DHHS Publication No. OHDS 80-30272). Washington, DC: Government Printing Office.

    This manual describes the guardian ad litem's role in representing an abused or neglected child in court.

6

Interviewing Skills

The dynamics surrounding child maltreatment cases require that mental health professionals possess special skills for use in interviewing the child, parents, witnesses or collateral resources, and the offender. Interviewing skills may be taught in practice courses, and mental health professionals probably will have acquired experience in using these skills. This chapter will assist in tuning these skills by applying them to working with child abuse and neglect. Reference will be made to the interviewer as a protective services worker because such individuals have primary responsibility for the assessment of child abuse and neglect cases. The information, however, applies to any human services professional working with child abuse and neglect.

❏ The Interview Relationship

To conduct effective interviews with individuals involved in child abuse and neglect, the protective services worker must be sensitive to two important components of the interview relationship: respect and empathy.

RESPECT

Respect is the cornerstone of the interview relationship. Communicating respect for the client's worth as a person is integral to the interviewing process. This is a familiar concept to human services professionals; however, at times this concept is difficult to implement, especially when working with child abuse and neglect. Respect is demonstrated, both verbally and nonverbally, with an awareness of the client's social and cultural uniqueness.

Respect, for example, is demonstrated at the initial contact with a client by addressing the latter as Mr., Mrs., or Ms., and by being direct and honest about the purpose of the interview. For example, the interview may begin as follows:

> Mrs. Roberts, I'm Janice Smith from the Department of Social Services. I would like to talk to you about Mike's bruises. My agency has received a report and is required to assess the report.

Being clear with clients regarding the purpose of the interview sets the stage not only for the interview process but also for any intervention that may be required later.

Focusing on the present and on an individual's strengths rather than deficiencies is a respectful approach to building the interview relationship and initiating change in the family. By setting this tone or climate, the interviewer encourages clients to share information about their private lives.

EMPATHY

The interviewer must communicate an understanding of the client rather than projecting judgment or blame. To communicate an understanding of the client's world, the interviewer must be able to get in contact with the client's world. This implies listening beyond the level of facts and attending to the feelings or emotions the client is sharing. This phenomenon is labeled as empathy, the process of feeling what the client is experiencing or feeling (Egan, 1990). Carl Rogers (1980) describes empathy as a basic quality that a skilled helper must have. He writes,

> It means entering the private perceptual world of the other and becoming thoroughly at home in it. It involves being sensitive, moment by moment to the changing felt meanings which flow in this other person, to the fear or rage or tenderness or confusion or whatever that he or she is experiencing. It means temporarily living in the other's life, moving about in it delicately without making judgments. (p. 142)

> To my mind, empathy is in itself a healing agent. It is one of the most potent aspects of therapy, because it releases, it confirms, it brings even the most frightened client into the human race. If a person is understood, he or she belongs. (p. 129)

Empathy is an important tool in working with an individual involved in child maltreatment, whether that person is the child victim, the parent, the offender, or a significant other. In most instances, abusive parents realize the deviancy of their behavior in maltreating a child. Parents attempt to cope with these feelings, to cover them, or to deny them by responding defensively with an uncooperative attitude, fear, and even anger toward whoever is discussing this issue with them and who insists that they must talk about what has happened. The interviewer can decrease or bypass these defenses through the use of empathy, that is, by recognizing, identifying, and verbalizing that the worker understands how the client must feel. Failing to recognize and impart understanding of the client's feelings or, even worse, responding in anger to the client will only heighten the client's defensive response.

Empathy helps gain cooperation.

Showing empathy does not mean that the protective services worker must abandon the role of protecting children. The worker can assess the alleged maltreatment effectively only if the client cooperates. Empathy helps gain cooperation. Showing empathy for parents who mistreat their children is difficult. To attempt to understand and be helpful to such parents requires a conscious and constant effort on the interviewer's part. Box 6.1 presents several suggestions for the use of empathy.

BOX 6.1

Suggestions for the Use of Empathy

1. Remember that empathy is, ideally, a way of being and not simply a professional role or communication skill.

2. Attend carefully, both physically and psychologically, and listen to the client's point of view.

3. Try to set your judgments and biases aside for the moment and walk in the shoes of the client.

4. As the client speaks, listen especially for the core message, that is, the message being expressed in terms of feelings, experiences, and behaviors that underlie what the client is saying.

5. Listen to both verbal and nonverbal messages and their content.

6. Respond fairly frequently, but briefly, to what the client is saying and feeling.

7. Be flexible and tentative enough that the client does not feel pinned down by your understanding of what he or she is feeling.

8. Be gentle, but keep the client focused on important issues.

9. Respond to the main features of all core messages—experiences, behaviors, and feelings—unless there is reason for emphasizing one over the others.

10. Gradually move toward the exploration of sensitive topics and feelings.

11. After responding with empathy, attend carefully to cues that either confirm or deny the effectiveness of your response.

12. Determine whether your empathic responses are helping the client remain focused while developing and clarifying important issues.

13. Note signs of client stress or resistance. Try to judge whether these arise because you are inaccurate or because you are too accurate in your judgments of what the client is feeling.

14. Keep in mind that the communication skill of empathy, however important, is a tool to help clients see themselves and their problem situations more clearly, with a view to managing them more effectively.

SOURCE: Adapted from *The Skilled Helper* (4th ed.) by Gerald Egan. Copyright © 1990, 1986, 1982, 1975 by Brooks/Cole Publishing Company, Pacific Grove, CA 93950, a division of International Thomson Publishing, Inc. By permission of the publisher.

Empathy does not mean that the worker agrees with the client or supports what the client says. Rather, the worker suspends personal judgment and tries to understand the client from the client's point of view. The use of empathy in exploring the client's feelings, together with knowledge of factors associated with child maltreatment identified earlier, will enable the worker to understand what was happening with the client when the maltreatment occurred. With that understanding, the worker will be able to intervene appropriately and effectively.

❏ Handling Resistance

One of the most difficult aspects of interviewing in child abuse and neglect is handling the resistance encountered from clients. This is especially true for protective services workers whose responsibility is to investigate reports of alleged child maltreatment. The protective services worker's very presence may be viewed as threatening; therefore, resistance must be anticipated.

The protective services worker may experience this resistance from a parent against whom a child maltreatment report has been filed, from the child as a victim, and from witnesses or other key individuals who may fear becoming involved in any way. Resistance may be expressed through anger, a refusal to cooperate, or denial. Resistance even may be expressed in verbal abuse directed against the worker. Such verbal abuse should not be taken as a personal attack. The hostility is against the *role* in which the protective services worker is functioning, not against the worker personally. To react to the resistance with anger or hostility, on the basis of the authority the worker has to assess the complaint, is the least effective response. Threats of retaliation from the worker will only increase resistance from the client and may even jeopardize the worker's personal safety.

The worker's task is to enable the client to lower his or her defenses and to feel as safe and comfortable as possible so that the goals of the visit can be accomplished. Warmth, sincerity, acceptance, and genuine interest should characterize the worker's attitude. Respect and courtesy extended to the client as well as a direct explanation of the interview's purpose will help to dispel the client's negative expectations of an unwelcome intruder in his or her life.

An empathic response flowing from genuine recognition of how the client is feeling at the moment will help reduce a client's resistance. This requires that workers place themselves in the position of clients and ask themselves, "How would I feel now if I were in the client's position?" Using the four basic feelings to be discussed later—sad, glad, mad, and scared—will be helpful in this process. The worker's verbalizations of these feelings, in a warm and understanding tone of voice, will convey a sense of caring and concern. For example,

Worker: Mrs. Roberts, I'm Janice Smith from the Department of Social Services. I would like to talk to you about Mike's bruises. My agency is required to assess reports of this nature.

Mrs. Roberts: If the damn teacher stuck to her teaching and didn't stick her nose into things that aren't any of her damn business, she would be a lot better off.

Worker: I know, Mrs. Roberts, my visit must make you very angry. However, I do need to talk with you about this matter.

In addition to empathy, the use of "I" statements is helpful in lowering resistance and in establishing a relationship with clients. "I" statements are encouraged in assertiveness training (a helpful course of study for protective services workers or anyone who works with child abuse and neglect) because they convey the speaker's observations, feelings, and concern. Such statements also allow clients greater flexibility in their responses and avoid giving the client a sense of being pressured or coerced. Notice the difference in feeling between the following two statements:

Worker Statement 1: You are very upset. You must really be angry.

Worker Statement 2: I realize this is very upsetting to you. I can imagine it makes you very angry that I am here.

Protective services workers may attempt to overcome clients' resistance by giving the impression that they are on the clients' side against the individual who filed the maltreatment report. Although this may be done in an attempt to demonstrate empathy, such behavior on the interviewer's part is not empathic. This is a dangerous position to take because the assessment may reveal that maltreatment did occur, which may require that the worker proceed with court action. Although the interviewer may have acquired the client's trust to secure needed information, the client will feel betrayed and distrustful of any further contacts with the worker.

The protective services worker must remain neutral in the assessment.

The protective services worker must remain neutral in the assessment. To be neutral does not mean to be cold and indifferent to the client. The worker's goal is to seek the facts. A neutral position with a generous expression of empathy that recognizes the client's feelings will assist in accomplishing this goal. Treating the client in a respectful and empathic manner also will provide the client with a new and constructive experience in human relationships.

❏ Facts and Feelings

Communication between persons occurs at two levels: the level of fact, called the cognitive component of communication, and the level of feeling, identified as the affective component. Figure 6.1 presents a pictorial image of these two communication components, using the imagery of a ship and an iceberg. A ship's captain recognizes that an iceberg represents greater danger than is immediately apparent because a large portion of the iceberg is hidden below the water. Thus, a captain who sights an iceberg in the distance realizes that the iceberg is much closer than it appears.

The portion of the iceberg above the water may be identified as conversation occurring when individuals are transmitting facts back and forth to each other. For example, in the scenario below, a social worker is interviewing a client for a social history.

Worker: Were you born here in Florida, Mrs. Troy?
Client: Yes, I have lived here all my life. I didn't even leave to attend college.
Worker: That's unusual. So many people living in Florida are from somewhere else. What about your husband? Was he born here?

Figure 6.1. Facts and Feelings

Client: He's from Georgia. We met when he was stationed here with the military.

In the above conversation, the two individuals are conversing primarily at the level of facts. Information is being exchanged between the two of them. Apart perhaps from the tone of voice either uses, it would be difficult to identify specific feelings attached to the facts the client is sharing. Facts are depicted in Figure 6.1 as the exposed part of the iceberg.

In many conversations, however, especially conversations occurring in the context of a helping relationship, many feelings are transmitted by the client in addition to the facts being exchanged. Feelings or emotions in communication are depicted in Figure 6.1 as the part of the iceberg hiding below the surface of the water.

Client: I know I shouldn't have lost my cool with Jimmy, but sometimes I just don't know what to do.
Worker: The pressures really build up at times.
Client: Yes, my husband doesn't send the child support. I can't afford to pay the baby-sitter; the landlord is on my back for the rent. Sometimes I don't know what is going to happen next. It's one thing after another.
Worker: I imagine this is very scary for you.
Client: Yes, and to add to it all I haven't been feeling well. The day I really lost my cool with Jimmy and hit him, I had been vomiting and couldn't go to work. (The client begins to cry.) I know I shouldn't have hit him. I didn't intend to hurt him. I feel so badly about this.

Worker: I sense you seem very sad about what happened.

In the example above, the worker and client are communicating at the level of facts. They are discussing information about the client's life situation and an abusive incident. More important, however, is the communication occurring at the level of feelings. Feelings or emotions are below the surface of what the client is saying, like the part of the iceberg that is hidden from view. The feelings component of communication is very important in understanding what the client is saying. The worker must strive to be sensitive to this communication component and respond accordingly. In doing so, the worker communicates that the client is being understood and that the worker cares and is concerned about the client.

Transactional analysis (TA) has created a helpful schema for identifying basic feelings a client may be sharing beneath the facts being communicated. In the same way that the colors red, blue, and yellow are the basic, or primary, colors and all other colors are blends of these, so TA theory suggests that there are four basic feelings or emotions (see Figure 6.2). All other feelings are blends of these four basic ones (T. Kahler, personal communication, June 20, 1990). The worker may use these four feelings as the basis for responding or reflecting to the client what is happening in regard to the client's feelings. A worker's use of these four basic feelings with clients when relating to the affective, or feeling, component of their communication also may help the clients to become sensitive to and cope with emotional states associated with their abusive behavior.

❏ Social and Cultural Considerations

The social and cultural background and uniqueness of each family must be considered when interviewing individuals and families during the assessment process. Social and cultural competence can be demonstrated by being sensitive to differences in lifestyles. For example, parenting practices may differ across various social and cultural groups, and religious values may influence parental behavior toward children.

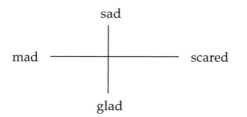

Figure 6.2. Four Basic Feelings

Case Example

Seven-year-old Toi's teacher suspected that he was a victim of child abuse and reported to the school counselor that the child had a large wound on his forearm that was reopened after it had begun to heal. When the teacher asked the child if he had picked off the scab, he responded that he had not, but that his mother had.

The school counselor met with the child's mother, a recent immigrant to the United States, and learned that a cultural practice in the family's country of origin was to rub a coin very hard on a child's forearm when the child was ill and to allow the abrasion to "breathe" for approximately a week. The mother had engaged in this practice following the child's being ill with the flu.

Cultural differences also may affect clients' responses to a worker's attempts to engage them in the assessment process. For example, a parent's failure to have eye contact with the worker may not be indicative of guilt or shame but rather may be in response to cultural proscriptions regarding interactions with strangers.

Demonstrating social and cultural competence through sensitivity to social and cultural issues does not imply that the worker condone child maltreatment when it occurs within these contexts. Rather, the worker must attempt to understand the context in which the maltreatment occurs and assist the client in gaining understanding of the dysfunctional aspects of the behavior. Child protective services workers can enhance their cultural competence by consulting with representatives of diverse social and cultural groups and through self-education from professional journals and conferences (Boyd-Franklin,

1989; DeVore & Schlesinger, 1981; Garbarino & Ebata, 1983; Ghali, 1982; Jenkins, 1981; Logan, Freeman, & McRoy, 1990; Watkins & Gonzales, 1982).

❏ **The Setting**

Providing a setting for interviewing is an important component in the engagement phase of the assessment process, the first step in working with parents, the victim, or other key individuals. As stated earlier, generally initial interviews with parents suspected of maltreatment occur in their home. The failure to structure the setting is an error that protective services workers frequently make when interviewing clients in their homes. Structuring a conducive setting includes interviewing the client without distractions and in confidence.

Protective services workers frequently encounter the problem of gaining access into the home so that an interview can be held in confidence. The worker must take the responsibility of ensuring that an effective interview can occur. For example, it is not inappropriate to ask tactfully if the interview might be conducted inside the home, rather than on the front porch or in the hallway of the apartment building where the client first meets the worker, unless the worker feels endangered by going into the home.

Case Example

Ms. Bradshaw from Child Protective Services was assigned to visit the home of Mr. and Mrs. James, who had been reported by a neighbor for "violently whipping" their 4-year-old son with a belt after he had walked through a flower bed Mr. James had planted recently. Ms. Bradshaw appeared at the James home, without an appointment, for an initial interview. Mrs. James responded to Ms. Bradshaw's knock on the front door.

"Good morning. I'm Katherine Bradshaw from the Child Protective Services Unit of the Department for Social Services. I would like to talk with you a few moments."

"About what?"

"About a complaint that has been filed with our office," replied Ms. Bradshaw.

"A complaint? I don't know what you mean," Mrs. James responded angrily.

"I know this is upsetting, Mrs. James; however, it is very important that I talk with you about this matter," Ms. Bradshaw commented. "Could I step into your living room so that we can discuss this privately?"

After Mrs. James reluctantly invited Ms. Bradshaw into the living room, the social worker was confronted with two additional problems. Another woman, a neighbor or friend, was sitting in Mrs. James's living room. Apparently Mrs. James and this lady had been drinking coffee while watching a soap opera. The television set was set at a high volume to compensate for the noises two small children were making as they ran through the living room on their way to a room in the back part of the house. As Ms. Bradshaw stepped into the living room, she became aware of Mrs. James's guest and the fact that they were watching television.

Ms. Bradshaw immediately said to Mrs. James, "I notice you have company. I'm sorry I couldn't phone you ahead of time to tell you I was coming, but apparently your phone is not in working order. It is very important that I see you at this time. Also, I'm sure you would like to know more about this. Could I meet with you alone?"

"I'm not a proud person. Anything you got to say you can say it here in front of Mabel, my friend," Mrs. James responded.

"I'm glad you feel that way; however, it is necessary for me to see you alone."

Apparently, Mrs. James's friend got the message and stood up, looking for her child as if she were about to leave.

"Come back in an hour, Mabel," Mrs. James said to her friend, "and just leave Jessica here so she and Billy can play. I'll keep an eye on 'em."

Ms. Bradshaw now had Mrs. James alone for a period of time to conduct an interview with her. Other problems confronted her, however: the blaring television set and the children running around. Mrs. James invited Ms. Bradshaw to sit on a chair near the door while she sat on the couch. As Ms. Bradshaw prepared to seat herself, she asked Mrs. James if she minded turning off the television, stating that she felt they could accomplish their business much more quickly if the set was off. Somewhat humorously, Ms. Bradshaw commented, "I don't often see that program myself, but I know how easily I can get hooked into watching it." Mrs. James said that she was hooked on the show but she would turn it off. (Turning the set off rather than just turning the sound down is more effective because, frequently, the silent picture can continue to distract the client and the worker.) Ms. Bradshaw said nothing about the two small children running in and out of the room occasionally, as she believed that their presence would give her an opportunity to observe how Mrs. James interacted with her son and his friend.

Toward the end of the interview, Ms. Bradshaw was sensitive to the fact that Mrs. James's friend, Mabel, left the house knowing that something was going to happen. Also, it was obvious from the state seal on the car Ms. Bradshaw was driving that this was official business of some kind, even if Mabel did not hear the initial conversation on the front porch between Ms. Bradshaw and Mrs. James. Ms. Bradshaw, prior to terminating the interview, thanked Mrs. James for her willingness to see her immediately, realizing that she had interrupted a visit with her friend and their viewing of a soap opera. Ms. Bradshaw asked Mrs. James how she would explain her visit to Mabel and volunteered to help in whatever way she could. Mrs. James did not seem concerned. She stated that the neighbors knew about her husband's temper and the way "he takes it out on Billy." Mrs. James thought she would simply tell Mabel who the visitor was.

❏ Positioning Behaviors

The setting for the interview also includes what Goldberg (1975) refers to as "positioning behaviors" of the worker and client. Positioning behaviors include the seating of the interviewer in relation to the client, the distance at which they position themselves, and eye contact. More possibilities for chair positioning exist in the worker's office than in clients' homes. The protective services worker is encouraged to sit at approximately a 60-degree angle to the client. This angle imparts to the client the nonverbal message, "I am with you." Compare this position of chairs to sitting directly across from a client, which may convey a message of confrontation. For example, interviewing a client from behind a desk with the client seated directly in front of the desk is reminiscent of a courtroom setting, with a client appearing before a judge. This is an appropriate seating position for a judge's role of making a judgment based on testimony. (The judge even may be seated at a level elevated from that of the client.) The protective services worker's role when assessing child abuse and neglect, however, is different. The worker must overcome barriers in communication such as the client's unwillingness to become involved, hostility, and perhaps embarrassment and shame for having maltreated a child.

In addition to sitting at an angle to the client, preferably the worker and client should be relatively close together rather than at a distance across the room. Anthropological research suggests that close seating is associated with personal communication and aids in conveying a message of caring and concern from the interviewer (Hall, 1959). Frequent, though not continual, eye contact with the client also assists in conveying this message. Parents who have been abusive may expect condemnation from others for their behavior, and they will be prepared to defend themselves against such feelings. Through body positioning behaviors, facial expression, and tone of voice, however, the worker can convey a message of care and concern to the client.

❏ Safety

The protective services worker must take into account personal safety when working with child abuse and neglect. Following a few simple guidelines will help to ensure this safety.

If an assessment is to occur in an apartment or house in a high-risk neighborhood and the worker feels endangered by going there, the worker should request that another worker accompany him or her. Workers also should keep their offices informed of their whereabouts, such as when they are entering and leaving a high-risk neighborhood.

Additional suggestions for personal safety include acting confident and assertive. These behaviors project an image that the worker knows where he or she is going rather than looking vulnerable and unsure. If a worker repeatedly must enter a high-risk neighborhood, such as a public housing project, the worker may wish to develop a relationship with certain community members. Key community persons in high-risk neighborhoods can meet a worker and accompany the worker into a building, and their residences or offices can provide places of retreat in the event of a crisis.

If a group of men or young people are congregated on a street corner or are blocking a sidewalk, the worker should avoid walking through the group. The worker should cross the street to pass them. A female social worker is advised not to carry her purse into high-risk areas but instead to lock the purse in the trunk of the car before entering the area. If a purse must be carried, the worker should keep her car keys in a pocket or accessible in her hand, but not in the purse. If car keys are kept in a purse and the purse is stolen, the worker has lost her transportation out of the neighborhood.

Workers are advised to trust their instincts. If, after reading a complaint the worker is to assess or upon arriving in a neighborhood, the worker feels that this is a highly risky situation in which personal safety may be jeopardized, the worker's instinct should be followed, thereby avoiding jeopardizing personal safety. Consultation with a supervisor and peers regarding how to approach the situation is appropriate rather than placing oneself in a highly vulnerable position (Griffin & Bandas, 1987).

The protective services worker may encounter a very angry client. Fighting anger with anger, an inappropriate use of authority, is the least effective response and one that may place the worker's safety in jeopardy. The worker must respond in a warm, authentic, and caring manner, being empathic and understanding of the client's hostile response.

The worker must attempt to understand the source of the anger. Is the anger based on the client's belief that the worker has no right to intervene? Is the client angry that someone reported alleged maltreatment? Is the client angry at the worker's authority? Or, is the anger a defense for the client's wounded self-esteem (American Humane Association, 1980)? Recognizing and responding to the source of the client's anger in an empathic and understanding manner, providing a calm, rational statement regarding the purpose of the visit, and expressing care and concern for the client rather than setting a climate of authority and judgment will assist in dissipating the anger.

> *The worker must attempt to understand the source of the anger.*

❏ **Interviewing Parents**

The adversarial nature of child protection assessment creates a difficult environment for conducting interviews. How well workers prepare, how they engage and join with the parent, and the way they frame questions will significantly influence parental responsiveness. Skillful planning in advance will help the worker achieve the purpose of the interview. The initial assessment interview plan may include

- The goal of the interview
- Whether to interview parents together or separately
- How to engage the parent
- The interview setting
- Social and cultural considerations
- Safety considerations

The goal of the interview is to determine if a child has been abused or neglected. The worker's role is to assess both past and present risks to the child as well as family functioning. The worker's role is not to accuse or determine someone's guilt but to offer services to protect and improve the family's functioning. It is imperative that the worker communicate this helping role to the family. Often, law enforcement personnel may be present during the initial assessment. Their presence may make it more difficult for the worker to communicate to the family that the protective services worker is in a "helping role" rather than the role of a criminal investigator. The protective services worker and law enforcement officer should discuss and clarify these respective roles, either through formal protocols both agencies have mutually established or through a planning session prior to the visit.

The decision of whether to interview parents together or separately may depend on the nature of the alleged maltreatment. Parents should be interviewed separately if a report alleges sexual abuse by one of them. In reports of child neglect, it is preferable to interview parents together. Whether the interviews are conducted separately or together, assessing parental and family attitudes, beliefs, and expectations is important. Paying attention to parents' nonverbal behavior can provide important information for the assessment. Framing comments and questions derived from observation can be helpful in promoting communication and in eliciting additional information. For example, the worker may comment, "Mr. Jones, I noticed that you were smiling when we were talking about your daughter's school activities. This must please you. Tell me more things about your daughter that please you."

This comment encourages the parent to look at the child's strengths rather than focusing on the child's deficient behavior or weaknesses. The parent's response to the comment also may provide the worker with information about his attitudes and expectations regarding the child.

Engaging the parents during the initial assessment interview requires demonstrating acceptance and respect for them, their situation, and their feelings. Managing the interview so that the parents understand who you are, the purpose of the interview, and why questions are being asked is the worker's first task in joining with parents in the assessment process. Eliciting the parents' view of the situation is helpful in the engagement process and allows the worker to acquire information about resources, abilities, and strengths. Following are two examples of ways to acquire information, one ineffective and one effective way. The question "Ms. Roberts, why did your son have those bruises?" will draw a different type of response from the question "Ms. Roberts, could you help me to understand how Mike got his bruises?" The latter approach is nonthreatening and nonaccusatory. Such an approach empowers parents to impart information in a way that is manageable for them.

Framing questions based on parental strengths provides affirmation and increased self-esteem for the individual. Even when interviewing an alleged perpetrator in a sexual abuse situation, this method may be used. For example,

> Mr. Brady, I believe Jane when she tells me you put your hand in her panties and then rub yourself between your legs. I know you love her and don't want to see her so sad and afraid to come home after school. Tell me about what has been happening when she comes home from school.

BOX 6.2

Helpful Hints in Interviewing Adults

- Maintain a neutral stance about the alleged abuse or neglect.
- Recognize the client's feelings, label the feelings, and verbalize these feelings.
- Focus on acquiring the facts, not on why the report was made.
- Be reassuring so that clients believe that you have their best interests at heart.
- Be sensitive to nonverbal communication.
- Interview family members separately and together as appropriate.
- If you do not understand a response, do not assume that you know what was meant. Ask for clarification.
- Convey a sense of caring and concern for the client's best interests.

SOURCE: Adapted from *Child Protective Services: A Guide for Workers* (DHEW Publication No. OHDS 79-30203), by Jenkins, Salus, and Schultze (1979). Reprinted with permission.

Mr. Brady probably will respond to the effect that nothing happens when his daughter comes home. The worker may then respond empathically.

> Mr. Brady, I know it is hard for you to talk about this. However, we must talk about what Jane told me. She drew a picture for me. As you can see, the figure she identifies as you has one hand in her panties and his other hand between his legs. I believe her and I believe this happened. I know you don't want to see her so sad and upset. Tell me what happens after school when she comes home.

Continuing the interview in this manner can facilitate an admission from the alleged perpetrator. In the above comments, the worker reinforces the parent's love for his child, not the abusive behavior. Acquiring an admission of guilt from the sexual abuse perpetrator is very important to the success of further treatment. Conducting this type of interview, however, requires special expertise and confidence and should not be attempted without adequate training and supervision.

Various techniques may help the protective services worker in gathering information from parents. The worker may need to shift from one approach to another to facilitate the task of gathering information for the assessment. Following are several interviewing techniques that can be used effectively to stimulate discussion, clarify facts and feelings, gather information, and in essence help the worker accomplish the goal of the interview (American Humane Association, 1980).

Open-ended questions. This format of questioning encourages the client to talk. An example is the question, "Could you please tell me what happened?" In contrast, closed-ended questions that can be answered with a "yes" or "no" restrict the client's response.

Probing questions. These questions, generally in open-ended format, explore information at progressively deeper levels. For example, "Earlier, Mr. Hall, you mentioned you became upset when you found that Mark did not clean up his room even though he said he had done so. What did you tell him at that time? What was his response? What did you do then?"

Immediate or retrospective clarification. Immediate clarification involves a request for additional information on the subject currently being discussed. For example, "You just said you hit Mark with a belt. Tell me how you were feeling at that moment?" Retrospective clarification involves returning to an earlier subject that may be related to the topic currently under discussion. For example, "Mr. Hall, you said earlier that you lose your cool with Mark at times. Tell me, when is that most likely to happen?"

Summarizing. This technique may be used to bring together aspects of a discussion with a client before moving on to a new topic. Summarizing allows a client to disagree with or correct an impression the worker holds. For example, "Mr. Hall, to summarize what we've been talking about, it seems that Mark not following through on what you expect him to do, and his covering up his failure to do so, is most upsetting to you."

Confrontation. This technique does not imply a harsh "hitting the client between the eyes" with what has been said. Rather, confrontation involves pointing out inconsistencies or contradictions in a client's comments or between what a client says and does, in a way that the client can accept without immediately becoming defensive.

Refocusing the interview. If a client talks incessantly, the worker may interrupt and refocus the interview to accomplish the interview goal.

❏ Interviewing Children

When interviewing a child victim, a protective services worker's first and primary objective is to determine if the child has been abused or neglected. The second objective is to assess risk for further harm to the child. Although allied professionals such as medical and school personnel play critical roles in this assessment, the protective services worker has primary responsibility for ensuring that a thorough investigation will be conducted. Individuals representing different agencies and serving in different roles may need to interview the child; for example, investigating law enforcement officers, the prosecuting and defense attorneys, and juvenile court personnel. The protective services worker, through careful planning, can coordinate those who must interview the child. This reduces the stress and additional trauma a child may experience in the assessment through repeated interviews with various individuals who essentially are seeking the same information. The interview plan should include

- Who is to be interviewed?
- When is the interview to occur?
- Who will conduct the interview?
- Where will the interview be conducted?
- What sequence should the interview follow?

In assessing reported cases of child sexual abuse, the following sequence for interviewing is suggested: the child victim, siblings, the nonoffending parent, and the alleged perpetrator (American Humane Association, 1980).

A helpful way of reducing a child victim's trauma and stress associated with multiple interviews is to videotape the interview. The use of videotaped material as admissible evidence in court, however, may vary on a state-by-state basis.

BOX 6.3

Helpful Hints in Interviewing Children

- Identify the feelings the child may have about talking with a stranger and verbalize these feelings with the child.
- Explain the purpose of the interview.
- Inform the child of the parent's permission for or knowledge of the interview.
- Do not take sides against the parents.
- Speak in language the child understands.
- Be aware of age-appropriate behavior.
- Be sensitive to nonverbal communication.
- Tell the child what will happen next, but do not overinform.

SOURCE: Adapted from *Child Protective Services: A Guide for Workers* (DHEW Publication No. OHDS 79-30203), by Jenkins, Salus, and Schultze (1979). Reprinted with permission.

Even when the alleged perpetrator is the parent, the parent still retains the right to be informed of what is happening with the child in the assessment process, unless the court has decreed otherwise. For example, if a physical examination is required of a child because of alleged physical or sexual abuse, parental consent must be obtained. If the parent refuses to allow the examination, the protective services agency will have an established protocol for seeking such authorization through a judge in the juvenile court.

Interviewing children who have been victims of physical and sexual maltreatment may provoke in the interviewer an array of feelings that may prompt the worker to identify with the child against the parent. The worker must remember that the mother and father are still "Mom" and "Dad" to the child, even though the child may have been maltreated by these individuals. Sometimes parents are the only persons the child can depend on, even though protective services workers may attempt to portray themselves to the child as rescuing them from their parents, who may have been abusive. If a child senses that the worker is talking against a parent, the child's defensiveness will be heightened, and he or she will find it difficult to trust the worker. In most instances, the child's parents will still be in that role long after the protective services worker is out of the scene.

The worker can avoid talking against the parent by keeping in mind the factors associated with various types of maltreatment, such as poverty, isolation, and a parental history of abuse or neglect. More often than not, at the conclusion of an assessment, the parent is found to be a person trying to do his or her best under difficult circumstances.

Relating on the child's level is important when interviewing children. This includes, for example, sitting next to a child rather than interviewing the child from across a desk or table. Using language a child understands also is important. In cases of sexual abuse, a child may refer to parts of the body with colloquial terms. To make the child more comfortable, the worker should adapt to these colloquialisms. Children, depending on age, experience, and development, will have varying verbal abilities. A child's limited verbal skills and the difficulty associated with talking about an abusive incident will complicate the interview process. In these situations, the worker should be prepared to use nonverbal means of communication such as drawings, dolls, or puppets to facilitate the interview.

Empathy can assist a worker in interviewing a child. The worker can put himself or herself in the place of the child and ask how he or she would feel at this moment. Another important self-directed question that gives clues for how to interview a child is, "If I were a child victim of abuse, how would I want an adult to relate to me?"

A helpful way to begin an interview with a child victim is to reassure the child that he or she is not in trouble. If the child reported the maltreatment, the child needs to be assured that this was the right thing to do. If the abuse was reported without the child's knowledge, the child should be assured that the abuse was not his or her fault and that he or she should not feel to blame. Also, when beginning an interview with a child, the social worker must explain carefully the purpose of the assessment interview, in a way the child will understand.

In interviews of children who are alleged to have been victims of sexual abuse, interview content should include an assessment of changes in behavior that have occurred. Such changes may be indicative of child sexual abuse. Changes may be assessed (Cage, 1988) in the following areas:

- Sleep habits, such as the occurrence of bed-wetting, nightmares, excessive sleeping, or the inability to fall asleep
- Changes in school performance
- Physical complaints, especially relative to anal and vaginal areas
- Changes noted in the child's emotional state, such as depression or mood swings
- Sexual behavior, for example, increased interest in sexual functioning
- The child's fears, such as being alone with certain adults or wanting to remain close to a parent or parents
- Unusual or delinquent behaviors in which the child engages, such as substance abuse, running away, or stealing

When the occurrence of these behaviors cannot be determined by interviews with the child, other sources such as parents and teachers should be consulted.

A child may exhibit many of the above behaviors because of trauma related to events other than sexual molestation, such as a serious illness, the separation of parents, or the death of a loved one. The presence of these symptoms, therefore, does not always indicate sexual abuse. The symptoms must be viewed in the perspective of the child's total functioning, with account taken of individual-related, family-related, and social and cultural factors affecting the child.

An interview with a child can be therapeutic to the child. The worker's verbal approach to the child in the interview can empower and validate the child. For example, the interviewer might state,

> Melissa, talking to your counselor about what Uncle Paul did was a very good decision to make. That was the correct thing to do, even though I'm sure you felt uncomfortable doing so.

The interviewer can validate the child's response and empathize with his or her feelings.

> John, telling your teacher the truth about your bruises was correct, even though it must have been awfully scary for you to do so.

Statements such as these let the children know that they have been able to make decisions. Thus, they begin not to feel so powerless in the abusive situation in which they find themselves, and their self-esteem also is enhanced.

A simple outline is suggested for interviewing children who may have been sexually abused. The outline focuses on the following key words and phrases: who, how, when, where, what happened, and did the child/victim tell anyone (Cage, 1988). The worker should avoid, however, asking leading questions relative to these key words that suggest a desired answer. Information acquired from asking leading questions can present problems for the worker later if the case goes to court.

Contradictory information may arise when nonleading questions are used. Note the difference in the following pairs of questions. The first question in each pair represents an open approach; the second a leading approach. The second question suggests an answer, generally a "yes" or "no" response, and cuts off additional information the child may be able to share.

> Mary, help me understand how this occurred.
>   Mary, were you tricked into doing this?
>
> Can you share with me when your uncle touched you?
>   Did your uncle touch you only that one time?
>
> Show me on this drawing where your uncle touched you.
>   Did he just touch you between your legs?

❏ Interviewing Other Key Individuals

Anyone living with the family, such as a grandparent, boarder, or boyfriend, is part of the victim's family system and may provide valuable information for the protective services worker in assessing the family. A tendency may occur for female child protective services workers to overlook interviewing male members of a household because of the primary role they assume that the mother plays for the child's care, the inaccessibility of males during daytime hours, and the worker's fear of the hostility that may be encountered in attempting to interview these persons (Jenkins et al., 1979). In cases of child sexual abuse as well as other types of child maltreatment, however, all members of the household should be interviewed.

Individuals living with the family, although perhaps loosely associated with the family, are part of the family system. Systems theory states that a balance exists in a system between the parts and the whole. Something affecting any part affects the whole system (Brill, 1985). Applying this theory to families as social systems implies that every family member, including individuals loosely attached to the family (a roomer, a baby-sitter, occasional live-in boyfriends), in some way affects the family system as a whole. Although these individuals may not be perpetrators of the maltreatment, they can assist the worker in assessing and understanding the dynamics operating in the family and later in developing appropriate treatment goals.

> *In cases of child sexual abuse all members of the household should be interviewed.*

❏ Types of Information

Two types of information that the protective services worker is seeking in the assessment of a child maltreatment complaint can be identified: primary and secondary. Primary information can be defined as information and observations the worker attains from interviews with the child, the parents, or other family members. The worker may make observations of a physical as well as an emotional nature. Included in the information and observations the worker makes of a physical nature would be indicators of abuse or neglect, such as bruises on the child's body, inadequate or soiled clothing, and the unkempt nature of the family home. Information and observations of an emotional nature would include the way family members interact with one another and the worker's evaluation of the emotional climate in the family. For example, how do the parents relate to the child? Do they show warmth and concern for the child?

Do the adult family members show respect for one another? Was the worker able to observe the way the parents disciplined the child?

The worker's observations of the way family members relate to one another may confirm or cast doubt on how they verbally describe the way they interact. For example, if the worker observes that the father does not seem involved with the family, this behavior would certainly not support a parent's description of the family as being "close-knit." Eye contact, facial expressions, tone of voice, the presence or absence of communication among family members, and the ability to express feelings may be additional important indicators of the emotional climate of the family (Jenkins et al., 1979).

Secondary sources of data include information the worker secures from medical evaluations and past medical records, school information and records, police records, photographs, and information from other community mental health or social services agencies with which the family has had contact. A protective services worker must check with an agency regarding procedures to be followed in securing information from secondary sources. Procedures may vary in different jurisdictions because of state law and interagency agreements regarding sharing information in child abuse and neglect cases.

❑ **Summary**

Working with child abuse and neglect requires that the protective services worker possess excellent interviewing skills. Respect and empathy are important tools for effectively interviewing child maltreatment victims, parents, the offender, and other concerned individuals. Respect for clients as individuals within their social and cultural context is an important element of effective interviewing. Through the use of empathy, the worker recognizes the diversity of emotions clients may be experiencing—such as anger, shame, or fear—and then communicates a caring and understanding attitude. This demonstrates to the client that the worker cares, is concerned, and is working in the client's best interest.

❏ Suggested Reading

Cage, R. (1988). Criminal investigation of child sexual abuse. In S. Sgroi (Ed.), *Vulnerable populations* (Vol. 1, pp. 187-227). Lexington, MA: Lexington Books.

This chapter presents guidelines and sample questions for interviewing victims and perpetrators of sexual abuse. Sample interviews are included.

DeLipsey, J., & Kelly, S. (1988). Videotaping the sexually abused child: The Texas experience, 1983-1987. In S. Sgroi (Ed.), *Vulnerable populations* (Vol. 1, pp. 229-254). Lexington, MA: Lexington Books.

This chapter presents the pros and cons of, as well as special problems connected with, the use of videotaping sexually abused children. See also Appendix 9-B and 9-C (pp. 257-264) for a sample protocol for videotaping testimony and a partial transcript of a videotaped interview.

Faller, K. (1988). *Child sexual abuse: An interdisciplinary manual for diagnosis, case management, and treatment.* New York: Columbia University Press.

Chapters 6, 7, and 8 focus on interviewing the child, interviewing the perpetrator, and interviewing the mother.

Jenkins, J., Salus, M., & Schultze, G. (1979). *Child protective services: A guide for workers* (DHEW Publication No. OHDS 79-30203). Washington, DC: National Center on Child Abuse and Neglect.

As the title implies, this manual is an excellent resource for protective services workers, covering the assessment and intervention phase with the family and providing helpful information on working with the courts.

MacFarlane, L., & Krebs, S. (1986). Techniques for interviewing and evidence gathering. In K. MacFarlane, J. Waterman, S. Conerly, L. Damon, M. Durfee, & S. Long (Eds.), *Sexual abuse of young children* (pp. 67-100). New York: Guilford.

This chapter provides helpful guidelines for the worker in interviewing sexually abused children.

Sgroi, S. (Ed.). (1982). *Handbook of clinical intervention in child sexual abuse.* Lexington, MA: Lexington Books.

Chapters by various writers provide valuable information for working with victims of sexual abuse in the assessment and treatment phases.

7

Child Abuse and Neglect Treatment

The protective services worker compiles the information gathered during the initial fact-finding interviews or assessment into a brief but comprehensive statement called the diagnostic summary. This statement reflects the worker's understanding of the maltreatment based on individual-related, family-related, and social and cultural factors. The diagnostic summary also serves as the basis for identifying goals to be accomplished in treatment. Depending on resources available, treatment may take place within the child protective services agency, or referrals may be made to other community mental health and social services agencies. When services are not available, the protective services worker may work in the role of advocate to encourage the establishment of needed community treatment resources.

When an agency initiates treatment with an abusive or neglectful family, the worker's diagnostic summary serves as an important initial statement in understanding the family's behavior. The worker responsible for treating the family, however, generally engages in a diagnostic assessment as the initial phase of the treatment process. This chapter opens with a discussion of the initial step in the treatment process, the diagnostic assessment. Emphasis will be given to a diagnostic assessment of child sexual abuse because of special problems associated with this form of child maltreatment. Next, the chapter will answer the question, "What is treatment?" General rules and principles governing treatment, as well as a range of treatment models, will be presented. The chapter will conclude with a discussion of treatment issues relative to race and culture.

❏ **Diagnostic Assessment in Treatment**

Although the diagnostic summary provides the worker responsible for treatment with an initial understanding of the case, further information generally is required. The worker obtains this information through a diagnostic assessment prior to implementing treatment.

PURPOSE

The purpose of the diagnostic assessment is to assist the worker in planning treatment. The assessment should identify specific target behaviors and issues to which treatment can be directed (Friedrich, 1990). Target behaviors and issues for treatment may include, for example, poor impulse control, inability to express anger, absence of prosocial behaviors between parent and child, inadequate or inappropriate parenting knowledge and skills, unsafe housing, absence of financial support, or inadequate supervision of a child during parental absence.

Social workers often mistakenly perceive assessment associated with treatment as focusing on the family members' intrapsychic dynamics. This may be one aspect of assessment; however, assessment is much broader. The diagnostic assessment must be viewed from an ecological perspective, taking into account individual-related, family-related, and social and cultural factors.

The diagnostic assessment culminates in a statement identified as the "treatment plan." The treatment plan identifies specific goals to be accomplished in treatment and interventive strategies for accomplishing these goals. The goals serve as the treatment focus and the basis, later, for evaluating treatment effectiveness (to be discussed in Chapter 9).

KNOWLEDGE AND SKILLS

The worker initially assessing the maltreatment report may not continue treating the family, or the family may be referred to another agency. In these instances, the family must become involved in a new helping relationship. This may present difficulties for the family and worker. This helping relationship, however, is critical to treatment effectiveness and sets the tone for all that follows. The family members must believe that the worker knows what to do and is invested in their welfare. The worker's task is to accept responsibility for the case and to demonstrate very early in the treatment process that services will be provided in a fair, nonjudgmental, and compassionate manner (Sgroi, 1982a).

An accurate and comprehensive diagnostic assessment is essential to good case management and for achieving treatment goals. The worker must bring to the case knowledge and skills necessary for understanding and responding to the nature, extent, and dynamics of the maltreatment. The worker's focus in the diagnostic assessment will be on the individual family members, the family as a social system, and social and cultural factors affecting the latter. At the individual level, for example, the worker must be sensitive to personality factors predisposing the parents to self-defeating behaviors contributing to their inability to adequately and appropriately function in their parental role. At the family level, the worker must analyze interactive patterns among family members that are abusive and that disregard the rights and needs of the family members. Such patterns may be intergenerational and resistant to change. Finally, social and cultural factors must be assessed; for example, environmental forces that may be denying the family access to services for meeting basic needs and that contribute to feelings of anxiety and powerlessness, or religious values that support the use of severe forms of corporal punishment.

The worker will be prepared to look beyond the family unit to other sources of information in the diagnostic assessment associated with treatment. While compiling the maltreatment assessment report, the protective services worker may have contacted teachers, school counselors, medical personnel, and others to assist in determining whether child maltreatment occurred and whether the child was at risk for further abuse. These individuals and the information they provided may serve as resources in the treatment assessment by helping the worker treating the family understand how the family functions. They also may identify individual and family strengths that the worker can build on in the treatment process.

As stated earlier, this information already may be available to the worker from the diagnostic summary, or the worker may wish to explore in depth specific areas of the clients' functioning as treatment is initiated. Assessment associated with treatment is not a one-time event, nor are diagnostic impressions cast in concrete. Rather, the diagnostic assessment is an ongoing and continual process. The social worker begins to know and understand the family from working with it. For example, a social worker conducting a parent education group for abusive parents found that a couple's marital problems were interfering with their ability to parent successfully. This was not apparent in the initial maltreatment report assessment. At the agency's request, the couple sought marital counseling. As more information is gained about clients, the worker's understanding of the family's dynamics may change, and treatment plans likewise may need to be changed or fine tuned.

ASSESSMENT TOOLS

Numerous tools are available to workers to assist them in the diagnostic assessment. The EcoMap and Family Genogram are two examples.

The EcoMap. The EcoMap is a diagram showing the relationship between a family as a social system and other social systems in the environment. This assessment tool, based on an ecological understanding of human behavior, may focus on the family, the family's composition, the relationships of individual family members to one another, and the relationship of the family as a unit to extended family members and to other systems in the community, such as those related to work, school, recreation, and health resources. The EcoMap assists the worker in understanding the balance that exists between a family and its environment and the stresses that affect the family. It also identifies the resources available within the family and its environment for coping with these stresses. When the worker uses an EcoMap, the family is provided with a visual, or graphic, view of its functioning as a social system in interaction with its environment. The EcoMap also will help the worker and family identify specific problem areas associated with the abuse to which treatment may be directed (Hartman, 1979).

The Family Genogram. Whereas the EcoMap demonstrates the family's relationship to its environment, the Family Genogram provides a historical perspective on the family (Hartman, 1979; McGoldrick & Gerson, 1985). Completing a Family Genogram may highlight dysfunctional family patterns occurring over time. For example, the Family Genogram may identify a pattern, over several generations, of suicides or hospitalizations for depression in response to stress. This assessment tool assists the worker and family in understanding how current functioning and sense of self have been shaped by the past. Family members may identify cultural and religious values affecting customs, traditions, and typical patterns of response to crises. As family members describe parents and grandparents and identify similarities and differences between themselves and these individuals, family values influencing parenting, family member roles, and issues surrounding sexuality will be brought into the open for discussion in treatment.

The EcoMap and Family Genogram bring together in a meaningful way information on boundaries among family members and around the family as a system, the family's interaction with other social systems, the way in which the family is structured, the nature of communication patterns in the family, and accepted, assumed, or unclear rules governing the family (Hartman, 1979; McGoldrick & Gerson, 1985; Satir, 1972). The process of completing an EcoMap or Family Genogram requires the participation of family members, thereby providing the worker an opportunity to observe family interactions when confronting a task and to see how the family resolves conflicts that may arise in the process.

The Family Assessment Form (FAF). The staff of the Children's Bureau of Los Angeles (n.d.) developed this instrument based on extensive experience in working with child abuse and neglect. The FAF views child maltreatment from an ecological perspective and provides the worker a comprehensive guide for assessing a family, planning services, and evaluating treatment effectiveness. The instrument may be used to collect information on individual family members' psychosocial functioning, the relationship of family members to one another, the functioning of the family as a unit or social system, the nature of the family's environment, and the family's interaction with this environment. Workers rate the family's functioning on a scale ranging from 1 to 5, with 1 indicating above-average functioning in the area and 5 indicating situations that endanger children's health, safety, or well-being. Detailed examples of observations, behaviors, or responses are provided for the rater. Workers complete the instrument following contacts with the family rather than using it as a guide for interviewing the family.

Information from the five substantive sections of the instrument are summarized and provide the basis for formulating a treatment plan. The instrument is completed at the initial assessment phase and again following the completion of treatment.

❏ Assessment for Treatment in Child Sexual Abuse

Special problems associated with child sexual abuse may require specific attention in assessment prior to initiating treatment.

GENERAL PRINCIPLES

Sexual victimization may significantly affect a child's normal psychosocial development. The diagnostic assessment for treatment must appraise the nature of this impact on the child's functioning. Sexual victimization may seriously impair a child's ability to trust others, including family members the child loves or authority figures the child respects. Initial disbelief when reporting the abuse and subsequent questioning by family members and social services and legal authorities may leave the child with the message that the abuse is partly the victim's fault. This self-blame may be seen in the child's self-esteem and self-worth. Through sexual victimization, the child is forced to experience adult sexuality without the cognitive or emotional maturity to respond to the premature eroticization (Yates, 1982). Such developmental derailment may result in a profound loss of childhood and may seriously interfere with the child's ability to master childhood tasks, including development of impulse control and a healthy autonomy (Adams-Tucker, 1982). Child sexual abuse also affects the family as a social system by creating role and boundary confusion. The shame and secrecy that surrounds incestuous relationships interferes with the family's ability to meet the psychosocial needs of its members and to protect the welfare of the victimized child and the family as a whole. These represent important areas for assessment and treatment in child sexual abuse.

The following are questions that can assist a social worker in assessing the nature, extent, and dynamics surrounding a child's sexual abuse.

What is the nature, extent, and history of the abuse; namely, what happened, when did the abuse begin, how long did it continue, and with what frequency?

What was the child's age, gender, and developmental stage when the abuse occurred? What are the age and developmental stage now, when treatment is beginning?

How vulnerable was the child at the time of the abuse? For example, were special factors operating relative to handicapping or developmental conditions, chronic lack of supervision, or the child being adopted or a foster child?

What was the child's relationship to the offender, including emotional relationship, degree of bonding, and offender's continued access to the child?

In what context did the abuse occur; for example, was there psychological or physical coercion or evidence of physical violence?

How did disclosure occur? Was it accidental or intentional?

What was the response of significant others to the disclosure? Were they supportive of the child? Did they refuse to believe the victim or blame or punish the victim? What was the response of the offender?

To what extent is the sexual abuse a current threat to the child's physical and/or emotional safety?

What is the nature of the child's current support system (immediate family, extended family, friends, neighbors)?

What are the medical and legal considerations of the sexual abuse—for example, results of a medical exam, criminal charges, or juvenile court proceedings?

INSTRUMENTS FOR THE DIAGNOSTIC ASSESSMENT OF SEXUAL ABUSE

The Traumatic Event Interview. This is a structured interview that can be used with children who have been sexually abused or who have experienced any violent event (Eth & Pyroos, 1985). The interview consists of three stages: opening stage, trauma stage, and closure stage.

The opening stage establishes the purpose or focus of the interview. The therapist greets the child, stating that he or she has talked with other children who have gone through a similar experience. The purpose of the opening stage is to inform children that they are not alone in having experienced this trauma. The child is given materials for drawing a picture and telling what happened. This activity involves the child in the diagnostic assessment and treatment rather than allowing the child to remain in a passive, helpless, or powerless state as a result of the trauma. The assumption is that the child will introduce the trauma in the drawing or accompanying story. The drawing and story provide the therapist information on how the child is experiencing the abuse, especially fears and anxieties associated with the trauma. The omission of significant features of the trauma may indicate aspects of the victimization that the child may not be able to express.

In the trauma stage, the therapist moves to an open or explicit discussion of the victimization. Something in a child's drawing or story may allow the therapist to shift to this stage. The child may react to the discussion of the event, an experience other family members may have stifled in the child, with an emotional outpouring. The child is asked to discuss details of the victimization, the worst moment of the experience, and even sensory experiences such as odors and physical pain. Toward the end of the trauma stage, the therapist shifts to a discussion of responsibility for the event: How could someone do something like this? If the child experiences self-blame for the sexual victimization, the therapist can respond from a realistic perspective. The therapist will encourage the child to discuss other reactions to the trauma, including anxiety, nausea, nightmares, and fear of revictimization.

> *The therapist moves to an open or explicit discussion of the victimization.*

In the third and final stage of the interview, closure is sought. As part of closure, the therapist focuses on the trauma's impact on current functioning; for example, family and peer relationships and school performance. Specific goals for treatment may be identified from assessing the child's functioning in these areas. The session is closed with the therapist encouraging the child to state what has been helpful or upsetting about the interview. By doing so, the therapist expresses interest in and respect for the child.

The Child Sexual Behavior Inventory. This instrument enables a worker to assess a child's sexual behavior problems linked to the occurrence of sexual abuse (Friedrich, 1990). Parents may find data from the instrument helpful in recognizing rather than ignoring the nature and extent of their child's sexual behavior stemming from the victimization. The instrument's author cautions, in connection with the use of this diagnostic tool, that beginning at age 2 and continuing to age 12, there is a steady decrease in overall sexual behavior at every age. The Child Sexual Behavior Inventory is available in Friedrich's *Psychotherapy of Sexually Abused Children and Their Families* (1990).

Assessment and Psychological Testing. A worker may wish to con-duct psychological testing as part of the assessment process associ-ated with treatment. A clinical psychologist knowledgeable of factors associated with sexual victimization and its impact on victims should do the testing. A worker should be clear on the reason psychological testing is being requested and communicate this to the psychologist so that test results will be meaningful and helpful to the assessment process. The psychologist can help the worker interpret the test results to ensure that they are properly understood and used in treatment.

❏ **Treatment:**
   Definition and Principles

Mental health professionals repeatedly refer to "treating clients." What is meant by the term "treatment"? A brief review of the concept will provide a foundation for later discussion of specific treatment models useful in working with child abuse and neglect.

Treatment may be defined as the application of interventions that help a client accomplish goals for positive change. Treatment, in essence, answers the following questions: How can clients change dysfunctional individual, family, and social and cultural factors associated with the maltreatment? How can workers intervene to help victims recover from the emotional pain they are experiencing as a result of their maltreatment? How can individuals and families be helped to prevent maltreatment from occurring again?

A mental health professional treats individuals and families within a context conceptualized as the helping relationship. Biestek (1957) identified seven principles governing the helping relationship: indi-vidualization, acceptance, nonjudgmental attitude, purposeful ex-pression of feelings, controlled emotional involvement, client self-determination, and confidentiality. *Individualization* means that the worker will view each client as a unique individual, despite similari-ties with other clients. *Acceptance* implies a respect for the client's innate dignity and personal worth, including strengths and weaknesses, congenial and uncongenial qualities, and constructive and destructive attitudes and behavior. A *nonjudgmental attitude* assumes that the worker begins by focusing on how to help the client rather than on assigning guilt or blame. The *purposeful expression of feelings* implies that the worker allows and encourages the client to talk about facts and feelings surrounding the maltreatment as well as life in general relative to what has happened. Individualization means that the worker respects the client and does not attempt to take over the client's life. The worker facilitates the achievement of, or helps the client to achieve, goals the client wishes to accomplish relative to changing circumstances and behaviors associated with the maltreatment. Thus, the worker exhibits *controlled emotional involvement* and allows the client choices and decisions, or *self-determination,* in changing the conditions and solving the problems associated with the maltreatment. Finally, the worker has an ethical obligation to respect information acquired from the client and to treat this information *confidentially.*

Treatment also may be conceptualized from the perspective of social roles. The therapist assumes different roles with clients when working with child abuse and neglect. These roles include broker, enabler, teacher, mediator, and advocate (Compton & Galaway, 1979).

Treatment occurs within certain parameters. The American Humane Association (1980) identifies these parameters as ten rules of practice that a worker should follow in working with child abuse and neglect (see Box 7.1).

❑ Effects of Maltreatment on the Victims

The effects of abuse on the victims will be discussed prior to the discussion of various treatment strategies for victims of child maltreatment. Numerous studies report the effects of child maltreatment on the victims shortly after the abuse has occurred as well as later in the survivors' adult lives. The results of these studies will be reviewed.

BOX 7.1

Rules of Practice When
Working With Child Abuse and Neglect

Rule 1: The child's safety and well-being are always a prerequisite in any treatment strategy.

Rule 2: Treatment must be goal oriented.

Rule 3: Treatment must be planned and must flow from the worker's diagnostic understanding of the case.

Rule 4: Treatment is purposeful and is based on goals or desirable outcomes to be achieved.

Rule 5: Treatment is selective in using the alternatives available and the client's ability to use them.

Rule 6: Treatment should be assertive, implying a positive attitude on the part of the worker that change can occur despite the severity of the client's problem and/or a client's lack of motivation.

Rule 7: Treatment must match the complexity of the problem and may require a range of treatment alternatives over an extended period of time.

Rule 8: The intent of treatment is for clients to take control of their own lives, to grow, and to become responsible.

Rule 9: Treatment is reality oriented and focuses on the here and now—what the clients can do now about their problems.

Rule 10: The client is the major resource, participant, and focal point in treatment. The therapist serves as a facilitator in the treatment process.

SOURCE: Adapted from *Helping in Child Protective Services: A Casework Handbook,* © copyright 1991 by the American Humane Association. Reprinted with permission.

EFFECTS OF NEGLECT AND
PHYSICAL AND EMOTIONAL ABUSE

The psychological functioning of a sample of children with case histories of at least 2 years of physical and emotional parental abuse (average age slightly over 10 years) was compared with a group of nonmaltreated children of a comparable age. The children were matched on socioeconomic characteristics and were from the same geographical communities. The abused children showed greater feelings of sadness as well as lower self-esteem and feelings of self-worth. Their lack of control over what had happened in their lives generated in the survivors a sense of helplessness toward life in general or more specifically about themselves, others, and the world (Cerezo & Frias, 1994).

In a study of school-aged and adolescent children who were physically abused or neglected, compared with a sample not maltreated, the maltreated children exhibited pervasive and severe academic and psychosocial problems, even when socioeconomic status was controlled in the two groups. The school functioning of the adolescent children was so poor that they were at high risk of dropping out of school. The abused children also showed more behavioral problems in the classroom when compared to their nonabused counterparts. Their anger, distractibility, anxiety, and lack of self-control made it virtually impossible for the maltreated children to achieve in school despite the excellence of the education program (Kurtz, Gaudin, Wodarski, & Howing, 1993).

Similarly, research shows that child abuse represents a significant risk factor for poor long-term intellectual and academic outcomes. Childhood victims of abuse and neglect showed lower levels of intellectual ability and academic achievement attained in young adulthood compared to matched controls (Perez & Widom, 1994; Wodarski, Kurtz, Gaudin, & Howing, 1990). Research has demonstrated that these effects of childhood victimization on intellectual and academic functioning extend even into adulthood. Although these effects often are thought to be associated with the lower economic status of the families in which abuse or neglect occurred, when socioeconomic status of families was controlled in the research, the differences in intellectual and academic functioning remained between the maltreated and nonmaltreated samples. The reasons for these effects are not clear; however, researchers suggest that early childhood abuse and neglect may lead to sequelae that have negative effects on subsequent cognitive and intellectual development. Certain forms of physical abuse, such as battering, may lead to developmental retardation, which can affect cognitive development (Perez & Widom, 1994).

Emotional maltreatment can affect the psychosocial functioning of children. In a study of 3,346 American parents with a child under age 18 living at home, researchers found that 63% reported one or more instances of verbal aggression, such as swearing and insulting the child. Children who experienced frequent verbal aggression from their parents, which could be classified as emotional abuse, showed

Disclosure of abuse can result in hostile and rejecting responses.

higher rates of physical aggression, delinquency, and interpersonal problems than did other children when measured on the Conflict Tactic Scales, an instrument used frequently in studies of family violence. The findings held for children in preschool, elementary school, and high school and for children of both genders (Vissing, Straus, Gelles, & Harrop, 1991).

EFFECTS OF SEXUAL ABUSE

Rejection. Disclosing to others that one has been sexually abused can affect the victim. Disclosure of abuse can result in hostile and rejecting responses from significant individuals in the victim's life. The process of disclosure can undermine the supportive relationship the victim may have with these individuals and place the disclosing victim in a socially isolated situation. A worsening of psychiatric symptomatology can occur at the time of disclosure for adult psychiatric patients (McNulty & Wardle, 1995).

Depression and Suicide. Children who have been sexually abused show high rates of depression as well as suicide attempts and suicidal ideation (Goodwin, 1981; Peters & Range, 1995; Smucker, Craighead, Craighead, & Green, 1986). In a study of sexually abused children seen for a psychological evaluation at a university clinic, researchers found that 37% of the sample had thought about suicide but indicated that they would not attempt it, and 5% reported that they wanted to kill themselves (Wozencraft, Wagner, & Pellegrin, 1991). Similarly, in a study of 266 college students, both women and men in the sample who had been sexually abused were more suicidal as adult college students than were their counterparts who had not experienced sexual abuse. Women reported degrees of suicidality similar to those of men, but they demonstrated greater survival and coping strategies and more fear of suicide than men. Those whose sexual abuse involved touching were more suicidal and felt less able to cope than nonabused students. Adults whose sexual abuse was exploitive but did not involve touch were not significantly different from nonabused adults. The researchers believed that the experience of being touched in a sexual way appeared to be more damaging than other kinds of unwanted sexual experiences in terms of suicidality and coping (Peters & Range, 1995). High rates of attempted suicide also were found in samples of adults who were sexually abused by a sibling when they were growing up (Wiehe, 1990b).

Children who are sexually abused often initially respond to their molestation by being depressed. The depression experienced by these children may be only the beginning of mental health problems that will occur as these children grow into adulthood (Koverola, Pound, Heger, & Lytle, 1993).

Psychological Problems. A study of 93 prepubertal children evaluated for sexual abuse and a comparison group of 80 nonabused children matched on age, gender, and race involved administering the Child Behavior Checklist (CBCL). The sexually abused children had significantly more behavior problems than the comparison group, including depression, aggression, sleep and somatic complaints, hyperactivity, and sexual problems (Dubowitz, Black, Harrington, & Verschoore, 1993).

In a study of 750 males age 18 to 27, 117 had experienced one or more unwanted sexual contacts as a child. Approximately one half of these individuals recalled experiencing multiple events of sexual abuse. The survivors were shown to have higher rates of current or recent depression, anxiety, and suicidal feelings and behavior. Those who had been sexually abused also demonstrated more sexual interest in or actual behavior involving minors when compared to their counterparts who had not experienced multiple incidents of sexual abuse as a youngster (Bagley, Wood, & Young, 1994).

High rates of posttraumatic stress disorder (PTSD) have been found in samples of sexually abused children and adult survivors of sexual abuse (Deblinger, McLeer, Atkins, Ralphe, & Foa, 1989; Greenwald & Leitenberg, 1990; Rowan, Foy, Rodriguez, & Ryan, 1994).

The symptoms experienced by these survivors include sleep disturbances, anxiety, and depression, which negatively affect their daily psychosocial functioning and for which many seek psychological help (McNew & Abell, 1995).

Dissociation is a problem often resulting from childhood sexual abuse (Gelinas, 1983; Goodwin, 1985; Herman, Russell, & Trocki, 1986; Young, 1992). Victims will dissociate themselves from the trauma occurring to them in sexual abuse and will deny the feelings that accompany the trauma as well as the trauma itself. Multiple personality disorder, a dissociative disorder, often is seen in sexual abuse survivors.

Substance Abuse. Women sexually abused as children often are found as adults to be drug and alcohol abusers (Boyd, Blow, & Orgain, 1993; Boyd, Guthrie, Pohl, Whitmarsh, & Henderson, 1994). Benward and Densen-Gerber (1975) reported that in a sample of female drug users, 44% had been victims of incest. Similarly, in a sample of 35 alcoholic women and a comparison group of nonalcoholics, researchers found that 34% of the alcoholics as compared to 16% of the nonalcoholics had experienced sexual abuse from a relative as a child (Covington & Kohen, 1984). Kovak (1986) found, in a group of 117 women attending Alcoholics Anonymous meetings who responded to a self-administered questionnaire, that nearly 25% of them had a childhood incest experience. Wiehe (1990b) likewise found that 25% of adult survivors of sibling abuse had been sexually molested as children by a sibling. In a study of recovering chemically dependent women living in a long-term treatment facility, the researchers found that 68% of the 60 respondents had been recipients of unwanted sexual contacts from perpetrators such as uncles, brothers, fathers, family friends, neighborhood boys, and strangers (Teets, 1995).

Substance abuse also can be a problem for men who have been sexually abused. In a study of men admitted for treatment of alcoholism to the Alcohol Rehabilitation Department at Camp Pendleton Naval Hospital, 30% admitted that they had been sexually victimized during childhood (Johanek, 1988).

The number of adult substance abusers who have been sexually abused as children may be higher than often reported because of the reluctance of adults to disclose earlier sexual victimization. Researchers found in a study investigating the rate of disclosure of childhood sexual abuse to staff in a treatment facility that initially only 20% of the women revealed abuse. After more extensive inquiry, however, the rate rose to 75% (Rohsenow, Corbett, & Devine, 1988).

Eating Disorders. Research shows a relationship between being sexually abused and experiencing eating disorders later in life. Being sexually abused can lead to self-denigratory beliefs that in turn lead to emotional instability. Sexual abuse survivors frequently use bingeing and purging, symptoms of anorexia and bulimia, to reduce these feelings (Lacey, 1990; Miller, McCluskey-Fawcett, & Irving, 1993; Waller, 1994). Seventy-two young adult women identified as having a high probability of suffering from bulimia nervosa were compared with matched controls who did not display bulimic symptoms. Both groups were given measures to determine if sexual abuse had occurred in their pasts. The women diagnosed as bulimic were found to have significantly greater rates of self-reported sexual abuse after the age of 12 with an adult relative as the perpetrator. Statistically nonsignificant but high rates of sexual abuse prior to age 12 also were found (Miller et al., 1993).

Health Problems. Having been abused as a child can have long-term health consequences for a woman. In a study of middle-class females in a gynecological practice, comparisons were made between those women who reported a history of physical, emotional, or sexual abuse on a self-administered, anonymous questionnaire and those not reporting having been abused. The abused women reported significantly more hospitalizations for illnesses, a greater number of physical and psychological problems, and lower ratings of their overall health. When the number of childhood abuses was considered—physical abuse, emotional abuse, and/or sexual abuse—the researchers found that the greater the number of childhood abuses, the poorer a woman's adult health was likely to be and the more likely she was to experience abuse as an adult. Divorce also was found to have occurred more frequently in the abused group as compared to the nonabused. In this highly educated sample of 668 middle-class women, an abuse rate of 19.8% was found (Moeller, Backmann, & Moeller, 1993).

Parenting Problems. Being a victim of sexual abuse, especially father-daughter incest, can affect the survivor's parenting ability. In one research study (Herman, 1981), three groups of women were studied: women with a history of father-daughter incest as children, comparison groups of women not sexually abused but whose fathers were alcoholic, and women who had not experienced sexual abuse as children. Researchers found that the women with a history of father-daughter sexual abuse exhibited difficulties in parenting their children adequately. These mothers felt less confident and less emotionally controlled as parents as compared to their counterparts. There were similarities with the mothers who had alcoholic fathers (Russell, 1986). It should be noted that alcohol was a significant problem in many of the families in which father-daughter incest had occurred, as has been found in other studies. Mothers who were childhood incest victims reported feeling a lack of confidence in their parenting responsibilities and seemed overwhelmed by the demands of parenting, especially in promoting autonomy in their children. Notable also were problems associated with parental consistency, organization, the appropriate assignment of responsibilities to the child, and the ability to parent with a firm and sure but sensitive manner (Cole, Woolger, Power, & Smith, 1992; Maccoby & Martin, 1983).

❏ Treatment Models

The social worker will select appropriate treatment resources based on an understanding of individual, family, and social and cultural factors associated with the maltreatment. An array of interventive resources, ranging from environmental change to psychotherapy, may be used. The worker's treatment choice may be limited by availability of treatment resources and the client's ability to use the resources.

Various treatment models will be presented in the following pages. More detailed information on these treatment models is available from national organizations associated with specific models and programs (see Appendix B).

TREATING CHILD NEGLECT

Project 12-Ways. Project 12-Ways demonstrates an ecobehavioral approach to treating child neglect using a wide range of community services (Lutzker, Frame, & Rice, 1982). The project provided 15 different services, based on individual or family need, to abusive and neglectful families in rural southern Illinois.

1. *Parent-child training.* This structured training helped parents reduce aversive behaviors in children and increase prosocial behaviors. For example, parents learned to use praise and time-out with their children rather than repeatedly resorting to "don't do" messages.
2. *Stress reduction.* Some parents were taught relaxation techniques as a way of reducing stress and anxiety.
3. *Assertiveness training.* Adults learned to be responsible and to express their feelings effectively through assertiveness training.
4. *Self-control.* Specific programs were designed to teach control over anger, weight, smoking, and other areas involving dysfunctional behavior.
5. *Basic skills.* Children and adults received training in basic life skills that neglectful families often lack. Basic skills included toilet training, bicycle riding, shoe tying, conversation, and family shopping.
6. *Leisure time.* Parents were given information and skills on simple and inexpensive ways to spend leisure time.
7. *Marital counseling.* Parents having difficulty in their marriage were referred for marital counseling.
8. *Substance abuse treatment.* Clients with substance abuse problems were referred to appropriate treatment resources.
9. *Social support.* Because child neglect often is associated with parents' social isolation, parent support groups were organized to encourage positive interactions with other adults.
10. *Employment.* Unemployed family members were assisted in finding employment. Employment helped to reduce the family's poverty, which was associated with their neglect.
11. *Money management.* Clients were taught simple tasks, such as economical shopping and budgeting, using protocols based on individual needs.
12. *Prevention.* Numerous social services were directed to potentially abusive or neglectful parents, such as teenage mothers, that assisted them in nutrition education, preparation for the birth of the child, infant care, safety, parent-child stimulation, and family planning.

13. *Health maintenance and nutrition.* Trained homemakers taught nutritious meal planning, shopping, cooking, and serving, using individualized training protocols.
14. *Home safety.* Parents were taught home safety procedures such as keeping children out of contact with poisons, weapons, and dangerous objects as well as avoiding fire and electrical hazards.
15. *Multiple-setting behavior management.* Project staff also worked with professionals in other settings, such as schools, day care centers, and foster homes, on helping these allied services to intervene effectively in the dysfunctional family systems.

Research evaluated this multifaceted, ecobehavioral approach to working with abusive and neglectful families as very effective. Treatment programs such as Project 12-Ways, which use an array of services tailored to the specific needs of an individual or family, are very costly. Evaluative research, however, documented the program's effectiveness and found the costs to be reasonable considering the program's impact. The program broke into families' intergenerational cycle of neglect, thereby preventing a continuing pattern of child maltreatment. These types of interventions are also cost effective when compared to the cost of providing substitute care for those children who may have been removed from their homes if this intervention had not been implemented.

Parents and Children Together (PACT). PACT represents another program model demonstrating a multifaceted approach to child neglect (Kropp, 1985). This home-based program intervened in abusive and neglectful families without removing children from the home. Parents' psychosocial functioning was diagnosed using an ecological approach to human development (Belsky, 1980; Bronfenbrenner, 1979). Three areas of functioning were assessed: the microsystem, or characteristics of the family; the exosystem, or characteristics of the neighborhood and the family's social supports; and ontogenic development, or the effects of the parents' history on present parenting practices. Workers then identified treatment strategies to counter deficiencies in these areas. Treatment strategies included homemaker services, parent education courses, job training, and referral to community social service agencies, mental health services, and legal services. When services were not available, the project staff assumed an advocacy role by working toward establishment of the needed services.

TREATING PHYSICAL
AND PSYCHOLOGICAL ABUSE

Community resources, such as day care centers, family counseling agencies, and child guidance clinics, are useful in treating a range of problems in living and also may be used in treating physical and psychological abuse. This section will describe two resources aimed specifically at treating physically and psychologically abusive families, namely, Parents Anonymous (PA) and parent education courses.

Parents Anonymous (PA). This program, operated primarily by parents, is available in many communities throughout the United States (Bornman & Lieber, 1984; Fritz, 1989; Lieber, 1983). PA groups follow a self-help model and meet once a week for 2 hours in a free meeting place, such as a church basement, YMCA/YWCA, or community center. The group leader is a parent, generally an individual who in the past has experienced problems in parenting and has been helped through Parents Anonymous or similar resources. Each PA group also has a sponsor, a volunteer professional who acts as a resource and consultant to the group. The sponsor, for example, may help the parent leader in understanding the group process occurring or may refer members to other community resources as necessary. The leader and sponsor serve as positive authority figures for group members. They represent individuals who care and are concerned about the best interests of the group participants as the latter struggle on a daily basis with the difficult task of parenting.

Group participants at PA meetings give identifying demographic information about themselves and their families; however, they may remain anonymous by using only first names. Group members generally share telephone numbers with other members so that they have someone to contact between meetings in the event of a crisis in their parenting. Participation with other parents in the weekly meetings and the sharing of telephone numbers results in the group becoming like an extended family to a member, thereby breaking down the social isolation often characterizing abusive families.

An open and accepting climate pervades PA meetings, with some members quietly listening while others actively discuss parenting problems encountered during the past week. The agenda of meetings generally is open, with participants determining topics for discussion based on their individual parenting needs. Group members positively evaluate their participation in a Parents Anonymous group. The following comments are typical. "These people understand me." "After we joined the group, we realized we weren't the only ones who had problems with their kids." "I found others who cared and could help me be a better mom."

Case Example

Tom, age 27, had difficulty with his temper, as seen in his frequent violent outbursts of anger toward his two small children when they did something that displeased him. A neighbor filed a complaint with the local protective services agency after witnessing Tom giving his 3-year-old daughter a severe beating. The protective services worker's assessment revealed that Tom frequently resorted to severe corporal punishment of his children. His wife, Susan, did not approve of Tom's disciplinary methods but was at a loss regarding how to intervene.

The treatment plan for Tom and Susan included participation in a local Parents Anonymous group. Although initially Tom did not participate verbally in the group, the sponsor thought that Tom's body language indicated that he was "with the group" and was profiting from listening to and observing the other participants.

During the third month of attending group sessions, Tom was on the verge of a violent episode with his daughter following her scratching of his truck when she was trying to help him wash it. Tom did not react violently, as he would have in the past, but walked away from the situation and later discussed the matter with his wife. In a subsequent PA session, Tom shared what had happened. Tom received support from the group in its discussion of this potentially abusive incident and how he averted what in the past would have resulted in a violent episode with his daughter and a distancing between him and Susan over their parenting styles.

Parent Education Courses. Parent education courses are offered in many communities under a variety of auspices, such as through adult education programs, child abuse councils, and community mental health agencies. Three examples of parent education courses are Systematic Training for Effective Parenting (STEP), Parent Effectiveness Training (PET), and the Nurturing Program.

Systematic Training for Effective Parenting (STEP) is a nine-session program, with sessions lasting 1½ to 2 hours. Each session includes discussion of a chapter from *The Parent's Handbook*, a video or audio presentation, and practice of the parenting skill learned. The sessions focus on helping parents understand children and communicate effectively with them. Parents are encouraged to apply at home with their children what they learn in the sessions. A detailed guide is available for group leaders of STEP courses.

Parent Effectiveness Training (PET) is a parent education program that has been field tested and evaluated extensively since its founding by Dr. Thomas Gordon in 1962. PET, an eight-session program, requires that an instructor be trained in the program by participating in a 5-day workshop. The program focuses on parenting skills, emphasizing effective disciplinary methods other than corporal punishment.

The Nurturing Program is a parent education course for parents and their children, ages 2 to 12. The program is designed to modify inappropriate parenting patterns. The Nurturing Program involves parents and their children on two levels of learning: the cognitive level, by learning new knowledge and skills, and the affective level, by experiencing positive healthy human interactions. Program content focuses on four parenting behaviors associated with child physical and psychological abuse: inappropriate developmental expectations of children, reversing parent-child roles, lack of empathic awareness of children's needs, and strong parental belief in the use of corporal punishment.

Parents and their children participate in separate sessions, meeting at the same time, for 2½ hours a week for 15 consecutive weeks. Weekly sessions for parents and children are based on specific learning goals and objectives. Children meet separately from parents in small, age-oriented groups (2-4 years, 5-8 years, and 9-12 years) learning nurturing and interaction skills. Parents and children meet together in a snack activity to share positive experiences. The program uses training manuals, filmstrips, and audiocassettes to teach parents new skills in behavior management. Effectiveness of this

program can be measured with the Adult Adolescent Parenting
Inventory (AAPI) (Bavolek, 1984).

Case Example

Mr. and Mrs. Troy, a couple in their mid-thirties and parents of two
children, ages 6 and 8, enrolled in a parent education class sponsored by
their local community mental health center. This action followed a report
of alleged abuse by a school nurse, who observed bruises on their older
child's arms. Although Mrs. Troy participated enthusiastically in
discussion and group exercises in the classes, Mr. Troy was reluctant to
participate verbally. During the sixth session, in a small-group discussion
with other men, he verbalized the anger he felt when, as a child, he had
been beaten by his father on numerous occasions. He stated that as the
oldest in the family, he often was unjustly accused of misbehaving when
in fact his siblings were at fault. The group leader was able to empathize
skillfully with Mr. Troy's feelings, which helped him become more open
in the group sessions.

In the ninth session, parents and children engaged in the task of
"tucking in," an exercise of closeness at bedtime between parents and
children. When Mr. Troy's 8-year-old son verbalized to his father during
this exercise that he loved him, Mr. Troy's voice cracked, and tears ran
down his cheek. Later, in the parents' discussion group, Mr. Troy
described how his son's comment "really hit me in the heart." Mr. Troy's
response to the group's support seemed to represent a turning point for
him. In the final session, he privately told the group leader that he and his
wife were planning on taking the course again when the children were
older and presented new challenges to them.

Family-Based Service. Family-based service is the name given to the
model of service delivery often used with physically abusive families. The goal of this method of service delivery is to preserve the
family unit through the provision of intensive services. Services are
provided to the family as a unit, and treatment often occurs in the
family home.

The Homebuilders program is an example of an intensive family
preservation program. The goal of the Homebuilders program is to
work intensively with the family for a brief period of time, 4 to 6
weeks, to avoid placement of the children outside the home. Thera-

pists carry a very small caseload of two families at a time and work from 10 to 20 hours a week with a family, providing multidimensional services including crisis intervention, family therapy, advocacy, home management, life skills training, and concrete assistance in meeting housing, food, clothing, and other needs (Bath & Haapala, 1993).

Home Visitation Programs. A less intensive supportive program in helping parents who have maltreated their children, and one that tends be more ongoing, involves the use of home visitors, individuals with a knowledge of parenting who meet regularly with the abusive parent or parents in their home. This is an effective intervention because maltreating families generally are not likely to seek treatment for themselves, not only because of low motivation and, frequently, transportation and child care problems but also because of the stigma of having been an abusive parent. Bringing services to the family in the privacy of the home can be very effective.

Home visits may occur weekly or less frequently, depending on the needs of the parents. The home visit provides the opportunity for a person with parenting knowledge to observe at first hand the home situation and stresses under which the parent may be operating. It also affords an opportunity to work in a concrete way with the parents on problems in parenting that may be occurring. The visit also allows for the introduction of other social and medical services based on the needs of the family (Wasik & Roberts, 1994). Home visitation may be regarded not only as an effective treatment resource but also as an example of tertiary prevention, which will be discussed in Chapter 8.

Stress Management. Because many abusive families operate under high degrees of stress, learning to manage stress effectively can be helpful for parents who have been abusive or are at high risk to abuse again. Research using laboratory experiments in which an infant crying was simulated for long periods of time found that mothers' anxiety was reduced after stress management training. The use of biofeedback was found especially helpful in the mothers' control of stress (Tyson & Sobschak, 1994).

❏ **Treating Child Sexual Abuse**

Prior to identifying models for treating sexual abuse, two related topics will be discussed: the appropriateness of treatment and issues on which treatment may focus.

APPRÓPRIATENESS OF TREATMENT

The seriousness of sexual abuse has been brought to public attention during recent years. A resultant, but at times erroneous, principle may follow that in all situations in which inappropriate sexual contact has occurred, treatment must follow. Nonaggressive sexual activity between children who are close in age may reflect nothing more serious than normal childhood exploration, calling for a calm and understanding response from caregivers. This situation does not necessarily require treatment.

Parents may exacerbate the trauma of sexual abuse by coercing children into treatment against their will or by insisting that children participate in treatment without sufficient reasons for doing so. Such parental behavior may compound the problem by making it more of an issue for the child than it really is (Faller, 1988b). For example, a 4-year-old girl is fondled by a 6-year-old neighbor boy, or two 3-year-old nursery school children of opposite sex are discovered exploring each other's genitals. These are nonaggressive sexually related incidents that do not necessarily require that the participants be treated. (Teaching the children age-appropriate sexual knowledge and the ability to discriminate between good touches and secret touches would be appropriate.) Forcing children into treatment may make them feel guilty and stigmatized for what happened. Treatment under such duress represents a form of coercion from the child's viewpoint.

When treatment is merited, a helpful way to present treatment to a child is to indicate that counseling presents an opportunity for the child to talk with someone who is knowledgeable about sexual abuse, who understands what the child has experienced, and who has been helpful to other girls and boys in similar situations. If the child chooses not to seek treatment, the child should be informed that whenever he or she wishes to talk with a therapist in the future about what happened, he or she may do so.

There are several indicators of when a child needs treatment for sexual abuse (Faller, 1988b). First, the abuse has been extensive in terms of duration, frequency, intrusiveness, and the number of perpetrators. Second, physical force was used with the child, or the child experienced physical harm, such as physical trauma occurring in anal intercourse. Third, psychological trauma is evident, as seen, for example, in fear, anger, guilt, sleep difficulties, withdrawn behavior, enuresis or encopresis, anxiety, depression, or problems at school or in interpersonal relationships. Fourth, inappropriate sexual behaviors are observed following the abuse, such as excessive masturbation, focusing on sexuality in conversation and play with other children, or inappropriate sexual behavior with adults.

TREATMENT ISSUES

Treatment with the victim may focus on the following issues, depending on the child's reaction to the abuse. First, the victim may experience a loss of trust toward other persons. This loss may be especially evident in intrafamilial abuse in which the offender was loved and trusted by the victim. Second, an altered body image may result if the child feels damaged or permanently impaired. This may occur as a result of physical trauma accompanying the sexual abuse. Third, the child may feel guilty and responsible for the abuse, even though realistically there were few alternatives to the child other than to acquiesce to the offender's wishes. These feelings may be especially pronounced in older children who experienced some sexual pleasure with the abuse. Fourth, the victim may need assistance in self-protection from further sexual abuse. Fifth, anger, depression, and self-destructive behavior may result from the sexual abuse.

Anger associated with sexual abuse is appropriate and expected. Victims may experience anger toward the offender for the abuse and toward family members for allowing the abuse. The goal in treatment is for victims to recognize the anger and direct it to appropriate targets, such as toward the perpetrator rather than toward themselves. Victims' self-directed anger may be found especially in intrafamilial abuse in which the victim's mother separates from the offender father following the abusive incident. The child may blame herself or himself for the family breakup. When anger is not expressed or is not recognized as a valid feeling and instead is turned in on the self, depression and self-destructive behavior may occur.

TREATMENT MODALITIES

Individual Therapy. Friedrich (1990), in a review of the literature on the use of individual therapy with sexually abused children, especially children experiencing intrafamilial abuse, concludes that little support exists for the use of this treatment modality. Sexually abused children often come from dysfunctional families with many problems existing prior to the appearance of sexual abuse. If treatment focuses on the child victim and ignores the family's multiple problems, there is little likelihood that the child's individual therapy will be effective. Individual treatment may be used appropriately with child sexual abuse victims when the family also is involved in treatment simultaneously. In these situations, behavioral change occurring with significant others in the family can support changes the child may be making (Friedrich, 1990).

When a child victim is treated individually, concurrently with the family seeking help, treatment may focus on the child's perception of the trauma and its impact on the child's life. The therapist can encourage the child to retell what happened. The therapist must try to understand from the child's perspective what happened and how the child perceives the trauma's impact on his or her life. The therapist's task then is to help the child reexamine the trauma from a reality perspective, correcting inappropriate conclusions involving guilt, self-blame, and responsibility for the abuse (Friedrich, 1990).

Play therapy is a helpful technique when treating children.

Play therapy is a helpful technique when treating children who are victims of sexual abuse. Dolls, toys, stories, drawings, and other means of play may be used to help children talk about their sexual victimization and its impact on their lives. Play becomes the means through which the therapist communicates to the child alternative solutions to conflicts the child may be experiencing as a result of the victimization (Marvasti, 1989). For example, storytelling may help lead children to talk about their sexual victimization. The therapist may begin a story about a small child, similar in age to the child in treatment, in which a scary event occurs. The therapist may ask the child to complete the story to determine how the child would handle a scary event, symbolic of the sexual abuse. An alternative approach is to ask the child to tell the scariest story possible, with the therapist completing the story, thereby informing the child of positive ways that traumatic events can be handled. Hand puppets or small rubber figures of people that can be bent into various positions also can be used as characters in storytelling. The figures may be children (representing peers and siblings), older persons (parents, grandparents, and other adult family members), a person from law enforcement or criminal justice (representing persons in authority such as the police, judge, attorney, social worker), and a witch or robber (perpetrator).

A child also may use drawings in play therapy as a means of projecting feelings about the abuse and its effect on the child's life. Groups of children may write a play script that they act out, expressing through the characters reactions to their victimization.

Bibliotherapy, or the use of children's literature in which the principal character in the book experienced some form of abuse, may be used in individual and group treatment of child sexual abuse. A child may read the book, listen while it is read by the therapist, or listen to a taped recording. A child receives the message from the book that other children have experienced sexual abuse and have coped with the trauma in various ways. Follow-up activities such as drawing pictures, writing a letter to the central character, or acting out the story with puppets provide the child with further opportunities to explore the victimization and its impact (Pardeck, 1990).

Box 7.2 presents a list of books useful in treating child abuse. The books are classified by general interest level and appropriate reading level.

Group Therapy. Research indicates that group therapy is the treatment of choice for latency and adolescent sexual abuse victims, and in some instances younger children (Berliner & Ernst, 1984; Friedrich,

BOX 7.2

Bibliotherapy Materials

Anderson, D., & Finne, M. (1986a). *Margaret's story*. Minneapolis: Dillon. 43 pages. Interest level: Ages 5-10. Reading level: Grade 4.

Margaret must go to court because her neighbor sexually abused her. Margaret was afraid to tell her parents because the neighbor told her not to tell anyone. She finds out that what her neighbor did was against the law.

Anderson, D., & Finne, M. (1986b). *Michael's story*. Minneapolis: Dillon. 43 pages. Interest level: Ages 5-10. Reading level: Grade 4.

Michael's parents make him feel bad about himself by yelling at him for being fat. His dad calls him stupid. After a fight at school, Michael ends up talking to a social worker. Treatment helps him deal with his anger and sadness.

Anderson, D., & Finne, M. (1986c). *Robin's story*. Minneapolis: Dillon. 43 pages. Interest level: Ages 5-8. Reading level: Grade 4.

Robin's mother often gets angry and spanks him. She spanks him with a board and cuts him with a cookie tin thrown at his head. He must go to the doctor because of the cut. Past physical abuse is discovered.

Bauer, M. (1977). *Foster child*. New York: Seabury. 98 pages. Interest level: Ages 11-18. Reading level: Grade 6.

Rennie, a 12-year-old, must defend herself from the sexual advances of her foster father. Feeling confused and ashamed, Rennie flees her foster home and seeks help from understanding adults.

Byars, B. (1977). *The pinballs*. New York: Harper & Row. 136 pages. Interest level: Ages 11-14. Reading level: Grade 5.5.

Three children, two teenagers who have been physically abused and a boy who was abandoned by his mother, live in a foster home. They share their feelings of hurt and rejection and begin to feel like a family.

Hunt, I. (1976). *The lottery rose*. New York: Scribner's. 185 pages. Interest level: Ages 11-14. Reading level: Grade 8.5.

After frequently being physically abused by his alcoholic mother and her boyfriend, 7-year-old Georgie is fearful and distrustful of adults. When the boyfriend brutally beats Georgie, he must be hospitalized and is then sent to a group care facility. There, he develops a positive relationship with counselors and other adults.

BOX 7.2

Continued

Kellogg, M. (1972). *Like the lion's tooth.* New York: Farrar, Straus, & Giroux. 148 pages. Interest level: Ages 11-14. Reading level: Grade 7.

Ben, an 11-year-old who has been sexually and physically abused by his father, is sent to a school for "problem children," mainly for his own protection. He tries to find his mother after running away from the school. He finally resigns himself to his situation and is befriended by other abused children at the school.

Mazer, H. (1978). *The war on Villa Street.* New York: Delacorte. 182 pages. Interest level: Ages 11-14. Reading level: Grade 5.

Willis, an 8-year-old boy, is beaten frequently by his alcoholic father, once almost to the point of unconsciousness. After Willis tries to strike back at his father, he runs away from home. He later returns, hoping that things will improve.

O'Hanlon, J. (1977). *Fair game.* New York: Dial. 94 pages. Interest level: Ages 11-18. Reading level: Grade 6.5.

Denise, a 14-year-old girl, is in turmoil after she discovers her stepfather watching her undress. When he makes sexual advances toward her younger sister and a friend, Denise tells her mother, who forces her husband to leave.

Orr, R. (1980). *Gunner's run.* New York: Harper & Row. 148 pages. Interest level: Ages 8-11. Reading level: Grade 3.5.

Gunner, a 9-year-old, is beaten frequently by his alcoholic father. Gunner runs away from home and develops a positive self-concept through his association with an elderly man who is dying.

Roberts, W. (1978). *Don's hurt Laurie.* New York: Atheneum. 172 pages. Interest level: Ages 11- 14. Reading level: Grade 6.

Since the age of 3, 11-year-old Laurie has been abused by her mother. Laurie is afraid to approach any adult about her situation but finally, with the encouragement of her stepbrother, tells her stepfather the truth. Her mother eventually receives treatment.

Smith, D. (1974). *Tough Chauncey.* New York: Morrow. 222 pages. Interest level: Ages 11-14. Reading level: Grade 5.5.

Thirteen-year-old Chauncey lives with his abusive grandfather and indifferent grandmother. After his mother gives legal custody of Chauncey to his grandparents, he runs away and decides to tell his story to a social worker.

SOURCE: Reprinted by special permission of the Child Welfare League of America from *Child Welfare, 69,* 1990, pp. 83-88.

Berliner, Urquiza, & Beilke, 1988; Lanktree & Briere, 1995; McGain & McKinzey, 1995; Nelki & Watters, 1989; Steward, Farquhar, Dicharry, Glick, & Martin, 1986). Group therapy can be less intensive and the group environment less threatening than individual treatment. The group also provides participants with a supportive feeling, counteracting the social isolation and alienation that children often experience as a result of their sexual victimization. Finally, as a sense of trust develops in the group, victims may be able to talk about the experiences of other group members. Frequently, they cannot recognize their own experiences or talk about them. Eventually, however, they may feel comfortable examining their own victimization and its impact on their psychosocial functioning.

The literature presents various group treatment models (Fowler, Burns, & Roehl, 1983; Mandell & Damon, 1989; Schiffer, 1984). For example, Nelki and Watters (1989) use a nine-session model with individual sessions focusing on specific subjects relative to sexual victimization such as touching, secrets, guilt, anger, and responsibility. Children's groups run parallel to a parents' or caregivers' group. The ninth and final session is a joint meeting of children, caregivers, and the therapists from both groups.

Corder, Haizlip, and DeBoer (1990) describe a structured, time-limited treatment group for sexually abused children ages 6 to 8. Techniques used in the group help children explore their reactions to their victimization and develop coping skills. These techniques include specially designed coloring books, therapeutic board games, drawings, and storytelling.

The Adolescent Sexual Abuse Treatment Program in Northampton, Massachusetts (Homstead & Werthamer, 1989), involves groups of seven adolescents ranging in age from 13 to 18 years who meet together 90 minutes per week for 20 weeks. A 4-week interlude occurs after 20 weeks, allowing members to leave treatment or to continue in another 20-week cycle with another group. Participants must agree to four rules when joining the group: confidentiality, respect and support of others, freedom regarding verbally participating in sessions or remaining silent, and promptness in attending sessions. The therapists use creative and flexible approaches to treatment based on participants' needs. For example, participants may be encouraged to keep journals as a way of recording reactions to their victimization. Sexual abuse education, an important feature of these groups, breaks down myths about sexual abuse, provides correct information, and increases participants' awareness of the various stages of the healing process. Cotherapists lead the groups. The use of two adults as group leaders provides participants the opportunity to observe and model the effective ways two adults can interact, disagree, and accomplish tasks. This is a corrective experience for many of the group participants who come from families in which parents interact dysfunctionally with each other.

Group therapy may be too intense for some sexual abuse victims, especially early in the treatment process (Friedrich, 1990). In these instances, group treatment may be deferred until after the initial disclosure/crisis is resolved and the victim has had the benefit of individual crisis intervention therapy.

Various issues may be discussed in group treatment, depending on the gender and age composition of the group and whether a structured or nonstructured approach is being used. Common issues are participants' victimization, including their anger, guilt, shame, helplessness, and self-blame; individual and family problems associated with the victimization; and the victims' need to develop a sense of mastery and competence in their lives (Friedrich, 1990; Nelki & Watters, 1989; Steward et al., 1986).

Family Therapy. Treating the family as a unit often poses problems for the therapist. The entire family often does not welcome the therapist's intervention and presence. Thus, family treatment may require a process of constant reengagement with family members. Initially, a family should not be seen together as a group. Individual family members initially may be involved in treatment, then mother and daughter together, and finally other siblings. The offender father in intrafamilial sexual abuse should not be introduced into family treatment until later in therapy, especially not until the offender has taken responsibility for his action.

Treating the family as a unit often poses problems for the therapist.

An important issue in family treatment of intrafamilial abuse is enhancing the mother's competence to function effectively in the family, especially if the offender father has been removed from the home. Ensuring the safety of the child victim is an important task facing the mother, especially if the father, though removed from the home, retains visiting rights to the children. Dysfunctional parent-child relationships also are significant issues in family therapy with sexually abusive families.

Although reunification may be a goal for some families, a precondition for reestablishing the family is the perpetrator taking responsibility for his behavior. Treatment involving the entire family is especially important after reunification occurs, so that the family is prevented from reestablishing former dysfunctional patterns of behavior. Treatment also helps the family examine alternative modes of interaction and problem solving (Friedrich, 1990).

VICTIM-OFFENDER COMMUNICATION

Victim-offender communication in the treatment of sexual abuse is a controversial and emotionally charged issue. Controversy surrounding this treatment technique focuses on the concern that revictimization can occur when communication takes place before the victim is ready to confront the offender. Revictimization may occur in very subtle ways when language used in the offender's communication is not sensitive to the victim's guilt and self-blame or when nonverbal language does not support the offender's verbalizations (Yokley & McGuire, 1990). Victim-offender communication, a technique stemming from sex offender treatment programs, is criticized for being used more often in the best interests of the offender's therapy rather than the victim's (Knopp & Stevenson, 1989).

Communication between victims and offenders can be classified according to different levels of intensity (direct and indirect) and the nature of the communication (personal and nonpersonal). Direct communication implies face-to-face contact between the victim and offender, generally in the presence of a therapist, in individual or group treatment settings. Indirect communication may occur through letters, videotape, voice recordings, or the telephone. Personal communication implies that the victim and the offender communicate with each other. Nonpersonal communication suggests that the victim and offender may not be known to each other. For example, an offender may appear before a treatment group of victims, even though the offender may not have sexually abused any of the group participants (Yokley, 1990).

Advocates for victim-offender communication indicate that the technique can be used effectively in sexual abuse treatment when victims' safety, needs, and rights are kept paramount. Communication between a victim and an offender may be beneficial in four ways, paralleling the Kübler-Ross (1969) reactive stages to death or loss (denial, anger, bargaining, depression, and acceptance). Reassurance of the reality of the abuse rather than denial occurs for the victim when the offender communicates an admission of the offense. Relief from guilt and self-blame may be facilitated for the victim when the offender communicates acknowledgment of full responsibility for the offense, including coercion and manipulation of the victim. Anger that the victim experiences toward the offender for the abuse and its impact on the victim's life may be expressed directly to the offender. A sense of power, self-control, and mastery of life events can result for the victim when an offender communicates responsibility for the offense (Yokley & McGuire, 1990).

As stated earlier, victim-offender communication must be in the victim's best interests. The victim's age, developmental stage, and reaction to the abuse are important factors to consider in using this technique. Victim-offender communication should be the victim's choice, and the victim should retain the right to terminate the communication at any time. Careful anticipatory preparation of both the victim and the offender should occur within the context of careful professional supervision and evaluation (Yokley & McGuire, 1990).

❑ **Treatment of Adult Childhood**
Sexual Abuse Survivors

Although some adult survivors of childhood sexual abuse engage in denial and suppression of the painful memories associated with their victimization, increasingly survivors are seeking help for the effects of their childhood sexual victimization as this social problem has been more openly discussed and treatment resources have become available (Leitenberg, Greenwald, & Cado, 1992). The problems for which adult survivors seek professional help include depression, somatic complaints, the inability to maintain effective interpersonal relationships, sexual dysfunction, and substance abuse (Kinzl, Traweger, & Biebl, 1995; Lowery, 1987). The depression adult survivors often experience is reflected in their high rates of attempted and completed suicides as compared to the general population (Peters & Range, 1995).

Several national organizations have established chapters throughout the United States to treat adult survivors of child sexual abuse. For example, VOICES in Action, Inc. (Victims of Incest Can Emerge Survivors) is a national organization of incest and child sexual abuse survivors dedicated to prevention and recovery through networking, support, and education. Similarly, Survivors of Incest Anonymous, Inc., with chapters throughout the United States, sponsors self-help groups for men and women 18 years of age or older. Treatment is based on the 12-step Alcoholics Anonymous model. Adult Survivors Abused as Children (ASAC) is another national organization sponsoring treatment groups for adult survivors of child sexual abuse. This program is patterned after the Parents Anonymous model. Parents United, Daughters and Sons United, and Adults Molested as Children United (Giaretto, 1982) are national organizations with more than 100 chapters providing guided self-help for sexually abusive parents and child/adult survivors of sexual abuse. (See Appendix B for addresses of some of these organizations.)

Groups for adult childhood sexual abuse survivors generally follow a self-help or peer-group treatment model. The groups provide a milieu, or environment, wherein adults can support one another as they awaken to the reality of their childhood sexual abuse, examine ways they have coped with this trauma, and learn new, more effective coping mechanisms. Treatment issues in these groups often focus on participants' memories and emotions associated with the trauma, problems in interpersonal relationships such as the inability to trust others based on the violation of trust they experienced, and anger toward the perpetrator (Bear & Dimock, 1988; Blake-White & Kline, 1985).

Five stages of recovery frequently occur in adult survivor treatment groups: acknowledging the reality of the abuse rather than continuing to deny it; overcoming secondary responses to the abuse, such as fear, anger, guilt, and a sense of being overwhelmed or out of control; forgiving oneself and thereby stopping self-punishment for the abuse; identifying and implementing effective coping behaviors to deal with the trauma; and relinquishing the identity of being a survivor of abuse and moving on in life (Sgroi, 1989b, 1989c).

❏ Treatment of Offenders

Offender treatment should be based on careful assessment of an offender's psychosocial history, past and present losses and stressors, and patterns of offense. This assessment is important for predicting the appropriateness and effectiveness of various treatment approaches and for determining if community-based treatment is admissible or if incarceration is warranted.

Sexual abuse offenders are generally typed as "regressed" or "fixated" (Groth, 1979). Although these types are not always clearly and discretely differentiated, the distinction is useful as a framework for assessing the motivation for the offense and for determining which treatment approach is most likely to deter further offenses. Intrafamilial sexual abuse perpetrators generally are identified as regressed offenders. The regressed offender has maintained a sexual relationship with an age-mate but, under personal or family stress, may turn to a daughter to meet his intimacy and emotional needs and/or to punish his estranged wife. The child serves as a substitute or surrogate mate for the offender. The prognosis for regressed offenders' treatment generally is positive.

The fixated offender or pedophile has a well-established preference for children. The fixated offender sees the child as an equal. Fixated offenders may relate to adult females sexually and even, in some instances, marry; however, generally these relationships are initiated by the other partner and may be a response to social pressures or a means to provide access to children (Groth, 1979). Fixated offenders often have multiple victims and may be involved in the publication and distribution of child pornography. Treatment prognosis for fixated offenders is poor. Intensive treatment must occur during incarceration and after release to control the sexual behavior and to avoid recidivism. Without treatment, incarceration is little more than a revolving door to continued crimes against children.

Three approaches to offender treatment can be identified: pharmacological treatment, behavior modification, and psychotherapy (Groth & Oliveri, 1989; Sgroi, 1989a). These treatment approaches, employed in community and prison-based programs, may be used individually or together. Pharmacological treatment is used with offenders who do not want to engage in sexually abusive behavior but find that they are unable to control their behavior (Groth & Oliveri, 1989). Drugs such as Depo-Provera (medroxyprogesterone acetate) lower testosterone levels and, in turn, decrease unwanted sexual fantasies and sexually aggressive behaviors. This treatment strategy requires careful medical supervision, because negative side effects can occur. Side effects may include a lowered sperm count or damaged sperm, breast development, diabetes, and hypertension (Meyer, Walker, Emory, & Smith, 1985). A disadvantage in using this treatment approach is that the offender relies on the drug as an external control and fails to learn internal controls for his sexually abusive behavior.

Treatment using behavior modification focuses on offenders' sexual arousal patterns. The offender's reaction to various sexual stimuli can be measured with a device attached to the penis known as a penile plethysmograph. Emphasis in treatment is placed on helping the offender gain greater control over dysfunctional behaviors in response to sexual stimuli (Sgroi, 1989a).

Intensive psychotherapy is a third offender treatment approach. Individual or group psychotherapy may be used; however, the latter generally is more effective. An innovative treatment approach involving family therapy also will be discussed. A goal in psychotherapy is helping offenders understand how past life experiences influence their sexually abusive behavior. To accomplish this goal, the perpetrator must first recognize, admit, and accept responsibility for the sexual abuse. Second, the perpetrator must recognize the antecedents to the abusive behavior and use this awareness as a way to control the behavior (Knopp, 1984).

Social learning theory often provides the theoretical basis for group treatment of sex offenders. The Barnert Hospital Mental Health Clinic, Juvenile Sexual Behavior Program (JSBP), an outpatient program in Paterson, New Jersey, provides an example of such a treatment program for juvenile offenders between the ages of 13 and 18 (Sermabeikian & Martinez, 1994). Sexual deviance in this program is viewed as behavior that was learned, observed, or experienced by the offender rather than behavior having a genetic or biological origin. The rationale for the intervention is to treat, disrupt, and prevent the sexually abusive behavior before it becomes a chronic or compulsive form of behavior. Following are the specific goals of the year-long group treatment program at the JSBP.

1. Personal responsibility for one's sexual behavior
2. Improvement of the ability to make good decisions
3. Increased acceptance of societal rules and persons in authority
4. A shift from exploitive to nonexploitive use of power and control in relationships
5. Development of healthy sexuality in peer relationships
6. Increased awareness of the interpersonal issues of adolescence and adulthood
7. An increase in control over impulsive behavior
8. Improvement in communication and assertive expression of feelings and needs
9. A decrease in distorted cognitions regarding relationships and sexuality
10. An increased awareness of the thoughts, feelings, and behaviors that lead to offending behavior (pp. 971-972)

In this treatment program, the group is co-led by a male and a female therapist who model prosocial and nonabusive behaviors between males and females. The group members also serve as models for one another when they display prosocial behaviors and do not follow previously held belief systems that supported their sexual offense. The group process is composed of a series of progressive components. The first stage focuses on the disclosure of the sexual offense and confrontation of denial or minimizing of the offense and its consequences. The next step involves group members examining cognitive distortions and irrational thinking that support the sexually offending behavior. From this phase of treatment, the adolescent should develop the ability to use judgment and self-observation before acting on impulses and engaging in dysfunctional behavior. Emphasis in this phase of treatment also is put on an empathic understanding of the effect of the offense on the victim. The final phases of treatment are aimed at helping the offenders to develop knowledge and skills to more effectively cope with a range of life situations they will face as they proceed through adolescence and become adults (Sermabeikian & Martinez, 1994).

An innovative treatment approach with offenders, supported by the family preservation philosophy, involves working with the offender and family as a unit (Skibinski, 1995). In this program, family therapy replaces prosecution or part of the offender's prison sentence. A pretrial conference is held to assess the offender's ability to benefit from treatment. If treatment is deemed feasible, the offender is charged, pleads guilty, and is diverted into a treatment program. A petition may be filed with the family court to provide protection and treatment for the victim and family. The offender enters a family-oriented treatment program that may involve family therapy, because sexual abuse in many instances is viewed as symptomatic of family dysfunctioning (Finkelhor, 1984a). If the offender completes treatment satisfactorily, as determined by mental health personnel, and completes all other pretrial conference stipulations, the guilty plea is vacated. If not, the offender is adjudged guilty and must serve the assigned sentence. Although this treatment approach has not been verified empirically, mental health professionals believe that the program is beneficial because the offender is not merely put in prison, where often no treatment occurs, but rather receives treatment. In addition, efforts are made to keep the family unit intact. The threat of imminent prosecution serves as a safety valve in the event the offender does not comply with the pretrial agreement.

❑ **Megan's Law**

In mid-October 1994 7-year-old Megan Konka was raped and murdered by a man living in her neighborhood who was a twice-convicted child molester. Residents of Hamilton Township, New

Jersey, where the crime occurred, were outraged that this convicted child molester was living with two other sex offenders in their community. As a result of public outcry over this incident, the state of New Jersey, in late October 1994, passed the Sexual Offender Registration Act, which has become known as Megan's Law.

This law requires prosecutors to notify neighborhoods of sex offenders returning from prison. It further requires sex offenders to register with the town's chief law enforcement officer whenever they move. More than 30 states have passed similar legislation. Courts in several states, however, have ruled such laws unconstitutional (Smith, 1995).

Insensitivity to issues of race and culture can be a barrier to effective treatment.

Differing views are held by mental health professionals regarding this legislation. The registration of sex offenders provides protection to children from being victimized; however, offenders who have been in therapy and wish to return to a normal life believe that such legislation violates their constitutional right to privacy and that the registration is tantamount to being punished twice for the same crime.

❑ Treatment Issues
Relative to Race and Culture

Therapists often treat clients of different racial and cultural backgrounds when working with child abuse and neglect. An insensitivity to issues of race and culture can be a barrier to effective treatment.

The influence of race in the presenting problem often is overlooked by white therapists (Robinson, 1989). Racism may not only affect clients' development of the problem but also place constraints on what they are able to do about the problem. Discussing the impact of race on treatment, Robinson (1989) states,

Whether the goals of intervention include change in behavioral patterns, intrapsychic restructuring, environmental changes, or change in interpersonal relationships, the presence of racist behaviors may contribute to difficulty in problem resolution. This realization allows the clinician to help the client acknowledge the complexity of the situation and clearly delineate the goals of treatment and the potential impact of planned interventions. Initiating a frontal attack on racist policies or behaviors usually is not appropriate or effective. It is extremely important for the clinician to have some ideas regarding the racial factors influencing a problem and attendant implications for the alternatives that the clinician considers as interventions. The clinician accrues this knowledge base as a result of an awareness of the community in which he or she practices. The clinician's affirmation of the contextual reality of the client tends to increase the intensity of the treatment alliance and the client's availability to consider his or her own contribution to problem maintenance. (p. 326)

Multiracial and multicultural analysis teams can help therapists develop sensitivity to issues of race and culture (Garbarino & Ebata, 1983). Multiracial and multicultural analysis teams may periodically review agency cases or may be available to workers on a consultative basis. When individuals representing racial and cultural groups are not involved in helping workers consider racial and cultural issues relative to clients in their caseloads, stereotyping can occur that often mistakenly is assumed to be sensitivity.

Mental health professionals must engage in self-examination regarding their covert and overt racist attitudes that would impede them from working effectively with clients of differing racial and cultural backgrounds. This introspection can occur, for example, for white workers working with African American clients by asking the following questions (Robinson, 1989):

- What is the history of my experience with African Americans (positive, negative, and neutral events and their outcomes)?
- What did my family of origin teach me regarding African Americans relative to the following areas: intelligence and intellectual capacity and potential, cleanliness of person and environment, hierarchical status vis-à-vis white people, truthfulness versus deceitfulness, sexual potency and restraint, sex role functioning in family interaction, personal worth and respect, inclination toward hostility, and the handling of aggression, such as attacking others or fighting?
- How have these teachings affected me over time? What have I done about these teachings?

- What is my personal style for dealing with diversity and conflict?
- How do I exercise authority and relate to the authority of others?
- How do I react in situations in which I observe African Americans being subjected to racist behaviors and ideology?
- What is the pervasive attitude in the agency regarding African American clients?

When treating African American clients or members of other racial and ethnic groups, white workers must be sensitive to their mistrust issues and the potential effect these may have on the helping relationship. Research indicates that when African Americans who are mistrustful of whites are assigned a white counselor, they tend to have diminished expectations for treatment and may find it difficult to discuss personal information, such as sexual behavior, that may be very relevant to child maltreatment. Mistrust of whites may stem from childhood socialization, from personal life experiences, or from parents' contacts with whites in the criminal justice, legal, and social services systems (Watkins, Terrell, Miller, & Terrell, 1989). Developing a sensitivity to racial and cultural issues will prevent workers from immediately viewing clients' behavior as psychopathological or indicative of resistance and the absence of motivation (Boyd-Franklin, 1989; Logan et al., 1990; Proctor & Davis, 1994).

❏ Summary

Various treatment modalities and techniques are available for treating child abuse victims, the family, and the offender. The worker's selection of a treatment modality will be based on an understanding of factors (individual, family, and social and cultural) related to the abuse and goals to be accomplished in treatment.

❏ Suggested Reading

Boyd-Franklin, N. (1989). *Black families in therapy*. New York: Guilford.

Logan, S., Freeman, E., & McRoy, R. (Eds.). (1990). *Social work practice with Black families*. White Plains, NY: Longman.

These books assist therapists in developing a sensitivity to the issue of race when working with African American clients.

Faller, K. (Ed.). (1981). *Social work with abused and neglected children: A manual of interdisciplinary practice*. New York: Free Press.

The subtitle of this book aptly describes its focus. Several chapters on treatment, emphasizing an interdisciplinary perspective, are included.

Friedrich, W. (1990). *Psychotherapy of sexually abused children and their families*. New York: W. W. Norton.

This comprehensive book focuses on the impact of sexual abuse on children, evaluating and planning for treatment, and the use of various treatment approaches.

MacFarlane, K., & Waterman, J. (Eds.). (1986). *Sexual abuse of young children*. New York: Guilford.

Includes chapters on treatment modalities and issues surrounding the treatment of young sexually abused children.

Polansky, N., Chalmers, M., Buttenwieser, E., & Williams, D. (1981). *Damaged parents: An anatomy of child neglect*. Chicago: University of Chicago Press.

This book, written from a personalistic theoretical perspective, discusses the etiology of neglect and treatment interventions.

Sgroi, S. (Ed.). (1988). *Vulnerable populations* (Vol. 1). Lexington, MA: Lexington Books.
Sgroi, S. (Ed.). (1989). *Vulnerable populations* (Vol. 2). Lexington, MA: Lexington Books.

These volumes contain chapters by various authors on an array of topics related to the treatment of sexual abuse, including the use of family therapy, treatment programs for sex offenders, and the treatment of adult childhood sexual abuse survivors.

8

Child Maltreatment Prevention

The previous chapters identify child maltreatment as a serious social problem. The victim may experience the effects of abuse and neglect not only at the time it occurs but also later, perhaps even years later. If child maltreatment could be prevented, the emotional pain and suffering associated with this social problem could be avoided.

An old adage states, "An ounce of prevention is worth a pound of cure." This bit of everyday philosophy is applicable to working with child abuse and neglect. This chapter will define the concept of prevention and will review examples of child maltreatment prevention programs.

❏ Prevention Defined

Human service professionals borrow their definition of prevention from the field of public health. Public health identifies three levels of prevention: primary, secondary, and tertiary (Leavell & Clark, 1958). Primary prevention consists of preventive activities undertaken before a malady strikes. In the public health model, this includes health promotion and efforts such as immunization to prevent disease from occurring. The polio vaccination programs of the 1950s and 1960s, in which people were immunized against this disease, serve as an example of primary prevention.

Secondary prevention focuses on identifying individuals at risk for certain illnesses and engaging in remedial efforts to prevent the onset of disease. Secondary prevention also may focus on the early diagnosis and prompt treatment of pathology in its incipient stages. An example of public health secondary prevention would be programs that attempt to identify individuals at risk of heart disease based on weight, eating and drinking habits, and smoking, and then make available remedial activities such as diets or smoking cessation programs (McMurtry, 1985). Tertiary prevention implies that the pathology already exists; the goal is to limit the extent and intensity of the pathology, such as through consultation with a physician, the use of pharmacological treatment, or surgery.

These three levels of prevention, based on a medical model, can be applied to child maltreatment. The medical analogy, however, becomes strained, because unlike diseases that may have few etiological factors associated with them, the different types and forms of child maltreatment may be associated with many etiological factors (individual, family, and social and cultural). We may not even be able to identify all the factors associated with child maltreatment (Giovannoni & Becerra, 1979; McMurtry, 1985).

Primary prevention in child maltreatment refers to programs or social policies that protect individuals or groups of individuals from the occurrence of abuse. Secondary prevention consists of programs and services targeted at individuals and groups who are at high risk for maltreatment. In tertiary prevention, maltreatment already has occurred, and preventive activities are aimed at treating the effects of the abuse or neglect or preventing the abuse from reoccurring (Daro, 1988).

Although the programs that follow will be related to one of the three prevention levels, in some instances a program may apply to more than one level. Information on these and other child abuse prevention programs that have been used effectively by social services agencies is available from the references cited and from the National Committee to Prevent Child Abuse, a national organization dedicated to the prevention of child maltreatment (see Appendix B).

❑ Primary Prevention

The goal of primary prevention programs is to prevent child abuse and neglect from occurring. The enactment of various public policies relevant to children's health and welfare may be viewed as examples of primary prevention. Nationwide efforts for states to adopt legislation prohibiting the use of corporal punishment in schools represents a current primary prevention example. Unfortunately, public policy often reinforces a residual rather than institutional perspective in the delivery of social services (Segal & Gustavsson, 1990). The residual view of social services focuses on adopting policies and implementing services after problems occur. An institutional perspective, or an "institutional preventive response," emphasizes policies and services ensuring the optimum psychosocial development of each child from birth through adolescence (Segal & Gustavsson, 1990).

A child's school years provide an excellent opportunity for primary preventive efforts, especially relevant to sexual abuse. For example, child abuse councils in many communities sponsor programs teaching children to "own" their bodies and to discriminate between good touches and secret touches. These programs also emphasize "empowerment" by teaching children that they have a right to privacy, the right to say no to hugs and touches they do not desire, the right to question adult authority when used in the context of sexual abuse, and the right to run, scream, and seek help when they are in potentially abusive situations. Box 8.1 identifies 10 principles underlying many child sexual abuse primary prevention programs.

An example of a primary prevention program is the "Bubbylonian Encounter," a three-character puppet play intended for elementary school children that was used widely in the Kansas City area (Borkin & Frank, 1986). This presentation focuses on the primary prevention principles in Box 8.1.

BOX 8.1

Principles Underlying Child-Centered
Sexual Victimization Prevention Programs

1. Give children correct terminology. It is important that children know the correct terminology for the sexual parts of their bodies, just as they know correct terms for other body parts. Correct misinformation whenever possible.

2. Help children identify different types of touching. There are good touches, confusing touches, and bad (secret) touches. Good touches include normal, loving interaction, such as a parent hugging a child when the child leaves for school in the morning, or a father "wrestling" with a child. A confusing touch might be incessant tickling by an adult that continues after the child has said "stop." Bad touches (secret touches) are touches on sexual or other body parts without the child's permission or that make the child feel uncomfortable and powerless in general. An example would be when an uncle lifts a young niece to his lap and puts his hand on or near her genitals.

3. Teach children that their bodies are their own private property. Children, rather than adults, should have control of their bodies.

4. Teach children that abuse is not their fault. Once children have learned that their bodies are their own personal property, they can be taught that they have the right to say "no" to bad (secret) types of touching, even touching by adults. One of the most difficult aspects of a prevention strategy is conveying to the child that children have the right to say "no" to adults. Children also must be taught, however, that abuse is not their fault whether they say "no" or not.

5. Teach children how someone might try to manipulate them into an abusive situation. Tell children that adults whom they know or those they do not know may try to bribe, trick, or force them into bad (secret) types of touching. Sexual abuse can, but rarely does, include the use of physical coercion; more often, it is initiated by verbal coercion such as promises of gifts. Moreover, the child needs to know that even seemingly warm, friendly adults may try to touch in a harmful way. Explain that bad (secret) touches could come from someone the child knows.

6. Encourage open communication. Children should be told that they never have to keep secrets from significant adults, even if the abuser made them promise or threatened to hurt them, a pet, or their parents in some way. Assure them that the parent or teacher will protect them and their pet.

BOX 8.1

Continued

7. Believe the child and investigate further. The best available evidence indicates that children almost never lie about being sexually abused when they, in fact, have not been. More often, the case is that the abused child will not tell anyone about being molested (Faller, 1984; Finkelhor, 1984a). In contrast to the child victim, the offender generally denies the fact of the molestation. Even nonvictimizing parents may have reasons for denying the existence of abuse, possibly in a misguided attempt to protect the child.

8. Foster appropriate attitudes in responsible adults. Help parents and teachers learn to indicate to children that there are approachable, askable, supportive, caring, and believing adults with whom every child can discuss touching problems.

9. Teach the child to keep telling. If the child tells his problem to one adult and gets no response or is not believed, he or she can go to another adult and another adult until someone believes (Hauser, 1984).

10. Make resources (films, books, and plays) available to parents and children to reinforce this message.

SOURCE: Adapted from "Child Sexual Abuse: A Review of Research and Theory With Implications for Family Life Educators," Hodson and Skeen, *Family Relations, 36,* p. 218, © copyright 1987 by the National Council on Family Relations, 3989 Central Ave. NE, Suite 550, Minneapolis, MN 55421. Reprinted with permission.

The Bubbylonian Encounter presents its message through puppet characters from the *Sesame Street* television show. The puppets demonstrate the sexual abuse prevention principles, and then discussion follows with the children. A follow-up program is presented approximately a month later. An information session for teachers and parents also is presented. When this program was evaluated, data revealed that children were more sensitive to inappropriate touching following program participation. Also, evaluative data revealed that 4- and 5-year-old children, as compared to 3-year-old participants, retained the information 4 to 6 weeks later (Borkin & Frank, 1986).

The Child Personal Safety Program, presented in Philadelphia day care centers, provides another example of a primary prevention program. The program's goal is to empower children at a very early age to keep themselves safe from sexual abuse. Creative programming techniques, including puppets and child-oriented videotapes, facilitate this goal. Program leaders believe that parents' support and participation in the program is critical to its effectiveness. Thus, parent workshops are held in conjunction with the children's program, with the goal of increasing parental knowledge about child sexual abuse, sharing information on the content of the Child Personal Safety Program, and enlisting parents' help to keep their children safe. Teachers, parents, and children have evaluated this program as an effective preventive effort (Spungen, Jensen, Finkelstein, & Satinsky, 1989).

A wealth of materials and information on primary prevention programs is available from the National Committee to Prevent Child Abuse (see Appendix B for address). A booklet titled *An Approach to Preventing Child Abuse* is available, as well as a publication titled *Database of Films and Videos on Child Abuse Prevention and Related Issues*. The latter publication contains a listing of numerous films and videos that can be used in prevention programs, where they are available, the cost, and a brief synopsis of each.

Information on programs and materials useful in designing primary child maltreatment prevention programs also can be obtained from the Committee for Children (see Appendix B for address). This organization publishes a free resource catalog including curricula, videos, and training materials. A VHS video for children Grades 2 through 6, *Yes, You Can Say No,* has received many awards, including an Emmy. The video presents 10-year-old David, who is being sexually exploited by a once-trusted adult. David's friends find out what is happening and demonstrate to him, as well as to the video audience, how he can handle the situation effectively by responding assertively.

A set of curricula on child abuse prevention for preschool through eighth grade, titled "Talking About Touching," is available from the Committee for Children. These curricula teach children the skills they need to protect themselves against exploitation using the three new Rs. They are "Recognize," "Resist," and "Report."

Primary prevention efforts against child sexual exploitation must begin early in a child's life, yet one study found that only 29% of 521 parents of children aged 6 to 14 in the Boston metropolitan area discussed sexual abuse with their child (Finkelhor, 1984b). Only 22% mentioned possible abuse by a family member. Most of the parents believed that the optimal age for discussing sexual abuse with a child was around 9. Unfortunately, many children, by that age, already have been victimized. Also, parents mistakenly assumed that any potential perpetrators would be strangers rather than family members. Similarly, Gilgun (1986) found from interviewing 20 sexually abused girls, ages 10 to 15, that they were provided with little or no sex education or information about sexual abuse. Neither parents nor schools provided this information. The researcher described their abuse as occurring in a knowledge vacuum. Because of their lack of knowledge, the victims did not understand what was happening. They lacked even an adequate vocabulary to discuss what had happened. The author concluded that provision of information about sexuality and child sexual abuse must begin at an early age. The provision of this information is not a one-time event but a process that occurs over a period of time relative to a child's psychosexual developmental stages (Gilgun, 1986).

Teaching children ownership of their bodies and strategies to prevent sexual victimization has been shown by evaluative research to be effective (Binder & McNiel, 1986; Kenning, Gallmeier, Jackson, & Plemons, 1987; Nibert, Cooper, & Ford, 1989). Some people express concern, however, that children exposed to such training may experience emotional or behavioral problems. The information may frighten younger children, or they may misinterpret appropriate touching and expressions of affection as aversive. Studies evaluating the impact of primary prevention programs do not support these ill effects (Finkelhor, Asdigian, & Dziuba-Leatherman, 1995; Miltenberger & Thiesse-Duffy, 1988; Nibert et al., 1989).

Provision of information about sexuality and child sexual abuse must begin at an early age.

Public service announcements providing guidelines or suggestions for good parenting are another example of primary child maltreatment prevention. Parenting courses offered by high schools or through community education programs, aimed at strengthening the anticipated or current parenting roles, also may help to prevent child abuse and neglect.

The argument often is made that parents want to take responsibility for educating their children about sex. The argument at times is extended to include educating children about preventing sexual abuse. Research shows, however, that parents are not knowledgeable about the extent and prevalence of child sexual abuse and thus cannot effectively accomplish this task. Although parents have good intentions in wanting to handle sexual abuse prevention education, the children would have received inaccurate or partial information and not some of the most essential information about preventing sexual abuse. The researchers concluded that parents clearly needed assistance, intervention, and realistic training to learn about sexual abuse and how to teach their children about this social problem (Elrod & Rubin, 1993).

❏ Secondary Prevention

Day care, a resource providing parents respite from stress associated with parenting, is an example of secondary child maltreatment prevention. Stress is a significant factor associated with the occurrence of child physical and psychological maltreatment. Day care is a valuable resource for reducing parental stress related to factors such as family size, physical or mental illness, lack of financial resources, physical or psychological absence of a mate, and social isolation. Child care programs also provide children at risk for abuse or neglect with opportunities to learn and develop social skills that they may not acquire in their home (Cohn, 1983).

Day care is a valuable resource for reducing parental stress.

Programs aimed at high-risk parents serve as secondary preventive efforts against child maltreatment. Examples are prenatal support programs sponsored by hospitals and public health clinics for

expectant teenage parents. Program goals include preparing participants for parenting roles and enhancing bonding between parents
and children.

Homemaker services are another example of secondary prevention. This type of service can assist parents in maintaining a home
and family when a high risk for abuse or neglect exists because of
parental psychosocial problems. Parental support groups provide a
similar service to parents who are socially isolated and at risk for
being abusive or neglectful.

The Good Start Program, developed by the Massachusetts Society
for the Prevention of Cruelty to Children, is an example of a secondary prevention program (Kowal et al., 1989). The program uses
home-based early interventions for enhancing parenting skills and
links mothers at risk to be abusive with needed services. It also
provides volunteer parent aides and other services to new mothers
identified to be at risk for child abuse and neglect of their newborn
infants.

❏ Tertiary Prevention

Community mental health and social services agencies, including
child protective services, and organizations working with victims of
child abuse and neglect represent tertiary prevention efforts. These
agencies focus on treating child maltreatment, thereby limiting the
impact of the problem on victims and their families. Telephone
hotlines serve a similar purpose, in that individuals can remain
anonymous while seeking help at times of crises involving child
maltreatment. Organizations working in child abuse and neglect
frequently operate child care centers for children who have experienced maltreatment. Parents also receive treatment through these
centers.

An example of a tertiary prevention program is provided by the
Children's Aid Society of Metropolitan Toronto. This agency established a series of treatment programs for abusive mothers, emphasizing nurturing skills (Breton, Welbourn, & Watters, 1981). The basic
premise underlying the programs was that abusive mothers could

not nurture their children because they never had been nurtured themselves. The programs addressed the mothers' need that they be given to without being asked to give anything in return. Hairdressing was selected as one way of accomplishing this. Hairdressing involved socially acceptable touching, and participants did not consider the activity as infantile or sexual. Later, problem-solving activities were added. Participation in the groups reduced the mothers' social isolation as they developed friendships, exchanged baby-sitting, and in general formed new social networks. As a result, they were better able to cope with their parenting responsibilities, thereby reducing abusive behavior.

The use of a time-limited, cognitive-behavioral, group treatment program for maltreating parents provides another example of tertiary prevention (Barth, Blythe, Schinke, & Shilling, 1983). A child protective services agency referred maltreating parents having problems with anger control to the group, sponsored by a multidisciplinary child development clinic. Parents met for eight twice-weekly group sessions led by social workers. Because disorganized families frequently have difficulty in attending regularly scheduled meetings, transportation was provided whenever necessary. Group leaders demonstrated parenting and anger-control skills by means of "live" performances or prerecorded videotapes. Role plays of participants' family problems provided group members with opportunities to rehearse new cognitive and behavioral responses to situations that might provoke aggression. As parents gained proficiency in the use of these skills, group leaders shifted to the role of coaching. To transfer the learning occurring in the group to the home, participants were given task assignments such as making one approval statement to each child between group meetings. Parents reported their experiences and received praise for accomplishing their tasks or assistance in overcoming problems encountered.

❏ **Summary**

Child maltreatment prevention can be implemented at three levels: primary, secondary, and tertiary. Programs at all three levels are occurring across the country. In many instances, existing prevention programs and curricula can be implemented effectively in other communities with minor modifications.

❑ **Suggested Reading**

Cohn, A. (1983). *An approach to preventing child abuse.* Chicago: National Committee to Prevent Child Abuse.

This booklet is available from the NCPCA (see Appendix B for address). In addition to discussing the concept of prevention in general, it identifies numerous preventive programs currently being used throughout the country.

McMurtry, S. (1985). Secondary prevention of child maltreatment: A review. *Social Work, 30,* 42-48.

This article discusses critical issues relative to secondary prevention of child maltreatment. The article focuses on the importance of screening individuals at high risk for child maltreatment and the effectiveness of programs directed to this target population.

9

Treatment Evaluation

Mental health professionals must evaluate their treatment to determine if it is effective. Evaluation involves using research methodology that you have studied in your research courses. This chapter will help you translate your general research knowledge for use specifically in evaluating treatment effectiveness when working with child abuse and neglect.

❏ Measuring Treatment Effectiveness

Although evaluation is identified as one of the last steps of the problem-solving process, in reality it begins much sooner. Evaluation begins when the worker identifies treatment goals for a family based on a diagnostic understanding of the family. These goals, found in the treatment plan, identify general outcomes the family should accomplish in treatment. When the worker begins treatment

188

with the family, these outcome statements must be reformulated into very specific goals that will serve as the basis for evaluating treatment effectiveness. The worker makes the treatment plan goals specific by stating the expected outcome in behavioral terms, thereby enabling the outcome to be measured; identifying a period of time in which the change will take place; and specifying how the change that is to occur will be accomplished.

The diagnostic summary and treatment plan from the Roberts's case, found in Chapter 4, provides an example. Three general goals composed the treatment plan. Mr. Roberts was to attend a therapy group for men to help him with anger control, and Mr. and Mrs. Roberts were to enroll in a parent education course and participate in Parents Anonymous meetings to improve their parenting knowledge and skills.

How will the Roberts's protective services worker be able to evaluate whether these goals were accomplished? Imagine, for example, that you are the social worker assigned to the Roberts family. You are scheduled to meet with an administrative review panel on the Roberts case 6 months following the case opening to determine if progress is being made in treatment. At the hearing, you briefly review the diagnostic summary and treatment plan with the committee and then state, "Treatment is progressing on target. Mr. Roberts is attending weekly therapy group meetings, Mr. and Mrs. Roberts have been attending Parents Anonymous meetings, and the Robertses have successfully completed the parent education course." A panel member asks, "How do you know the Robertses received help in their parenting from the parent education course?" You stutter a bit and reply that the course instructor told you that the Roberts family was present at every session except one, when Mrs. Roberts's aunt died. Also, Mr. and Mrs. Roberts told you during a recent home visit that the course was helpful. As you say this, however, the thought flashes through your mind that as part of your graduate education, you took a statistics course and attended every session, but at the end of the course you still did not understand statistics, as your grade unfortunately reflected. Also, you recall the term "response bias" from your research course. You remember that sometimes people respond in ways they think they should or in ways that will make them look good.

A	B	C
Client at pretreatment stage	Treatment	Client at posttreatment stage

Figure 9.1. A Model for Treatment Effectiveness Evaluation

How can you satisfy the panel's concern that the parent education course made an impact on Mr. and Mrs. Roberts? Obviously, you need some data. Your responses to the panel are going to be very subjective unless you have collected some objective data. To do this, you should have implemented an evaluative process prior to the time the Robertses began the parent education course. Figure 9.1 depicts this process.

Prior to implementing treatment, a client's knowledge, attitudes, or behaviors that are to be changed in treatment must be appraised (Stage A). These data may be referred to as "baseline" or "before treatment" data. Treatment is implemented at Stage B. (The term "treatment" is being used comprehensively to imply an array of interventions, such as a client finding employment, securing adequate housing, arranging day care, attending a parent education course, or joining a therapy group.) Stage C represents treatment completion, or when treatment effectiveness is measured. (Measurements also may be made during treatment, allowing the worker to change the treatment or fine-tune it to meet a client's needs.) Data collected following treatment may be identified as "after treatment data." The difference between stages A and C represents change occurring in the client.

The measurement of change occurring between stages A and C will be very vague and subjective unless the worker identifies, prior to implementing treatment, client knowledge, attitudes, or behavior to be changed and how such change will be measured. If the client is to be referred to another worker within the protective services agency or to a worker in another agency, then the referring worker and the worker responsible for treatment must determine the changes the client is expected to make and how these changes will be measured. Simply referring a client to another agency and having the client participate in the service that agency offers does not constitute documenting treatment effectiveness. The protective services worker making the referral has primary responsibility for determining, with the treatment resource, how treatment effectiveness will be measured.

❑ Identifying Goals of Treatment

Evaluating treatment effectiveness is made easier if the treatment plan is translated into specific goals. Thus, each treatment plan goal must be reformulated into a measurable goal when treatment begins. The goal will identify the way or ways the clients' knowledge, attitudes, or behavior will differ at Stage C in Figure 9.1 as compared to Stage A, the time period in which this will take place, and how the change will occur.

Being able to write measurable goals is critical to evaluating treatment effectiveness. Goals are statements of intent. They help clients organize their lives. Goals channel energy. The way goals are conceptualized and stated is important to their accomplishment and to the entire evaluation process. Vague and unclear goals cannot be measured and most likely will not be accomplished. This means that goals must be stated in behavioral terms. Behavior here refers to any visible activity displayed by the client (Mager, 1962).

Goals have been defined as statements of intent, namely, what the social worker and client want to happen following treatment. This assumes that treatment programs designed for maltreating parents have clear goals, or intended occurrences following program completion. If treatment programs within protective services agencies or in community social services and mental health agencies do not identify how clients will be helped after using the service, then there is little hope that the treatment will be effective. (This does not mean that every client will experience the results intended. Other factors, such as the client's lack of motivation or the program's failure to produce intended results, may prevent the program's effectiveness.) A match must occur between what a client needs and what a treatment program identifies that it can accomplish (Mager, 1972). For example, following are program goals for a parent education program an agency is implementing for physically abusive parents. At the end of this parent education course, participants should be able to

1. Identify three ineffective methods of discipline and state why they are ineffective
2. Describe the use of "time-out"
3. Role-play the use of "time-out" with another group participant, who will play a misbehaving child

The worker for the Roberts family could have used these program goals as the basis for formulating treatment goals the family would accomplish by attending the parent education course. If this had been done, the worker would have been able to respond effectively to the panel's concern regarding what the Robertses learned from the parent education course. The worker could have cited their performance on each of these goals, thereby providing the panel with performance data rather than relying on attendance information and the Robertses own evaluation of their participation.

Goals not written in behavioral terms are vague, imprecise, and open to many interpretations (Mager, 1962). The choice of words used in writing precise goals is important. Phrases such as "to know," "to understand," and "to improve" are vague and, consequently, are not measurable. Compare these phrases to more precise ones such as "to list," "to identify," and "to state." Goals written with the latter phrases are measurable.

Following is a goal written with a verb open to many interpretations: "At the end of this parent education course, the participant should know ways to discipline other than corporal punishment." The next goal uses verbs specifying measurable behaviors open to fewer interpretations: "At the end of this parent education course, the participant should be able to identify and describe three disciplinary methods other than corporal punishment."

Notice the difference in the verbs used in the first and second goals. The verb *know* in the first goal is ambiguous in the sense that it does not specify a *behavior* or *activity* in which the participant will engage. Rather, *knowing* is an internal state of affairs. One cannot look into another individual's mind to determine whether that person knows something. In the second goal, the verbs *identify* and *describe* refer to activities. These are measurable outcomes.

Measurable activities may be verbal or nonverbal. Individuals may be asked, orally or in writing, to demonstrate the skill identified in the goal. Although a client may be able to compare different types of discipline verbally, this does not mean that the client necessarily will use these methods. This introduces a problem familiar to mental health professionals focusing on the linkage between knowledge, attitudes, and behavior. As part of their participation in a parent education course, parents practice, through role-play, skills they are learning in the course. If parents have the opportunity to practice these skills, the likelihood is much greater that they will use these skills with their children.

This introduces the problem of recidivism in child abuse and neglect. A therapist cannot ever state with certainty that a client will never again maltreat a child or recidivate. If measurable (behavioral) goals are set and attained by a client in treatment, however, a therapist can document with greater certainty what a client has gained from treatment as compared to merely reporting a client's attendance at treatment.

The goals of treatment should include criteria or minimum acceptable performance standards for their completion. For example, a 6-year-old child frequently misses school because the mother fails to awaken the child early enough to meet the school bus. In the treatment plan, the worker intends to help mother and child improve school attendance by their waking early enough for the child to board the bus. Following is a goal the client and worker formulated: "To ensure that my child meets the school bus every day for 30 consecutive school days, my child and I will each set an alarm clock for an hour prior to the bus arriving." This goal, written in behavioral or measurable terms, specifies the criterion that must be met for accomplishing the goal. The mother must successfully wake the child in time for the child to board the school bus for 30 consecutive school days.

The goals of treatment should include criteria or minimum acceptable performance standards.

The literature on goal setting emphasizes that the person who is going to fulfill the goal must participate in the goal-setting process. This is referred to as "clients owning a goal." If a client does not "own" a goal (in which case the worker has forced the goal on the client), there is little likelihood that the client will accomplish the goal. Clients' involuntary involvement with child protective services agencies creates difficulties relative to participating in goal setting. Protective services workers may be tempted simply to use their authority to inform clients what they *must* do. Through their interviewing skills, however, combined with an appropriate use of authority, they can encourage maltreating parents to participate in the goal-setting process. The use of empathy, discussed in an earlier chapter, can be helpful in this process.

❏ Research Designs

The worker must determine a strategy for evaluating treatment effectiveness following goal identification. This strategy is known as the research design. Various research designs are available for evaluating treatment effectiveness. Several such designs will be discussed briefly. You may also wish to review material from your research courses on single-subject, experimental, and quasi-experimental designs, including factors influencing the internal and external validity of these designs.

SINGLE-SUBJECT DESIGNS

Single-subject designs may be used with individual clients to determine client behavioral change over a period of time. The worker and client determine a target behavior to be changed. Using the example referred to earlier, the baseline would be meeting the school bus so that the child can attend school. A baseline would be determined reflecting the number of times the child attended school for a month prior to initiating treatment. The mother and/or school should be able to provide the worker with this information. The intervention represents the treatment period when the worker is working with the mother and child on setting alarms to wake early enough for the child to board the school bus. This is known as an AB design, with the A signifying the baseline and the B the intervention, or treatment.

Charts can be used to keep a record of progress in single-subject designs and to provide the client (and worker) with visual feedback on the effectiveness of the intervention. Using our case example, the mother can record on a chart each day whether the child boards the school bus and attends school that day. The worker can verify this information, if necessary, from the school.

Advantages in using a single-subject design include the worker being able to shape the intervention directly to the specific need of the client, so that both the worker and the client are able to follow the progress toward meeting the established goal. Charting provides the client with visual feedback that can be a motivating force as the client begins to experience a sense of mastery over a problem (Bloom & Fischer, 1982; Royse, 1990).

EXPERIMENTAL DESIGNS

Several research designs are available for evaluating treatment effectiveness with groups of clients. The classical experimental design involves the random assignment (R) of subjects either to an experimental group that receives the treatment (X) or to a control group that does not. Measurement of subjects' behavior to be changed occurs on a pretest (O_1, or first observation) and posttest (O_2, or second observation) basis. This design may be diagrammed as follows:

$$R \qquad O_1 \qquad X \qquad O_2$$
$$R \qquad O_1 \qquad \qquad O_2$$

Although this is an optimum design because of its control of internal and external validity factors, research with clients in agency settings usually does not permit the use of such a rigorous design. A worker may not have access to a control group or, if one is available, cannot randomly assign clients to an experimental or control group. Also, the worker ethically cannot withhold treatment from a client or group of clients for a period of time for research purposes. Thus, less rigorous designs may more appropriately be used when working with groups of clients using agency services, such as in group therapy or in parent education courses.

PRE-EXPERIMENTAL DESIGNS

Pre-experimental designs are easier to implement and are more adaptable to situations therapists face when evaluating treatment effectiveness. Because clients must be provided services when they seek help from an agency, random assignment to treatment or control groups cannot occur. A pre-experimental design may be diagrammed in the following way:

$$O_1 \qquad X \qquad O_2$$

This design will indicate for the therapist that improvement has occurred following treatment; however, the design will not rule out alternate explanations for what may have caused the change other than the treatment (internal validity factors). A control group would be necessary to determine the effect of such extraneous factors.

In some instances, pretest data may not be available to the worker. To merely measure the clients after the introduction of treatment $(X\,O_1)$, a posttest-only design, tells nothing about the treatment impact on the clients because there is no baseline behavioral measurement. Pretest data, however, may be collected in other ways.

A variation of this design, known as the posttest-only design with nonequivalent groups, may help the worker determine baseline behavioral rates even though they could not be measured. The design is diagrammed as follows:

$$X \qquad\qquad O_1$$
$$O_1$$

In this design, pretest data are not available for the group of clients being treated. Data from a similar group, however, are available. For example, a protective services agency receives complaints on abusive and neglectful families. Following the assessment, families are given several treatment options. One option is participation in a parent education course. This becomes the treatment group, or the first group in the above diagram. Some clients chose not to take the course but, rather, to work on their parenting problems in interviews with their social worker. This is the nonequivalent comparison group, or the second group in the diagram. Later, the agency attempts to appraise client recidivism as a way of evaluating effectiveness of various treatment strategies. If the data indicate that parent education participants showed a lower recidivism rate than did those undergoing other types of treatment, a logical conclusion would be that this difference is a result of the intervention, namely, the parent education course. One cannot conclude this with certainty, however, because the two groups may not have been similar and there was no random assignment of clients to one treatment or the other. Subjects may have self-selected themselves for a specific treatment that may, in turn, have affected the results achieved (Royse, 1990).

QUASI-EXPERIMENTAL DESIGNS

Quasi-experimental designs are more rigorous than pre-experimental designs, but they do not approach experimental design rigor. Frequently in agency settings, random assignment of clients to one of several treatment strategies is not possible. The nonequivalent control group design makes use of pre- and posttest measurements and a comparison group receiving another type of treatment (Y). This design is diagrammed as follows:

$$O \qquad\qquad X \qquad\qquad O_2$$
$$O \qquad\qquad Y \qquad\qquad O_2$$

For example, a worker may wish to evaluate the effectiveness of parents attending a parent education course as compared to participating in Parents Anonymous meetings. Pre- and posttest data may be collected in both groups. Although the two groups are similar in that both are composed of parents who have engaged in abusive behavior with their children, the groups are not necessarily equivalent. Although attempts may be made to match the two groups on demographic variables such as gender, age, education, and socioeconomic status, matching is very difficult because of the large number of variables to be matched and uncertainty regarding whether all influential variables are being controlled. Again, the factor of self-selection affects the results of this design. Factors influencing clients to choose one intervention over another are unknown, and these factors may have affected the treatment effectiveness.

Choose the most rigorous design possible.

Researchers generally regard pre-experimental and quasi-experimental designs as weak, especially if more rigorous designs are available. When selecting a research design for evaluating treatment effectiveness, choose the most rigorous design possible. Unfortunately, however, in some instances implementing rigorous designs may not be possible because of time constraints, the way agency services are provided, or the lack of comparison or control groups.

❑ Using a Research Consultant

Therapists working with clients involved in child maltreatment may believe that they do not have the time or expertise to design studies measuring treatment effectiveness. A helpful way for an agency to initiate treatment evaluation is to seek consultation from someone who is knowledgeable and experienced in research. In the same way that agencies use psychological or psychiatric consultation for selected cases, so agencies may use research consultation to begin evaluating treatment effectiveness. Once evaluative strategies are designed for various treatment programs, they may be used repeatedly and can become a regular part of agency service delivery. Child maltreatment literature contains many program evaluation examples. Workers may adapt these examples for use in their own agencies. Some examples of treatment/prevention program evaluations include the evaluation of treatment groups for adult female sexual abuse survivors (Alexander, Niemeyer, Follette, Moore, & Harter, 1989), evaluation of a social learning approach to treatment with abusive mothers (Lorber et al., 1984), evaluation of a sexual abuse prevention program with preschool children (Nibert et al., 1989) and school-age children (Wurtele, Saslawsky, Miller, Marrs, & Britcher,

1986), evaluation of a parent training program (Rickel, Dudley, & Berman, 1980), and evaluation of family preservation services (Bath & Haapala, 1994; Wells, 1994).

❑ Summary

To work effectively with child abuse and neglect clients, one must evaluate the impact or effectiveness of interventions. Evaluation, although identified among the final steps of the problem-solving process, must begin in the initial case assessment phase as goals for treatment are determined with the client. These goals must be translated into measurable statements at the initiation of treatment so that the worker can later evaluate if treatment has been effective. Various research designs may be used in the evaluation process. Evaluating treatment effectiveness is an essential and critical aspect of working with child abuse and neglect.

❑ Suggested Reading

Bloom, M., & Fischer, J. (1982). *Evaluating practice: Guidelines for the accountable professional.* Englewood Cliffs, NJ: Prentice Hall.
   This book, focusing primarily on the use of single-subject designs, will assist a therapist in evaluating treatment interventions with individual clients.

Royse, D. (1995). *Research methods in social work.* Chicago: Nelson-Hall.
   This introductory text on social work research includes a wealth of information for mental health professionals wishing to evaluate their practice, including chapters on designs, the construction of instruments, and instruments available for use.

Appendix A:
The Child Abuse Prevention and Treatment Act (Public Law 93-247)

To provide financial assistance for a demonstration program for the prevention, identification, and treatment of child abuse and neglect, to establish a National Center on Child Abuse and Neglect, and for other purposes.

Be it enacted by the Senate and House of Representatives of the United States of America in Congress assembled, That this Act may be cited as the "Child Abuse Prevention and Treatment Act."

❑ The National Center on Child Abuse and Neglect

Sec. 2. (a) The Secretary of Health, Education, and Welfare (hereinafter referred to in this Act as the "Secretary") shall establish an office to be known as the National Center on Child Abuse and Neglect (hereinafter referred to in this Act as the "Center").

(b) The Secretary, through the Center, shall—

    (1) compile, analyze, and publish a summary annually of recently conducted research on child abuse and neglect;

    (2) develop and maintain an information clearinghouse on all programs, showing promise of success, for the prevention, identification, and treatment of child abuse and neglect;

    (3) compile and publish training materials for personnel who are engaged or intend to engage in the prevention, identification, and treatment of child abuse and neglect;

    (4) provide technical assistance (directly or through grant or contract) to public and nonprofit private agencies and organizations to assist them in planning, improving, developing, and carrying out programs and activities relating to the prevention, identification, and treatment of child abuse and neglect;

    (5) conduct research into the causes of child abuse and neglect, and into the prevention, identification, and treatment thereof; and

    (6) make a complete and full study and investigation of the national incidence of child abuse and neglect, including a determination of the extent to which incidents of child abuse and neglect are increasing in number or severity.

❏ Definition

Sec. 3. For purposes of this Act the term "child abuse and neglect" means the physical or mental injury, sexual abuse, negligent treatment, or maltreatment of a child under the age of eighteen by a person who is responsible for the child's welfare under circumstances which indicate that the child's health or welfare is harmed or threatened thereby, as determined in accordance with regulations prescribed by the Secretary.

❏ Demonstration Programs and Projects

Sec 4. (a) The Secretary, through the Center, is authorized to make grants to, and enter into contracts with, public agencies or nonprofit private organizations (or combinations thereof) for demonstration programs and projects designed to prevent, identify, and treat child abuse and neglect. Grants or contracts under this subsection may be—

(1) for the development and establishment of training programs for professional and paraprofessional personnel in the fields of medicine, law, education, social work and other relevant fields who are engaged in, or intend to work in, the field of the prevention, identification, and treatment of child abuse and neglect; and training programs for children, and for persons responsible for the welfare of children, in methods of protecting children from child abuse and neglect;

(2) for the establishment and maintenance of centers, serving defined geographic areas, staffed by multidisciplinary teams of personnel trained in the prevention, identification, and treatment of child abuse and neglect cases, to provide a broad range of services related to child abuse and neglect, including direct support and supervision of satellite centers and attention homes, as well as providing advice and consultation to individuals, agencies, and organizations which request such services;

(3) for furnishing services of teams of professional and paraprofessional personnel who are trained in the prevention, identification, and treatment of child abuse and neglect cases, on a consulting basis to small communities where such services are not available;

(4) for such other innovative programs and projects, including programs and projects for parent self-help, and for prevention and treatment of drug-related child abuse and neglect, that show promise of successfully preventing or treating cases of child abuse and neglect as the Secretary may approve.

Not less than 50 per centum of the funds under this Act for any fiscal year shall be used only for carrying out the provisions of this subsection.

(b) (1) Of the sums appropriated under this Act for any fiscal year, not less than 5 per centum and not more than 20 per centum may be used by the Secretary for making grants to the States for the payment of reasonable and necessary expenses for the purpose of assisting the States in developing, strengthening, and carrying out child abuse and neglect prevention and treatment programs.

(2) In order for a State to qualify for assistance under this subsection, such State shall—

(A) have in effect a State child abuse and neglect law which shall include provisions for immunity for persons reporting instances of child abuse and neglect for prosecution under any State or local law, arising out of such reporting;

(B) provide for the reporting of known and suspected instances of child abuse and neglect;

(C) provide that upon receipt of a report of known or suspected instances of child abuse or neglect an investigation shall be initiated promptly to substantiate the accuracy of the report, and upon a finding of abuse or neglect, immediate steps shall be taken to protect the health and welfare of the abused or neglected child, as well as that of any other child under the same care who may be in danger of abuse or neglect;

(D) demonstrate that there are in effect throughout the State in connection with the enforcement of child abuse and neglect laws and with the reporting of suspected instances of child abuse and neglect, such administrative procedures, such personnel trained in child abuse and neglect prevention and treatment, such training procedures, such institutional and other facilities (public and private), and such related multidisciplinary programs and services as may be necessary or appropriate to assure that the State will deal effectively with child abuse and neglect cases in the State;

(E) provide for methods to preserve the confidentiality of all records in order to protect the rights of the child, his parents or guardians;

(F) provide for the cooperation of law enforcement officials, courts of competent jurisdiction, and appropriate State agencies providing human services;

(G) provide that in every case involving an abused or neglected child which results in a judicial proceeding a guardian ad litem shall be appointed to represent the child in such proceedings;

(H) provide that the aggregate of support for programs or projects related to child abuse and neglect assisted by State funds shall not be reduced below the level provided during fiscal year 1973, and set forth policies and procedures designed to assure that Federal funds made available under this Act for any fiscal year will be so used as to supplement and to the extent practicable, increase the level of State funds which would, in the absence of Federal funds, be available for such programs and projects;

(I) provide for dissemination of information to the general public with respect to the problem of child abuse and neglect and the facilities and prevention and treatment methods available to combat instances of child abuse and neglect; and

      (J) to the extent feasible, ensure that parental organizations combating child abuse and neglect receive preferential treatment.

    (3) Programs or projects related to child abuse and neglect assisted under part A or B of title IV of the Social Security Act shall comply with the requirements set forth in clauses (B), (C), (E), and (F) of paragraph (2).

(c) Assistance provided pursuant to this section shall not be available for construction of facilities; however, the Secretary is authorized to supply such assistance for the lease or rental of facilities where adequate facilities are not otherwise available, and for repair or minor remodeling or alteration of existing facilities.

(d) The Secretary shall establish criteria designed to achieve equitable distribution of assistance under this section among the States, among geographic areas of the Nation, and among rural and urban areas. To the extent possible, citizens of each State shall receive assistance from at least one project under this section.

❏ Authorization

Sec. 5. There are hereby authorized to be appropriated for the purposes of this Act $15,000,000 for the fiscal year ending June 30, 1974, $20,000,000 for the fiscal year ending June 30, 1975, and $25,000,000 for the fiscal year ending June 30, 1976, and for the succeeding fiscal year.

❏ Advisory Board on Child Abuse and Neglect

Sec. 6. (a) The Secretary shall, within sixty days after the date of enactment of this Act, appoint an Advisory Board on Child Abuse and Neglect (hereinafter referred to as the "Advisory Board") which shall be composed of representatives from Federal agencies with responsibility for programs and activities related to child abuse and neglect, including the Office of Child Development, the Office of Education, the National Institute of Education, the National Institute of Mental Health, the National Institute of Child Health and Human Development, the Social and Rehabilitation Service, and the Health Services Administration. The Advisory Board shall assist the Secretary in coordinating programs and activities related to child abuse and neglect administered or assisted under this Act with such programs or activities administered or assisted by the Federal agencies whose representatives are members of the Advisory Board. The Advisory Board shall also assist the Secretary in the development of Federal standards for child abuse and neglect prevention and treatment programs and projects.

(b) The Advisory Board shall prepare and submit, within eighteen months after the date of enactment of this Act, to the President and to the Congress a report on the programs assisted under this Act and the programs, projects, and activities related to child abuse and neglect administered or assisted by the Federal agencies whose representatives are members of the Advisory Board. Such report shall include a study of the relationship between drug addiction and child abuse and neglect.

(c) Of the funds appropriated under section 5, one-half of 1 per centum, or $1,000,000 whichever is the lesser, may be used by the Secretary only for purposes of the report under subsection (b).

❑ Coordination

Sec. 7. The Secretary shall promulgate regulations and make such arrangements as may be necessary or appropriate to ensure that there is effective coordination between programs related to child abuse and neglect under this Act and other such programs which are assisted by Federal Funds.

Approved January 31, 1974.

Appendix B: Resources and National Organizations Concerned With Child Maltreatment

American Academy of Pediatrics
141 Northwest Point Blvd.
P.O. Box 927
Elk Grove Village, IL 60009-0927
(800) 433-9016

American Bar Association Center on Children and the Law
1800 M Street, NW, Suite 200
Washington, DC 20036
(202) 331-2250

American Humane Association
American Association for Protecting Children
63 Inverness Dr. East
Englewood, CO 80112
(303) 792-9900
(800) 227-5242

American Medical Association
Health and Human Behavior Department
535 N. Dearborn
Chicago, IL 60610
(312) 645-5066

American Public Welfare Association
810 First St., NE
Suite 500
Washington, DC 20002-4205
(202) 682-0100

Child Welfare League of America
440 First St., NW
Suite 310
Washington, DC 20001
(202) 638-2952

Childhelp USA
6463 Independence Ave.
Woodland Hills, CA 91367
Hotline: (800) 4-A-CHILD or (800) 422-4453

Clearinghouse on Child Abuse and Neglect Information
P.O. Box 1182
Washington, DC 20013
(703) 385-7565
(800) FYI-3366

Committee for Children
2203 Airport Way South, Suite 500
Seattle, WA 98134-2027
(206) 343-1223
(800) 634-4449

National Association for Family-Based Services
1513 Stoney Point Rd., NW
Cedar Rapids, IA 52405
(319) 396-4829

National Association of Social Workers
750 First St., NE, Suite 700
Washington, DC 20002-4241
(202) 408-8600

National Black Child Development Institute
1023 15th St., NW, Suite 600
Washington, DC 20005
(202) 387-1281

National Center for Child Abuse and Neglect (NCCAN)
Children's Bureau
Administration for Children, Youth and Families
Office of Human Development Services
Department of Health and Human Services
P.O. Box 1182
Washington, DC 20013
(202) 245-8586

National Center for Missing and Exploited Children
2101 Wilson Blvd., Suite 550
Arlington, VA 22201
(703) 235-3900
(800) 843-5678

National Child Abuse and Neglect Clinical Resource Center
Henry Kempe Center for Prevention and Treatment of Child Abuse
and Neglect
1205 Oneida St.
Denver, CO 80220
(303) 321-3963

National Committee to Prevent Child Abuse
332 S. Michigan Ave., Suite 1600
Chicago, IL 60604
(312) 663-3520

National Council of Juvenile and Family Court Judges
P.O. Box 8970
Reno, NV 89507
(702) 784-6012

National Council on Child Abuse and Family Violence
1050 Connecticut Ave., NW, Suite 300
Washington, DC 20036
(800) 222-2000

National Resource Center on Child Abuse and Neglect
American Humane Association
63 Inverness Dr. East
Englewood, CO 80112
(800) 2-ASK-AHA

National Resource Center on Child Sexual Abuse
2204 Whitesburg Dr., Suite 200
Huntsville, AL 35801
(205) 534-6868
(800) KIDS-006

National Resource Center on Family Based Services
The University of Iowa School of Social Work
Oakdale Campus, N240OH
Oakdale, IA 52319
(319) 335-4123

National Runaway Switchboard Metro-Help, Inc.
2080 N. Lincoln
Chicago, IL 60657
(312) 880-9860
(800) 621-4000

Nurturing Program
Family Development Resources, Inc.
3160 Pinebrook Rd.
Park City, UT 84060
(801) 649-5822

Parent Effectiveness Training (PET)
Effectiveness Training Inc.
531 Stevens Ave.
Solana Beach, CA 92075
(619) 481-8121

Parents Anonymous
675 W. Foothill Blvd., Suite 220
Claremont, CA 91711
(909) 621-6184

Parents United
Daughters and Sons United
Adults Molested as Children United
615 15th St.
Modesta, CA 95354
(205) 572-3446

Safer Society Press
P.O. Box 340
Brandon, VT 05733-0340
(802) 247-3132

Survivors of Incest Anonymous, Inc.
P.O. Box 21817
Baltimore, MD 21222-6817

Systematic Training for Effective Parenting (STEP)
American Guidance Service
P.O. Box 99
Circle Pines, MN 55014-1796
(800) 328-2560

VOICES in Action, Inc.
(Victims of Incest Can Emerge Survivors)
P.O. Box 148309
Chicago, IL 60614
(312) 327-1500
(800) 786-4238

Appendix C:
Canadian Provincial and Territorial Agencies Concerned With Child Abuse

Alberta
Child Welfare Services Department of Family and Social Services
9th Floor, 7th Street Plaza
10030-107th St.
Edmonton, Alberta T5J 3E4

British Columbia
Family and Children's Services
Ministry of Social Services and Housing
Parliament Buildings
Victoria, British Columbia V8W 3A2

Manitoba
Child and Family Services
Department of Family Services
114 Garry St., 2nd Floor
Winnipeg, Manitoba R3C 1G1

New Brunswick
Department of Health and Community Services
P.O. Box 5100
Fredericton, New Brunswick E3B 5G8

Newfoundland
Department of Social Services
Confederation Building
P.O. Box 8700
St. John's, Newfoundland
A1B 4J6

Nova Scotia
Family and Children's Services
Department of Community Services
P.O. Box 696
Halifax, Nova Scotia B3J 2T7

Ontario
Children's Services Branch
Ministry of Community and Social Services
80 Grosvenor St.
S.W. 355, Hepburn Block
Toronto, Ontario M7A 1E9

Prince Edward Island
Department of Health and Social Services
P.O. Box 2000
Charlottetown, Prince Edward Island C1A 7N8

Quebec
Services des programmes à la jeunesse
Direction générale de la prévention et des services communautaires
Ministère de la Santé et des Services sociaux
1075, chemin Ste-Foy, 6ᵉ étage
Quebec (Quebec) G1S 2M1

Saskatchewan
Family Services Division
Saskatchewan Social Services
1920 Broad St.
Regina, Saskatchewan 34P 3V6

Northwest Territories
Family and Children's Services
Department of Social Services
7th Floor, Precambrian Building
Yellowknife, Northwest Territories X1A 2L9

Yukon Territory
Family and Children's Services
Department of Health and Social Services
Box 2703
Whitehorse, Yukon Territory Y1A 2C6

References

Ackley, D. (1977). A brief overview of child abuse. *Social Casework, 58,* 21-24.

Adams-Tucker, C. (1982). Proximate effects of sexual abuse in childhood. *American Journal of Psychiatry, 139,* 1252-1256.

Agosta, C., & Loring, M. (1988). Understanding and treating the adult retrospective victim of child sexual abuse. In S. Sgroi (Ed.), *Vulnerable populations* (Vol. 1, pp. 115-135). Lexington, MA: Lexington Books.

Alderette, P., & deGraffenried, D. (1986). Nonorganic failure-to-thrive syndrome and the family system. *Social Work, 31,* 207-211.

Alexander, P., Niemeyer, R., Follette, V., Moore, M., & Harter, S. (1989). A comparison of group treatments of women sexually abused as children. *Journal of Consulting and Clinical Psychology, 57,* 479-483.

American Bar Association Center on Children and the Law. (1988). *1988 annual report.* Washington, DC: Author.

American Humane Association. (1980). *Helping in child protective services.* Englewood, CO: Author.

American Humane Association. (1991). *Helping in child protective services: A casework handbook.* Englewood, CO: Author.

American Humane Association. (1992). *Helping in child protective services: A competency based casework handbook.* Englewood, CO: Author.

American Humane Association. (1995). *Fact sheet #1: Child abuse and neglect data.* Englewood, CO: Author.

Anderson, D., & Finne, M. (1986a). *Margaret's story.* Minneapolis: Dillon.

Anderson, D., & Finne, M. (1986b). *Michael's story.* Minneapolis: Dillon.

215

Anderson, D., & Finne, M. (1986c). *Robin's story*. Minneapolis: Dillon.

Ayalon, O., & Van Tassel, E. (1987). Living in dangerous environments. In M. Brassard, R. Germain, & S. Hart (Eds.), *Psychological maltreatment of children and youth* (pp. 171-184). Elmsford, NY: Pergamon.

Azar, S., Robinson, D., Hekimian, E., & Twentyman, C. (1984). Unrealistic expectations and problem-solving ability in maltreating and comparison mothers. *Journal of Consulting and Clinical Psychology, 52*, 687-691.

Bagley, C., Wood, M., & Young, L. (1994). Victim to abuser: Mental health and behavioral sequels of child sexual abuse in a community survey of young adult males. *Child Abuse & Neglect, 18*, 683-697.

Baily, T., & Baily, W. (1986). *Operational definitions of child emotional maltreatment.* Washington, DC: National Committee on Child Abuse and Neglect.

Baldwin, J., & Oliver, J. (1975). Epidemiology and family characteristics of severely abused children. *British Journal of Preventive Social Medicine, 29*, 205-221.

Barth, R., Blythe, B., Schinke, S., & Shilling, R. (1983). Self-control training with maltreating parents. *Child Welfare, 62*, 314-324.

Barth, R., & Sullivan, R. (1985). Collecting competent evidence in behalf of children. *Social Work, 30*, 130-136.

Bateson, G. (1972). *Steps to an ecology of mind*. New York: Chandler.

Bath, H., & Haapala, D. (1993). Intensive family preservation services with abused and neglected children: An examination of group differences. *Child Abuse & Neglect, 17*, 213-225.

Bath, H., & Haapala, D. (1994). Family preservation services: What does the outcome research really tell us? *Social Service Review, 68*, 386-404.

Bauer, M. (1977). *Foster child*. New York: Seabury.

Bavolek, S. (1984). *Handbook for the Adult-Adolescent Parenting Inventory (AAPI)*. Park City, UT: Family Development Resources.

Bavolek, S. (1989). Assessing and treating high-risk parenting attitudes. In J. Pardeck (Ed.), *Child abuse and neglect: Theory, research and practice* (pp. 97-110). New York: Gordon & Breach.

Bear, E., & Dimock, P. (1988). *Adults molested as children: A survivor's manual for women and men*. Orwell, VT: Safer Society Press.

Behling, W. (1979). Alcohol abuse as encountered in 51 instances of reported child abuse. *Clinical Pediatrics, 18*, 87-91.

Bell, C., & Mylniec, W. (1974). Preparing for a neglect proceeding: A guide for the social worker. *Public Welfare, 32*, 26-37.

Belsky, J. (1980). Child maltreatment: An ecological integration. *American Psychologist, 35*, 320-335.

Benward, J., & Densen-Gerber, J. (1975). Incest as a causative factor in antisocial behavior: An exploratory study. *Contemporary Drug Problems, 4*, 322-340.

Berg, P. (1976). Parental expectations and attitudes in child-abusing families (Doctoral dissertation, University of Southern California, 1976). *Dissertation Abstracts International, 37*, 1889B.

Berkowitz, C. (1987). Sexual abuse of children and adolescents. *Advances in Pediatrics, 34*, 274-312.

Berliner, L., & Ernst, E. (1984). Group work with preadolescent sexual assault victims. In I. Stuart & J. Greer (Eds.), *Victims of sexual aggression* (pp. 105-123). New York: Van Nostrand Reinhold.

Biestek, F. (1957). *The casework relationship*. Chicago: Loyola University Press.

Binder, R., & McNiel, D. (1986). *Evaluation of a school-based sexual abuse prevention program: Cognitive and emotional effects.* Paper presented at the annual meeting of the American Psychiatric Association, Washington, DC.

Blake-White, J., & Kline, C. (1985). Treating the dissociative process in adult victims of childhood incest. *Social Casework, 66,* 394-402.

Bloom, M., & Fischer, J. (1982). *Evaluating practice: Guidelines for the accountable professional.* Englewood Cliffs, NJ: Prentice Hall.

Borkin, J., & Frank, L. (1986). Sexual abuse prevention for preschoolers: A pilot program. *Child Welfare, 65,* 75-81.

Bornman, L., & Lieber, L. (1984). *Self-help and the treatment of child abuse.* Chicago: National Committee for Prevention of Child Abuse.

Boyd, C., Blow, F., & Orgain, L. (1993). Gender differences among African-American women substance abusers. *Journal of Psychoactive Drugs, 25,* 301-305.

Boyd, C., Guthrie, B., Pohl, J., Whitmarsh, J., & Henderson, D. (1994). African-American women who smoke crack cocaine: Sexual trauma and the mother-daughter relationship. *Journal of Psychoactive Drugs, 26,* 243-247.

Boyd-Franklin, N. (1989). *Black families in therapy.* New York: Guilford.

Brassard, M., & Gelardo, M. (1987). Psychological maltreatment: The unifying construct in child abuse and neglect. *School Psychology Review, 16,* 127-136.

Brassard, M., Germain, R., & Hart, S. (Eds.). (1987). *Psychological maltreatment of children and youth.* Elmsford, NY: Pergamon.

Breton, M., Welbourn, A., & Watters, J. (1981). A nurturing and problem-solving approach for abuse-prone mothers. *Child Abuse & Neglect, 5,* 475-480.

Briere, J., & Runtz, M. (1989). University males' sexual interest in children: Predicting potential indices of "pedophilia" in a nonforensic sample. *Child Abuse & Neglect, 13,* 65-75.

Brill, N. (1985). *Working with people.* New York: Longman.

Bronfenbrenner, U. (1979). *The ecology of human development.* Cambridge, MA: Harvard University Press.

Bullard, D., Glaser, G., Heagarty, M., & Pivchik, E. (1967). Failure to thrive in the "neglected" child. *American Journal of Orthopsychiatry, 37,* 680-690.

Burgess, R., & Conger, R. (1977). Family interaction patterns related to child abuse and neglect: Some preliminary findings. *Child Abuse & Neglect, 1,* 269-277.

Burrell, B., Thompson, B., & Sexton, D. (1994). Predicting child abuse potential across family types. *Child Abuse & Neglect, 18,* 1039-1049.

Byars, B. (1977). *The pinballs.* New York: Harper & Row.

Caffey, J. (1946). Multiple fractures in the long bones of infants suffering from chronic subdural hematoma. *American Journal of Roentgenology, Radium Therapy and Nuclear Medicine, 56,* 163-173.

Cage, R. (1988). Criminal investigation of child sexual abuse. In S. Sgroi (Ed.), *Vulnerable populations* (Vol. 1, pp. 187-227). Lexington, MA: Lexington Books.

Carey, T. (1994). "Spare the rod and spoil the child": Is this a sensible justification for the use of punishment in child rearing? *Child Abuse & Neglect, 18,* 1005-1010.

Caudill, H. (1963). *Night comes to the Cumberlands.* Boston: Little, Brown.

Caulfield, B., & Horowitz, R. (1987). *Child abuse and the law: A legal primer for social workers.* Chicago: National Committee for Prevention of Child Abuse.

Cerezo, M., & Frias, D. (1994). Emotional and cognitive adjustment in abused children. *Child Abuse & Neglect, 18,* 923-932.

Chan, Y. (1994). Parenting stress and social support of mothers who physically abuse their children in Hong Kong. *Child Abuse & Neglect, 18*, 261-269.

Child Welfare League of America. (1989). *Standards for services for abused or neglected children and their families.* New York: Author.

Children's Bureau of Los Angeles. (n.d.). *Family Assessment Form.* (Available from Children's Bureau of Los Angeles, 2824 Hyans St., Los Angeles, CA 90026)

Chilman, C. (1973). [Review of *Roots of Futility.*] *Social Work, 18*, 115-116.

Clark, K. (1975). Knowledge of child development and behavior interaction patterns of mothers who abuse their children (Doctoral dissertation, Wayne State University, 1975). *Dissertation Abstracts International, 36*, 5784B.

Cohn, A. (1983). *An approach to preventing child abuse.* Chicago: National Committee to Prevent Child Abuse.

Cohn, A. (1987). How do we deal with research findings? *Journal of Interpersonal Violence, 2*, 228-232.

Cole, P., Woolger, C., Power, T., & Smith, K. (1992). Parenting difficulties among adult survivors of father-daughter incest. *Child Abuse & Neglect, 16*, 239-249.

Compton, B., & Galaway, B. (1979). *Social work processes.* Homewood, IL: Dorsey.

Conger, R., Burgess, R., & Barnett, C. (1979). Child abuse related to life change and perceptions of illness: Some preliminary findings. *Family Coordinator, 58*, 73-77.

Connelly, C., & Straus, M. (1992). Mother's age and risk for physical abuse. *Child Abuse & Neglect, 16*, 709-718.

Corder, B., Haizlip, T., & DeBoer, P. (1990). A pilot study for a structured, time-limited therapy group for sexually abused pre-adolescent children. *Child Abuse & Neglect, 14*, 243-251.

Covington, S., & Kohen, J. (1984). Women, alcohol, and sexuality. *Advances in Alcohol and Substance Abuse, 4*, 41-56.

Daro, D. (1988). *Confronting child abuse.* New York: Free Press.

Deblinger, E., McLeer, S., Atkins, M., Ralphe, D., & Foa, E. (1989). Post-traumatic stress in sexually abused, physically abused, and nonabused children. *Child Abuse & Neglect, 18*, 403-408.

DeLipsey, J., & Kelly, S. (1988). Videotaping the sexually abused child: The Texas experience, 1983-1987. In S. Sgroi (Ed.), *Vulnerable populations* (Vol. 1, pp. 229-264). Lexington, MA: Lexington Books.

DeMause, L. (1976). *The history of childhood.* London: Souvenir.

Demos, J. (1986). *Past, present and personal.* New York: Oxford University Press.

DeVore, W., & Schlesinger, E. (1981). *Ethnic sensitive social work practice.* St. Louis, MO: C. V. Mosby.

Downs, A., & Gowan, D. (1980). Sex differences in reinforcement and punishment on prime-time television. *Sex Roles, 6*, 683-694.

Driver, E. (1989). An introduction. In E. Driver & A. Droisen (Eds.), *Child sexual abuse: A feminist reader* (pp. 1-68). New York: New York University Press.

Driver, E., & Droisen, A. (Eds.). (1989). *Child sexual abuse: A feminist reader.* New York: New York University Press.

Drotar, D., Eckerle, D., Satola, J., Pallotta, J., & Wyatt, B. (1990). Maternal interactional behavior with nonorganic failure-to-thrive infants: A comparison study. *Child Abuse & Neglect, 14*, 41-51.

Dubowitz, H., Black, M., Harrington, D., & Verschoore, A. (1993). A follow-up study of behavior problems associated with child sexual abuse. *Child Abuse & Neglect, 17*, 743-754.

Duquette, D., & Ramsey, S. (1986). Using lay volunteers to represent children in child protection court proceedings. *Child Abuse & Neglect, 10,* 293-308.

Edna McConnell Clark Foundation. (1985). *Keeping families together: The case for family preservation.* New York: Author.

Egan, G. (1990). *The skilled helper* (4th ed.). Pacific Grove, CA: Brooks/Cole.

Elmer, E. (1960). Abused children seen in hospitals. *Social Work, 5,* 98-102.

Elrod, J., & Rubin, R. (1993). Parental involvement in sexual abuse prevention education. *Child Abuse & Neglect, 17,* 527-538.

Eth, S., & Pyroos, R. (1985). Psychiatric interventions with children traumatized by violence. In D. Schetky & E. Benedek (Eds.), *Emerging issues in child psychiatry and the law* (pp. 285-309). New York: Brunner/Mazel.

Ethier, L., Lacharite, C., & Couture, G. (1995). Childhood adversity, parental stress, and depression of negligent mothers. *Child Abuse & Neglect, 19,* 619-632.

Evans, D., Bowie, M., Hansen, J., Moodie, A., & van der Spuy, H. (1980). Intellectual development and nutrition. *Journal of Pediatrics, 97,* 358-363.

Evans, S., Reinhart, J., & Succop, R. (1972). Failure to thrive. *Journal of the American Academy of Child Psychiatry, 2,* 440-457.

Faller, K. (Ed.). (1981). *Social work with abused and neglected children: A manual of interdisciplinary practice.* New York: Free Press.

Faller, K. (1984). Is the child victim of sexual abuse telling the truth? *Child Abuse & Neglect, 8,* 473-481.

Faller, K. (1988a). *Child sexual abuse: An interdisciplinary manual for diagnosis, case management, and treatment.* New York: Columbia University Press.

Faller, K. (1988b). Decision-making in cases of extrafamilial child sexual abuse. *American Journal of Orthopsychiatry, 58,* 121-128.

Faller, K., Bowden, M., Jones, C., & Hildebrandt, H. (1981). Types of child abuse and neglect. In K. Faller (Ed.), *Social work with abused and neglected children: A manual of interdisciplinary practice* (pp. 13-31). New York: Free Press.

Faller, K., & Ziefert, M. (1981). Causes of child abuse and neglect. In K. Faller (Ed.), *Social work with abused and neglected children: A manual of interdisciplinary practice* (pp. 32-51). Elmsford, NY: Free Press.

Famularo, R., Kinscherff, R., & Fenton, T. (1992). Parental substance abuse and the nature of child maltreatment. *Child Abuse & Neglect, 16,* 475-483.

Famularo, R., Stone, K., Barnum, R., & Wharton, R. (1986). Alcoholism and severe child maltreatment. *American Journal of Orthopsychiatry, 56,* 481-485.

Feshbach, N., & Feshbach, S. (1969). The relationship between empathy and aggression in two age groups. *Developmental Psychology, 1,* 102-107.

Feshbach, S. (1964). The function of aggression and the regulation of aggressive drive. *Psychological Review, 71,* 257-272.

Finkelhor, D. (1979). *Sexually victimized children.* New York: Free Press.

Finkelhor, D. (1984a). *Child sexual abuse: New theory and research.* New York: Free Press.

Finkelhor, D. (1984b). The prevention of child sexual abuse: An overview of needs and problems. *SIECUS Report, 13,* 1-5.

Finkelhor, D., Asdigian, N., & Dziuba-Leatherman, J. (1995). The effectiveness of victimization prevention instruction: An evaluation of children's responses to actual threats and assaults. *Child Abuse & Neglect, 19,* 141-153.

Finkelhor, D., Hotaling, G., Lewis, I., & Smith, C. (1990). Sexual abuse in a national survey of adult men and women: Prevalence, characteristics, and risk factors. *Child Abuse & Neglect, 14,* 14-28.

Flynn, C. (1994). Regional differences in attitudes toward corporal punishment. *Journal of Marriage and the Family, 56,* 314-324.

Fontana, V. (1968). *The maltreated child: The maltreatment syndrome in children.* Springfield, IL: Charles C Thomas.

Fowler, C., Burns, S., & Roehl, J. (1983). The role of group therapy in incest counseling. *International Journal of Family Therapy, 5,* 127-135.

Friedrich, W. (1990). *Psychotherapy of sexually abused children and their families.* New York: W. W. Norton.

Friedrich, W., Berliner, L., Urquiza, A., & Beilke, R. (1988). Brief diagnostic group treatment of sexually abused boys. *Journal of Interpersonal Violence, 3,* 331-343.

Fritz, M. (1989). Commentary: Full circle or forward. *Child Abuse & Neglect, 13,* 313-318.

Frodi, A. (1981). Contribution of infant characteristics to child abuse. *American Journal of Mental Deficiency, 85,* 341-349.

Frodi, A., & Lamb, M. (1980). Child abusers' responses to infant smiles. *Child Development, 51,* 238-241.

Garbarino, J. (1976). A preliminary study of some ecological correlates of child abuse: The impact of socioeconomic stress on mothers. *Child Development, 47,* 178-185.

Garbarino, J., & Ebata, A. (1983). The significance of ethnic and cultural differences in child maltreatment. *Journal of Marriage and the Family, 45,* 773-783.

Garbarino, J., Guttman, E., & Seeley, J. (1986). *The psychologically battered child.* San Francisco: Jossey-Bass.

Garbarino, J., & Vondra, J. (1987). Psychological maltreatment: Issues and perspectives. In M. Brassard, R. Germain, & S. Hart (Eds.), *Psychological maltreatment of children and youth* (pp. 25-44). Elmsford, NY: Pergamon.

Gardner, L. (1972). Deprivation dwarfism. *Scientific American, 227,* 76-82.

Gelinas, D. (1983). The persisting negative effects of incest. *Psychiatry, 46,* 312-329.

Gellert, G., Maxwell, R., Durfee, M., & Wagner, G. (1995). Fatalities assessed by the Orange County Child Death Review Team, 1989-1991. *Child Abuse & Neglect, 19,* 875-883.

Gelles, R., & Straus, M. (1987). Is violence toward children increasing? *Journal of Interpersonal Violence, 2,* 212-222.

Germain, C., & Gitterman, A. (1980). *The life model of social work practice.* New York: Columbia University Press.

Ghali, S. (1982). Understanding Puerto Rican traditions. *Social Work, 27,* 98-102.

Giaretto, H., (1982). *Integrated treatment of child sexual abuse.* Palo Alto, CA: Science and Behavior Books.

Gil, D. (1970). *Violence against children: Physical child abuse in the United States.* Cambridge, MA: Harvard University Press.

Gilgun, J. (1986). Sexually abused girls' knowledge about sexual abuse and sexuality. *Journal of Interpersonal Violence, 1,* 309-325.

Giovannoni, J., & Becerra, R. (1979). *Defining child abuse.* New York: Free Press.

Giovannoni, J., & Billingsley, A. (1970). Child neglect among the poor: A study of parental adequacy in families of three ethnic groups. *Child Welfare, 49,* 196-204.

Goldberg, G. (1975). Breaking the communication barrier: The initial interview with an abusing parent. *Child Welfare, 54,* 274-282.

Gonzalez, L., Waterman, J., Kelly, R., McCord, J., & Oliveri, M. (1993). Children's patterns of disclosures and recantations of sexual and ritualistic abuse allegations in psychotherapy. *Child Abuse & Neglect, 17,* 281-289.

Goodwin, J. (1981). Suicide attempts in sexual abuse victims and their mothers. *Child Abuse & Neglect, 5*, 217-221.

Goodwin, J. (1985). Post-traumatic symptoms in incest victims. In S. Eth & R. Pynoos (Eds.), *Post-traumatic stress disorder in children* (pp. 155-168). Washington, DC: American Psychiatric Press.

Goodwin, J., Sahd, D., & Rada, R. (1982). False accusations and false denials of incest: Clinical myths and clinical realities. In J. Goodwin (Ed.), *Sexual abuse: Incest victims and their families* (pp. 17-26). Boston: John Wright.

Green, A., Gaines, R., & Sandgrund, A. (1974). Child abuse: Pathological syndrome of family interaction. *American Journal of Psychiatry, 131*, 882-886.

Greenwald, E., & Leitenberg, H. (1990). Post-traumatic stress disorder in a nonclinical and nonstudent sample of adult women sexually abused as children. *Journal of Interpersonal Violence, 5*, 691-703.

Greven, P. (1977). *The Protestant temperament*. New York: Knopf.

Griffin, W., & Bandas, J. (1987). *Social worker safety*. Chapel Hill, NC: Brendan Associates & National Child Protective Workers Association.

Groth, N. (1979). *Men who rape*. New York: Plenum.

Groth, N., Hobson, W., & Gary, T. (1982). The child molester: Clinical observation. In J. Conte & D. Shore (Eds.), *Social work and child sexual abuse* (pp. 129-144). New York: Haworth.

Groth, N., & Oliveri, F. (1989). Understanding sexual offense behavior and differentiating among sexual abusers: Basic conceptual issues. In S. Sgroi (Ed.), *Vulnerable populations* (Vol. 2, pp. 309-327). Lexington, MA: Lexington Books.

Hall, E. (1959). *The silent language*. Greenwich, CT: Fawcett.

Hally, C., Polansky, N. A., & Polansky, N. F. (1980). *Child neglect: Mobilizing treatment*. Washington, DC: National Center on Child Abuse and Neglect, Children's Bureau.

Hart, S., & Brassard, M. (1987). A major threat to children's mental health: Psychological maltreatment. *American Psychologist, 42*, 160-165.

Hartman, A. (1979). *Finding families: An ecological approach to family assessment in adoption*. Beverly Hills, CA: Sage.

Hauser, R. (Producer). (1984). *Strong kids, safe kids* [VCR Film]. Hollywood, CA: Paramount Home Video, Paramount Pictures Corporation.

Hawkins, W., & Duncan, D. (1985). Perpetrator and family characteristics related to child abuse and neglect: Comparison of substantiated and unsubstantiated reports. *Psychological Reports, 56*, 407-410.

Herman, J. (1981). *Father-daughter incest*. Cambridge, MA: Harvard University Press.

Herman, J., Russell, D., & Trocki, K. (1986). Long-term effects of incestuous abuse in childhood. *American Journal of Psychiatry, 143*, 1293-1296.

Homstead, K., & Werthamer, L. (1989). Time-limited group therapy for adolescent victims of child sexual abuse. In S. Sgroi (Ed.), *Vulnerable populations* (Vol. 2, pp. 65-84). Lexington, MA: Lexington Books.

Howze-Browne, D. (1988). Factors predictive of child maltreatment. *Early Child Development and Care, 31*, 43-54.

Hunt, I. (1976). *The lottery rose*. New York: Scribner's.

Jaudes, P., Ekwo, E., & Voorhis, J. (1995). Association of drug abuse and child abuse. *Child Abuse & Neglect, 19*, 1065-1075.

Jenkins, J., Salus, M., & Schultze, G. (1979). *Child protective services: A guide for workers* (DHEW Publication No. OHDS 79-30203). Washington, DC: National Center on Child Abuse and Neglect.

Jenkins, S. (1981). *The ethnic dilemma in social services.* New York: Free Press.

Johanek, M. (1988). Treatment of male victims of child sexual abuse in military service. In S. Sgroi (Ed.), *Vulnerable populations* (Vol. 1, pp. 103-113). Lexington, MA: Lexington Books.

Johnson, B., & Morse, H. (1968). Injured children and their parents. *Children, 15,* 147-152.

Johnson, R., & Shrier, D. (1987). Past sexual victimization by females of male patients in an adolescent medicine clinic population. *American Journal of Psychiatry, 144,* 650-652.

Jones, D. (1994). Editorial: The syndrome of Munchausen by Proxy. *Child Abuse & Neglect, 18,* 769-771.

Jones, D., & McGraw, J. (1987). Reliable and fictitious accounts of sexual abuse to children. *Journal of Interpersonal Violence, 2,* 27-45.

Jones, R., & Jones, J. (1987). Racism as psychological maltreatment. In M. Brassard, R. Germain, & S. Hart (Eds.), *Psychological maltreatment of children and youth* (pp. 146-158). Elmsford, NY: Pergamon.

Kadushin, A., & Martin, J. (1988). *Child welfare services.* New York: Macmillan.

Kamerman, S., & Kahn, A. (1976). *Social services in the United States.* Philadelphia: Temple University Press.

Katz, L. (1990). Effective permanency planning for children in foster care. *Social Work, 35,* 220-226.

Kaufman, I., Peck, A., & Tagiuri, L. (1954). The family constellation and overt incestuous relations between father and daughter. *American Journal of Orthopsychiatry, 24,* 266-279.

Kaufman, J., & Zigler, E. (1987). Do abused children become abusive parents? *American Journal of Orthopsychiatry, 57,* 186-192.

Kellogg, M. (1972). *Like the lion's tooth.* New York: Farrar, Straus, & Giroux.

Kelly, R., & Scott, M. (1986). Sociocultural considerations in child sexual abuse. In K. MacFarlane & J. Waterman (Eds.), *Sexual abuse of young children* (pp. 151-163). New York: Guilford.

Kempe, H., Silverman, F., Steele, H., Droegemueller, W., & Silver, H. (1962). The battered-child syndrome. *Journal of the American Medical Association, 181,* 17-24.

Kenning, M., Gallmeier, T., Jackson, T., & Plemons, S. (1987). *Evaluation of child sexual abuse prevention programs: A summary of two studies.* Paper presented at the National Conference on Family Violence, Durham, NC.

Kinzl, J., Traweger, C., & Biebl, W. (1995). Sexual dysfunctions: Relationship to childhood sexual abuse and early family experiences in a nonclinical sample. *Child Abuse & Neglect, 19,* 785-792.

Knopp, F. (1984). *Retraining adult sex offenders: Methods and models.* Syracuse, NY: Safer Society Press.

Knopp, F., & Stevenson, W. (1989). *Nationwide survey of juvenile and adult sex-offender treatment programs and models, 1988.* Orwell, VT: Safer Society Press.

Kotch, J., Browne, D., Ringwalt, C., Stewart, P., Ruina, E., Holt, K., Lowman, B., Jung, J., & Libow, J. (1995). Risk of child abuse or neglect in a cohort of low-income children. *Child Abuse & Neglect, 19,* 1115-1130.

Kottmeier, P. (1987). The battered child. *Pediatric Annals, 16,* 344-345.

Kovak, J. (1986). Incest as a treatment issue for alcoholic women. *Alcoholism Treatment Quarterly, 3,* 1-15.

Koverola, C., Pound, J., Heger, A., & Lytle, C. (1993). Relationship of child sexual abuse to depression. *Child Abuse & Neglect, 17*, 393-400.

Kowal, L., Kottmeier, C., Ayoub, C., Komives, J., Robinson, D., & Allen, J. (1989). Characteristics of families at risk of problems in parenting: Findings from a home-based secondary prevention program. *Child Welfare, 68*, 529-538.

Kravitz, R., & Driscoll, J. (1983). Expectations for childhood development among child-abusing and nonabusing parents. *American Journal of Orthopsychiatry, 53*, 336-344.

Kropp, J. (1985, March). *Ecologically-based intervention with abusive and neglectful families*. Paper presented at the Fifth Annual Symposium on the Future of Parenting, Chicago, IL.

Kübler-Ross, E. (1969). *On death and dying*. New York: Macmillan.

Kurtz, P., Gaudin, J., Wodarski, J., & Howing, P. (1993). Maltreatment and the school-aged child: School performance consequences. *Child Abuse & Neglect, 17*, 581-589.

Lacey, J. (1990). Incest, incestuous fantasy and indecency: A clinical catchment area study of normal-weight bulimic women. *British Journal of Psychiatry, 157*, 399-403.

Landau, H., Salus, M., Stiffarm, T., & Kalb, N. (1980). *Child protection: The role of the courts* (DHHS Publication No. OHDS 80-30256). Washington, DC: Government Printing Office.

Lanktree, C., & Briere, J. (1995). Outcome of therapy for sexually abused children: A repeated measures study. *Child Abuse & Neglect, 19*, 1145-1155.

Lawson, L., & Chaffin, M. (1992). False negatives in sexual abuse disclosure interviews. *Journal of Interpersonal Violence, 7*, 532-542.

Leavell, H., & Clark, E. (1958). *Preventive medicine—for the doctor and his community*. New York: McGraw-Hill.

Leitenberg, J., Greenwald, E., & Cado, S. (1992). A retrospective study of long-term methods of coping with having been sexually abused during childhood. *Child Abuse & Neglect, 16*, 399-407.

LeTourneau, C. (1981). Empathy and stress: How they affect parental aggression. *Social Work, 26*, 529-538.

Lieber, L. (1983). The self-help approach: Parents Anonymous. *Journal of Clinical Child Psychology, 12*, 288-291.

Logan, S., Freeman, E., & McRoy, R. (Eds.). (1990). *Social work practice with Black families: A culturally specific perspective*. White Plains, NY: Longman.

Lorber, R., Felton, D., & Reid, J. (1984). A social learning approach to the reduction of coercive processes in child abusive families: A molecular analysis. *Advanced Behavior Research Therapy, 6*, 29-45.

Lowery, M. (1987). Adult survivors of childhood incest. *Journal of Psychosocial Nursing, 25*, 27-31.

Lukianowicz, N. (1972). Incest. *British Journal of Psychiatry, 120*, 301-313.

Lutzker, J., Frame, R., & Rice, J. (1982). Project 12-Ways: An ecobehavioral approach to the treatment and prevention of child abuse and neglect. *Education and Treatment of Children, 5*, 141-155.

Lystad, M. (1975). Violence in the home: A review of the literature. *American Journal of Orthopsychiatry, 45*, 328-345.

Maccoby, E., & Martin, J. (1983). Socialization in the context of the family: Parent-child interaction. In P. H. Mussen (Ed.), *Handbook of child psychology* (4th ed., pp. 1-101). New York: John Wiley.

MacFarlane, L., & Krebs, S. (1986). Techniques for interviewing and evidence gathering. In K. MacFarlane, J. Waterman, S. Conerly, L. Damon, M. Durfee, & S. Long (Eds.), *Sexual abuse of young children* (pp. 67-100). New York: Guilford.

MacFarlane, K., & Waterman, J. (Eds.). (1986). *Sexual abuse of young children.* New York: Guilford.

MacFarlane, K., Waterman, J., Conerly, S., Damon, L., Durfee, M., & Long, S. (1986). *Sexual abuse of young children.* New York: Guilford.

Mager, R. (1962). *Preparing instructional objectives.* Belmont, CA: Fearon.

Mager, R. (1972). *Goal analysis.* Belmont, CA: Fearon.

Maisch, R. (1973). *Incest.* London: Andre Deutsch.

Mamay, P., & Simpson, R. (1981). Three female roles in television commercials. *Sex Roles, 7,* 1223-1232.

Mandell, J., & Damon, L. (1989). *Group treatment for sexually abused children.* New York: Guilford.

Margolin, L. (1992). Child abuse by mothers' boyfriends: Why the overrepresentation? *Child Abuse & Neglect, 16,* 541-551.

Marshall, P., & Norgard, K. (1983). *Child abuse and neglect: Sharing responsibility.* New York: John Wiley.

Marvasti, J. (1989). Play therapy with sexually abused children. In S. Sgroi (Ed.), *Vulnerable populations* (Vol. 2, pp. 1-42). Lexington, MA: Lexington Books.

Masson, J. (1990). *Final analysis.* Reading, MA: Addison-Wesley.

Mazer, H. (1978). *The war on Villa Street.* New York: Delacorte.

McCann, J., Voris, J., Simon, M., & Wells, R. (1990). Comparison of genital examination techniques in prepubertal girls. *Pediatrics, 85,* 182-187.

McCrea, R. (1910). *The humane movement.* New York: Columbia University Press.

McGain, B., & McKinzey, R. (1995). The efficacy of group treatment in sexually abused girls. *Child Abuse & Neglect, 19,* 1157-1169.

McGoldrick, M., & Gerson, R. (1985). *Genograms in family assessment.* New York: Norton.

McMurtry, S. (1985). Secondary prevention of child maltreatment: A review. *Social Work, 30,* 42-48.

McNew, J., & Abell, N. (1995). Posttraumatic stress symptomatology: Similarities and differences between Vietnam veterans and adult survivors of childhood sexual abuse. *Social Work, 40,* 115-126.

McNulty, C., & Wardle, J. (1995). Adult disclosure of sexual abuse: A primary cause of psychological distress? *Child Abuse & Neglect, 19,* 549-555.

Mehrabian, A., & Epstein, N. (1972). A measure of emotional empathy. *Journal of Personality, 40,* 525-543.

Meier, E. (1964). Child neglect. In N. Cohen (Ed.), *Social work and social problems* (pp. 153-200). New York: National Association of Social Workers.

Meiselman, L. (1978). *Incest: A psychological study of causes and effects with treatment recommendations.* San Francisco: Jossey-Bass.

Meyer, W., Walker, P., Emory, L., & Smith, E. (1985). Physical, metabolic and hormonal effects on men of long-term therapy with medroxyprogesterone acetate. *Fertility and Sterility, 43,* 102-109.

Miller, A. (1983). *For your own good: Hidden cruelty in child-rearing and the roots of violence.* New York: Free Press.

Miller, D., McCluskey-Fawcett, K., & Irving, L. (1993). The relationship between childhood sexual abuse and subsequent onset of bulimia nervosa. *Child Abuse & Neglect, 17,* 305-314.

Miltenberger, R., & Thiesse-Duffy, E. (1988). Evaluation of home-based programs for teaching personal safety skills to children. *Journal of Applied Behavior Analysis, 21,* 81-87.

Minuchin, S. (1974). *Families and family therapy.* Cambridge, MA: Harvard University Press.

Moeller, T., Backmann, G., & Moeller, J. (1993). The combined effects of physical, sexual, and emotional abuse during childhood: Long-term health consequences for women. *Child Abuse & Neglect, 17,* 623-640.

Murphy, J., Jellinek, M., Quinn, D., Smith, G., Poitrast, F., & Goshko, M. (1991). Substance abuse and serious child mistreatment: Prevalence, risk, and outcome in a court sample. *Child Abuse & Neglect, 17,* 623-640.

National Center on Child Abuse and Neglect. (1988a). *Executive summary: Study of national incidence and prevalence of child abuse and neglect: 1988* (DHHS Publication No. 20-01095). Washington, DC: Author.

National Center on Child Abuse and Neglect. (1988b). *Study findings: Study of national incidence and prevalence of child abuse and neglect: 1988* (DHHS Publication No. 20-01093). Washington, DC: Author.

National Resource Center on Child Abuse and Neglect. (1995). *Childhood fatalities due to child abuse and neglect: Information sheet.* Denver, CO: Author.

Nelki, J., & Watters, J. (1989). A group for sexually abused young children: Unravelling the web. *Child Abuse & Neglect, 13,* 369-377.

Nelson, B. (1984). *Making an issue of child abuse: Political agenda setting for social problems.* Chicago: University of Chicago Press.

Nibert, D., Cooper, S., & Ford, J. (1989). Parents' observations of the effect of a sexual-abuse prevention program on preschool children. *Child Welfare, 68,* 539-546.

Nurse, S. (1964). Familial patterns of parents who abuse their children. *Smith College Studies in Social Work, 35,* 11-25.

O'Hanlon, J. (1977). *Fair game.* New York: Dial.

Oliver, J., & Taylor, A. (1971). Five generations of ill-treated children in one family pedigree. *British Journal of Psychiatry, 119,* 473-480.

Orr, R. (1980). *Gunner's run.* New York: Harper & Row.

Pardeck, J. (1990). Children's literature and child abuse. *Child Welfare, 69,* 83-88.

Parke, R., & Collmer, C. (1975). Child abuse: An interdisciplinary analysis. In E. M. Hetherington (Ed.), *Review of child development research* (pp. 509-590). Chicago: University of Chicago Press.

Patterson, G. (1979). A performance theory for coercive family interaction. In R. Cairns (Ed.), *The analysis of social interactions: Methods, issues, and illustrations* (pp. 119-162). Hillsdale, NJ: Lawrence Erlbaum.

Patterson, G. (1982). *Coercive family process.* Eugene, OR: Castalia.

Paulson, M., & Chaleff, A. (1973). Parent surrogate roles: A dynamic concept in understanding and treating abusive parents. *Journal of Clinical and Consulting Child Psychology, 38,* 129-134.

Pelton, L. (1978). Child abuse and neglect: The myth of classlessness. *American Journal of Orthopsychiatry, 43,* 608-617.

Perez, C., & Widom, C. (1994). Childhood victimization and long-term intellectual and academic outcomes. *Child Abuse & Neglect, 18,* 617-633.

Peters, D., & Range, L. (1995). Childhood sexual abuse and current suicidality in college women and men. *Child Abuse & Neglect, 19,* 335-341.

Peters, J. (1976). Children who are victims of sexual assault and the psychology of offenders. *American Journal of Psychotherapy, 30,* 598-642.

Polansky, N. (1986). "There is nothing so practical as a good theory." *Child Welfare, 65,* 3-15.

Polansky, N., Borgman, R., & DeSaix, C. (1972). *Roots of futility.* San Francisco: Jossey-Bass.

Polansky, N., Borgman, R., DeSaix, C., & Sharlin, S. (1971). Verbal accessibility in the treatment of child neglect. *Child Neglect, 50,* 349-356.

Polansky, N., Chalmers, M., Buttenwieser, E., & Williams, D. (1981). *Damaged parents: An anatomy of child neglect.* Chicago: University of Chicago Press.

Pollack, L. (1983). *Forgotten children.* Cambridge, England: Cambridge University Press.

Powell, G., Brasel, J., & Blizzard, R. (1967). Emotional deprivation and growth retardation simulating idiopathic hypopituitarism. *New England Journal of Medicine, 276,* 1271-1278.

Proctor, E., & Davis, L. (1994). The challenge of racial difference: Skills for clinical practice. *Social Work, 39,* 314-323.

Rada, R. (1976). Alcoholism and the child molester. *Annals of the New York Academy of Science, 273,* 492-496.

Reid, J. (1978). *A social learning approach to family intervention: Vol. 2. Observation in home settings.* Eugene, OR: Castalia.

Reid, J., Taplin, P., & Lorber, R. (1981). A social interactional approach to the treatment of abusive families. In R. Stuart (Ed.), *Violent behavior: Social learning approaches to prediction, management and treatment* (pp. 83-101). New York: Brunner/Mazel.

Reschly, D., & Graham-Clay, S. (1987). Psychological abuse from prejudice and cultural bias. In M. Brassard, R. Germain, & S. Hart (Eds.), *Psychological maltreatment of children and youth* (pp. 137-145). Elmsford, NY: Pergamon.

Rickel, A., Dudley, G., & Berman, S. (1980). An evaluation of parent training. *Evaluation Review, 4,* 389-403.

Roberts, W. (1978). *Don's hurt Laurie.* New York: Atheneum.

Robinson, J. (1989). Clinical treatment of Black families: Issues and strategies. *Social Work, 33,* 323-329.

Rogers, C. (1980). *A way of being.* Boston: Houghton Mifflin.

Rohsenow, D., Corbett, R., & Devine, D. (1988). Molested as children: A hidden contribution to substance abuse. *Journal of Substance Abuse Treatment, 5,* 13-18.

Rowan, A., Foy, D., Rodriguez, N., & Ryan, S. (1994). Posttraumatic stress disorder in a clinical sample of adults sexually abused as children. *Child Abuse & Neglect, 18,* 51-61.

Royse, D. (1990). *Research methods for social workers.* Chicago: Nelson-Hall.

Royse, D. (1995). *Research methods in social work.* Chicago: Nelson-Hall.

Rudin, M., Zalewski, C., & Bodmer-Turner, J. (1995). Characteristics of child sexual abuse victims according to perpetrator gender. *Child Abuse & Neglect, 19,* 963-973.

Rush, F. (1980). *The best kept secret.* New York: Prentice-Hall.

Russell, D. (1986). *The secret trauma.* New York: Basic Books.

Sabotta, E., & Davis, R. (1992). Fatality after report to a child abuse registry in Washington State, 1973-1986. *Child Abuse & Neglect, 16,* 627-635.

Satir, V. (1972). *Peoplemaking.* Palo Alto, CA: Science & Behavior Books.

Schene, P. (1987). Is child abuse decreasing? *Journal of Interpersonal Violence, 2,* 225-227.

Schiffer, M. (1984). *Children's group therapy: Methods and case histories.* New York: Free Press.

Schmitt, B., & Mauro, R. (1989). Nonorganic failure to thrive: An outpatient approach. *Child Abuse and Neglect, 13*, 235-248.

Schreier, H., & Libow, J. (1993). *Hurting for love: Munchausen by Proxy syndrome.* New York: Guilford.

Sedlack, A. (1990). *Technical amendment to the study findings—National Incidence and Prevalence of Child Abuse and Neglect: 1988.* Rockville, MD: Westat.

Segal, E., & Gustavsson, N. (1990). The high cost of neglecting children: The need for a preventive policy agenda. *Child and Adolescent Social Work, 7*, 475-485.

Sermabeikian, P., & Martinez, D. (1994). Treatment of adolescent sexual offenders: Theory-based practice. *Child Abuse & Neglect, 18*, 969-976.

Sgroi, S. (1982a). An approach to case management. In S. Sgroi (Ed.), *Handbook of clinical intervention in child sexual abuse* (pp. 81-108). Lexington, MA: Lexington Books.

Sgroi, S. (Ed.). (1982b). *Handbook of clinical intervention in child sexual abuse.* Lexington, MA: Lexington Books.

Sgroi, S. (Ed.). (1988). *Vulnerable populations* (Vol. 1). Lexington, MA: Lexington Books.

Sgroi, S. (1989a). Community-based treatment for sexual offenders against children. In S. Sgroi (Ed.), *Vulnerable populations* (Vol. 2, pp. 351-393). Lexington, MA: Lexington Books.

Sgroi, S. (1989b). Healing together: Peer group therapy for adult survivors of child sexual abuse. In S. Sgroi (Ed.), *Vulnerable populations* (Vol. 2, pp. 131-166). Lexington, MA: Lexington Books.

Sgroi, S. (1989c). Stages of recovery for adult survivors of child sexual abuse. In S. Sgroi (Ed.), *Vulnerable populations* (Vol. 2, pp. 111-130). Lexington, MA: Lexington Books.

Sgroi, S. (Ed.). (1989d). *Vulnerable populations* (Vol. 2). Lexington, MA: Lexington Books.

Shubin, C. (1984). Child abuse and neglect: The physician's role. *Maryland State Medical Journal, 33*, 46-50.

Silver, L., Dublin, C., & Lourie, R. (1969). Does violence breed violence? Contributions from a study of the child abuse syndrome. *American Journal of Psychiatry, 126*, 404-407.

Sirles, E., & Franke, P. (1989). Factors influencing mothers' reactions to intrafamily sexual abuse. *Child Abuse & Neglect, 13*, 131-140.

Skibinski, G. (1995). The influence of the family preservation model on child sexual abuse intervention strategies: Changes in child welfare worker tasks. *Child Welfare, 74*, 975-989.

Smith, D. (1974). *Tough Chauncey.* New York: Morrow.

Smith, R. (1995, September). What to do with the serial abuser? *NASW News,* p. 3.

Smucker, M., Craighead, W., Craighead, L., & Green, B. (1986). Normative and reliability data for the Children's Depression Inventory. *Journal of Abnormal Child Psychology, 14*, 25-39.

Sorensen, T., & Snow, B. (1991). How children tell: The process of disclosure in child sexual abuse. *Child Welfare, 70*, 3-15.

Spungen, C., Jensen, S., Finkelstein, N., & Satinsky, F. (1989). Child personal safety: Model program for prevention of child sexual abuse. *Social Work, 34*, 127-131.

Steele, B. (1975). Working with abusive parents: A psychiatrist's view. *Children Today, 4*, 3.

Steinberg, L., Catalano, R., & Dooley, D. (1981). Economic antecedents of child abuse and neglect. *Child Development, 52*, 975-985.

Steward, M., Farquhar, L., Dicharry, D., Glick, D., & Martin, P. (1986). Group therapy: A treatment of choice for young victims of child abuse. *International Journal of Group Psychotherapy, 36,* 261-277.

Straus, M. (1979). Measuring intrafamily conflict and violence: The Conflict Tactics (CT) Scales. *Journal of Marriage and the Family, 41,* 75-88.

Straus, M. (1981, July). *Societal change and change in family violence.* Paper presented at the National Conference for Family Violence Researchers, University of New Hampshire.

Straus, M., & Gelles, R. (1986). Societal change and change in family violence from 1975 to 1985 as revealed by two national surveys. *Journal of Marriage and the Family, 48,* 465-479.

Straus, M., & Gelles, R. (1988). How violent are American families? Estimates from the National Family Violence Resurvey and other studies. In G. Hotaling, D. Finkelhor, J. Kirkpatrick, & M. Straus (Eds.), *Family abuse and its consequences: New directions in research* (pp. 14-36). Newbury Park, CA: Sage.

Straus, M., Gelles, R., & Steinmetz, S. (1980). *Behind closed doors: Violence in the American family.* Garden City, NY: Anchor.

Sturm, L., & Drotar, D. (1989). Prediction of weight for height following intervention in three-year-old children with early histories of nonorganic failure to thrive. *Child Abuse & Neglect, 13,* 19-28.

Summit, R. (1983). The child sexual abuse accommodation syndrome. *Child Abuse & Neglect, 7,* 177-193.

Summit, R., & Kryso, J. (1978). Sexual abuse of children: A clinical spectrum. *American Journal of Orthopsychiatry, 48,* 237-251.

Teets, J. (1995). Childhood sexual trauma of chemically dependent women. *Journal of Psychoactive Drugs, 27,* 231-238.

Telzrow, C. (1987). Influence by negative and limiting models. In M. Brassard, R. Germain, & S. Hart (Eds.), *Psychological maltreatment of children and youth* (pp. 121-136). Elmsford, NY: Pergamon.

Tierney, K., & Corwin, D. (1983). Exploring intra-familial child sexual abuse: A systems approach. In D. Finkelhor, R. Gelles, G. Hotaling, & M. Straus (Eds.), *The dark side of families: Current family violence research* (pp. 102-116). Beverly Hills, CA: Sage.

Tsai, M., & Wagner, N. (1978). Therapy groups for women sexually molested as children. *Archives of Sexual Behavior, 7,* 417-427.

Tyson, P., & Sobschak, K. (1994). Perceptual responses to infant crying after EEG biofeedback assisted stress management training: Implications for physical child abuse. *Child Abuse & Neglect, 18,* 933-943.

U.S. Department of Health and Human Services. (1980). *Representation for the abused and neglected child: The guardian ad litem and legal counsel* (DHHS Publication No. OHDS 80-30272). Washington, DC: Government Printing Office.

Van Den Bergh, N., & Cooper, B. (Eds.). (1986). *Feminist visions for social work.* Washington, DC: National Association of Social Workers.

Vissing, Y., Straus, M., Gelles, R., & Harrop, J. (1991). Verbal aggression by parents and psychosocial problems of children. *Child Abuse & Neglect, 15,* 223-238.

Waldby, C., Clancy, A., Emetchi, J., & Summerfield, C. (1989). Theoretical perspectives on father-daughter incest. In E. Driver & A. Droisen (Eds.), *Child sexual abuse: A feminist reader* (pp. 88-106). New York: New York University Press.

Waller, G. (1994). Childhood sexual abuse and borderline personality disorder in the eating disorders. *Child Abuse & Neglect, 19,* 97-101.

Wasik, B., & Roberts, R. (1994). Survey of home visiting programs for abused and neglected children and their families. *Child Abuse & Neglect, 18,* 271-283.

Watkins, C. E., Terrell, F., Miller, F., & Terrell, S. (1989). Cultural mistrust and its effects on expectational variables in Black client-white counselor relationships. *Journal of Counseling Psychology, 36,* 447-450.

Watkins, S. (1990). The Mary Ellen myth: Correcting child welfare history. *Social Work, 35,* 500-503.

Watkins, T., & Gonzales, R. (1982). Outreach to Mexican Americans. *Social Work, 27,* 68-73.

Wells, K. (1994). A reorientation to knowledge development in family preservation services: A proposal. *Child Welfare, 73,* 475-488.

Wells, S., Stein, T., Fluke, J., & Downing, J. (1989). Screening in child protection services. *Social Work, 34,* 45-48.

Whipple, E., & Webster-Stratton, C. (1991). The role of parental stress in physically abusive families. *Child Abuse & Neglect, 15,* 279-291.

Wiehe, V. (1987). Empathy and locus of control in child abusers. *Journal of Social Service Research, 9,* 17-30.

Wiehe, V. (1990a). Religious influence on parental attitudes toward the use of corporal punishment. *Journal of Family Violence, 5,* 173-186.

Wiehe, V. (1990b). *Sibling abuse.* Lexington, MA: Lexington Books.

Wiehe, V. (1992). Abusive and nonabusive parents: How they were parented. *Journal of Social Service Research, 15,* 81-93.

Wodarski, J., Kurtz, P., Gaudin, J., & Howing, P. (1990). Maltreatment and the school-age child: Major academic, socioemotional and adaptive outcomes. *Social Work, 35,* 506-513.

Wolock, I., & Horowitz, B. (1979). Child maltreatment and maternal deprivation among AFDC recipient families. *Social Service Review, 53,* 175-194.

Woodling, B., & Heger, A. (1986). The use of the colposcope in the diagnosis of sexual abuse in the pediatric age group. *Child Abuse & Neglect, 10,* 111-114.

Wozencraft, T., Wagner, W., & Pellegrin, A. (1991). Depression and suicidal ideation in sexually abused children. *Child Abuse & Neglect, 15,* 505-511.

Wurtele, S., Saslawsky, D., Miller, C., Marrs, S., & Britcher, J. (1986). Teaching personal safety skills for potential prevention of sexual abuse: A comparison of treatments. *Journal of Consulting and Clinical Psychology, 54,* 688-692.

Yates, A. (1982). Children eroticized by incest. *American Journal of Psychiatry, 139,* 482-485.

Yokley, J. (Ed.). (1990). *The use of victim-offender communication in the treatment of sexual abuse: Three intervention models.* Orwell, VT: Safer Society Press.

Yokley, J., & McGuire, D. (1990). Introduction to the therapeutic use of victim-offender communication. In J. Yokeley (Ed.), *The use of victim-offender communication in the treatment of sexual abuse: Three intervention models* (pp. 7-22). Orwell, VT: Safer Society Press.

Young, L. (1964). *Wednesday's children: A study of child neglect and abuse.* New York: McGraw-Hill.

Young, L. (1992). Sexual abuse and the problem of embodiment. *Child Abuse & Neglect, 16,* 89-100.

Index

About the Author

Vernon R. Wiehe is Professor in the College of Social Work at the University of Kentucky at Lexington. After he received a master's degree from the University of Chicago, he did postgraduate work in the Program of Advanced Studies in Social Work at Smith College. He received his doctorate from Washington University in St. Louis. He is the author of numerous articles in professional journals as well as the following books: *Sibling Abuse: The Hidden Physical, Emotional, and Sexual Trauma*; *Perilous Rivalry: When Siblings Become Abusive*; *Working With Child Abuse and Neglect*; *Intimate Betrayal: Understanding and Responding to the Trauma of Acquaintance Rape*; and *The Brother/Sister Hurt: Recognizing the Effects of Sibling Abuse*. Dr. Wiehe has appeared on numerous television and radio talk shows discussing family violence, including *Phil Donahue* and *Sonya Live*. He is a frequently cited author on the subject of family violence.